GIANTS
Along My Path

My Fifty Years in the Ministry
---

by DALE OLDHAM

WARNER PRESS
anderson, indiana

Library of Congress Cataloging in Publication Data

Oldham, W. Dale

Giants along my path; my fifty years in the ministry.

1. Oldham, Dale.   I. Title.

BX7027.Z804   269'.2'0924 [B]   73-16413

Paperbound Edition: ISBN 0   87162   162   2

Clothbound Edition: ISBN 0   87162   165   7

Printed in the United States of America.

Douglas L. Talley

Dedication

My beloved "Polly," to whom I have been married (without a dull moment) for nearly fifty years, joins in dedicating this story of love, life, and work to our son, Douglas Reed Oldham, whose new heart-song keeps his parents singing.

CONTENTS

Introduction

What a gracious privilege it is to serve the Lord! One avoids a thousand pitfalls and a thousand heartaches when his life is totally committed to Christ. One receives confidence to move ahead when he knows he is being led by a divine hand. Long roads are shortened, heavy burdens made lighter, as our Friend locks step with ours.

Since August of 1921 I have given full time to gospel work. Thirty-four years were spent in pastorates and the rest in evangelistic work.

It has been an interesting life, with never a dull moment. Rewarding, too. As I look back over half a century, the satisfactions far outnumber the regrets. I would echo the words of the hymn writer:

It pays to serve Jesus, it pays every day,
It pays every step of the way.
Though the pathway to glory may sometimes be drear,
You'll be happy each step of the way.

Yours and His!

W. Dale Oldham

Eustis, Florida
May 1, 1973

Chapter One

In Old Kentucky

"**I NEVER DID** think the Lord would call a man just to do a little dab of singing." Thus commented my good friend, the Reverend W. F. Chappel (*Brother* Chappel to all of us in those days), after I confessed that the Lord had put it on my heart to preach the gospel. The time was November of 1922; the place, the little village of Camargo, Kentucky, where the Chappels lived. We were in the midst of a two weeks' series of evangelistic meetings in the church there. Brother Chappel was preaching, his seventeen-year-old son John was playing the piano, and I was in charge of the music. The "highway" connecting Mount Sterling and Frenchburg passed the church and was rutted and muddy. Churchgoers within walking distance usually stayed with the bluegrass along the fences to avoid the mud.

The Chappels lived down a lane a quarter of a mile from the church. Their comfortable country home was surrounded by rolling, bluegrass-covered hills. Twenty miles to the south the mountains began. It was a great country for white-faced Hereford cattle. Over toward Lexington and Winchester were the large, beautifully fenced bluegrass farms where some of the fastest horses in the world were to be found.

The bluegrass sections of old Kentucky were reminiscent of the early days of American independence and self-sufficiency. In Paris, Lexington, Winchester, and Richmond could be found remnants of a bluenosed aristocracy, but they were not necessarily the people who now owned the land. All through central Kentucky

9

big, pillared mansions were contrasted by log cabins and plainer houses. It seemed to me there were just two classes, the rich and the poor.

W. F. Chappel was to become one of my best friends. He had migrated over the mountains from North Carolina where he had been brought up with an axe in his hand. During his teens he had worked as a logger in the big woods of the Tar Heel state and had developed a rugged body. He was big-chested and strong, with a rugged, manly physique. His parents were religious people—Baptists, I believe—and Brother Chappel used to tell of travelers whom they entertained during his childhood. They were an assorted group, with a good sprinkling of preachers among them. Some were itinerant evangelists on their way to or from a preaching engagement. So as a growing boy, Brother Chappel was exposed to a great deal of conversation about a world which lay far out beyond the circle of his immediate experience. He found these visitors, for the most part, to be quite interesting.

There in the mountains the latchstring of hospitality was almost invariably extended to travelers who happened along. If evening caught one far from town, all he had to do was shout from the road, "Hello, the house!" Someone would appear in the doorway to return the greetings and more often than not would add, "Get down, stranger, and come in." Or perhaps it would be, "Hitch your horse and light." The traveler would be welcomed to the supper table and afterward, as all sat around the open fire, he would share whatever news he thought would be of interest to his host and family. More often than not he would find that he knew someone they knew. In fact, it was not unusual to discover that he was distantly related to those whose hospitality he was sharing. The conversation would center on the weather, crops, cattle, horses, the tobacco market, and finally religion in the community.

Before the group retired for the night, like as not, someone would go to the root cellar and bring in a pan of red, juicy apples. Apples never taste better than when shared thus before a crackling fire. About nine o'clock the host would reach for a Bible, ask the traveler to read a chapter, and then lead out in prayer. With devo-

10

tions over, someone would bring in a short ladder, and the stranger would be shown to his husk-mattress bed in the loft above.

How many of those "spare bedrooms" I occupied during the early days of my singing ministry in Kentucky and West Virginia! If it wasn't a loft, it was a spare bedroom indeed, often shut off from the rest of the house and never heated in winter. Heat came only from the living room fireplace and the kitchen range. I vividly remember those cold, cold bedrooms! I would hurriedly change into pajamas and jump into bed. The straw ticks were often chilly and damp. I would put my head under the covers and breathe there for a while to warm the sheets. The Kentucky people were most hospitable. During an evangelistic meeting they would have had me sleeping in a different bed every night had I been willing to change about.

Brother Chappel and I walked the lane toward his home that night after I had told him of my call to preach. There was silence for a time and then he stunned me by saying, "You must bring the message tomorrow night." A shiver went over me, a chill. I preach? Tomorrow night? I was nineteen years old, with two years of high school and two years of Bible Training School behind me. The previous summer I had begun my work as an evangelistic singer. But preach? When some minister now and then had asked if I did not feel a call to preach, my stock reply had been, "You do the preaching, I'll do the singing, and we'll get along just fine." But on this particular night things were different. Brother Chappel had preached a moving sermon. Several persons had responded to the invitation and had come to kneel at the old-fashioned altar, petitioning the Lord for forgiveness. But this night the invitation had been for me as well as for them. All during the evening a heavy burden had been on my heart for my own needs. Ordinarily at the conclusion of the invitation I would have gone to pray with those who had come forward. This time, however, I knelt in back of the pulpit, all alone, and there and then made a complete surrender of my life to the will of God. I said, "Father, if you really want me to preach, I will do it." But I was frightened at the prospect and doubly frightened when Brother Chappel said, "You must bring the message tomorrow night."

I prayed for a longer time than usual that night before sleeping, and next morning I was up with the sun. It was a beautiful, frosty dawn. After a breakfast of eggs, fluffy light biscuits, bacon, and cream gravy, I walked out into a little grove not far from the house and gave myself to meditation and prayer. Finally the Lord seemed to suggest the text which speaks of the strait gate and the narrow way. Immediately I began to work out an outline for the evening message. I use the word *work* advisedly because that is exactly what it was. In fact, for the first several years sermon preparation was the hardest, most taxing, most frustrating part of my job.

My training in the Bible Training School had been rather rudimentary. Also, I had been only seventeen when taking my only course in homiletics. Finally, I finished my outline, and then went back over it with many misgivings. Was this really a sermon outline? Would it support me when I stood before the people? Were my illustrations fitting and appropriate? I was worried. Suddenly I was also shaken by another feeling of uncertainty. Was my "call" the real thing? I thought it was, but I had to be sure. With Gideon and the fleece in mind, I turned again to prayer. "Father, if you are really calling me to preach, please grant that at least one person may find Christ as Savior at the conclusion of tonight's service." This was a rather foolish thing to ask of the Lord, but I didn't know any better. God doesn't force anyone to serve him. I continued, "Lord, I'm willing to preach a dozen sermons after tonight with no response, but please let at least one person come forward tonight. I will take this as a seal of my calling."

Time for the evening service arrived, and, finally, with knees trembling, I delivered the message the Lord had given me out there among the saplings. To my delight, six persons responded to the invitation and found Christ as Savior. I preached several times after that before there were any more conversions, but, from that night forward I never doubted my call to preach. It gave me a good solid feeling about the ministry, especially during times when the going was rough. God still calls people to preach the gospel, and those who feel divinely called do a better job because of the certainty that the hand of the Lord is upon them.

Not that the ministry was a strange vocation to me. I am a P.K. (preacher's kid) and was born and reared in a parsonage. In spite of my resistance for a time, I think I had always known that some day I would preach. At the age of five I felt I was going to be a preacher. At fifteen, although not living as I should, I remember filling out a high school vocational questionnaire for the teacher in which I indicated that I was preparing for the ministry.

Chapter Two

Oklahoma - - Indian Territory

I AM A "SOONER." I was born in Indian Territory down along the banks of the red, muddy Cimmaron River, near the little village of Ripley in Payne County. The date was March 30, 1903, and Oklahoma would not become a state for another four years. Mother said it was a dark, rainy, Monday morning when I appeared on the scene. My father was William Harrison Oldham, and my mother, Myrtle (Elmore) Oldham. I was a rather sickly infant and nearly died before my first birthday. In 1903 Oklahoma was pioneer country. There was no courthouse, and so no birth records were kept. Actually, I can't prove I was ever born! There were no hospitals, and few doctors were willing to face the rigors, poverty, and privations of that new country.

You have read various stories about the opening up of the Cherokee Strip for settlement in the early 90s. The land-hungry people came in buggies, wagons, on horseback, and afoot. The advertised hour arrived, a gun was fired, and the race for homesteads was on.

Both of my grandfathers entered that race and each obtained a farm, but on opposite sides of the Cimmaron. When Grandfather J. F. Oldham arrived at the claim he had earlier chosen, it was to find it already taken. He offered the occupant fifty dollars to move on and the offer was accepted.

These efforts to obtain homesteads were colorful and sometimes dangerous. Racing vehicles sometimes collided and were overturned. Rightful claimants were sometimes forcibly ejected from their land by ruffians who silenced them with threats. Since most of the claims were without buildings of any kind, there were no shelters into which one could move his family and possessions.

Tents and covered wagons had to do until houses could be built. Wells were few and far between. Water was scarce and typhoid common. At nineteen, my father almost died from it. Dozens of other illnesses plagued the poorly fed, undoctored people. Summers were hot and crop failures common.

Grandfather J. R. Elmore planted cotton, put in a big garden, and set out an orchard. Grandfather Oldham farmed, but he also opened a school on his place, putting his oldest daughter, Mattie, in charge as teacher. He built a two-story brick building in Ripley, opened a general store, and lived in the second floor apartment. A sign painter blocked off *Oldham Mercantile Company* in letters two-feet high along the upper wall of the building.

Grandfather Oldham helped organize and finance the town's only bank and later bought an interest in a local cotton gin. There was no bridge across the muddy Cimmaron at Ripley, but about 1900 a suspension bridge was erected to connect Ripley with Ingalls and Stillwater. Soon Ripley was a town of 3,000 persons.

But the bridge had not yet been built when my father began courting Myrtle Elmore. The two had met quite by chance at a revival meeting, but getting together afterward was a problem because of the intervening river. Neither a bridge nor a boat was available. But love conquers all. Dad used to tell how he would undress in a thicket on the river bank and then fold trousers and underwear carefully. Making a pile of these and his shoes, he then tied the whole thing on top of his head with a bandanna. After swimming the river, he would dress and go on to his date. He said you really had to be in love in those days!

The situation reminded me of the fellow who wrote to his girl, "I love you more than life itself. I'd climb the highest mountain, swim the deepest river, cross the hottest desert, just to be at your side." With heart palpitating with emotion he signed the letter and then added, "P.S. I'll be over to see you Saturday night if it doesn't rain."

I was born in the country but while still an infant in arms our family moved into Ripley to occupy a little corner cottage. A lane ran by it leading to a large pasture where now and then one could catch sight of a Texas longhorn.

Every day my father walked that lane and disappeared among the shrubs and trees of the pasture. This worried me because I was afraid of the cattle. One day, however, he took me by the hand and we walked down the lane, through the gate, and into the pasture. A few hundred feet farther was a huge stump half-hidden by shrubs and saplings. It turned out to be my father's private chapel.

Falling on his knees, with one arm around me, he began to pray. He thanked the Lord for his family, for the little church of which he was the pastor. Then he prayed for the unconverted of the community. And last he prayed for me, asking the Lord to help me to be a good boy and obedient to my parents. Then he asked me to pray and I did as best I could.

The experience made quite an impression on me and in later years helped to explain the secret of my father's humility and saintliness. There was a gentleness, a tenderness about him. All through my growing up years I felt the warmth of his love for me. Fortunate is the lad who has a reverent father, and doubly fortunate is he if he can regularly hear that father pray.

As my two older sisters and I walked down the pasture lane one day, we heard the bellowing of an angry steer. Something abnormal about it frightened us. My sisters nearly lifted me off the ground as they ran for the house. We made it just in time. The steer had "gone loco" and was on quite a rampage, running the people off the streets. With hearts still palpitating, we watched from the safety of our living room window as cowboys lassoed the steer, snubbed him to a tree, and shot him. It was quite an experience for a child, but that was Oklahoma in the pioneer days.

Some of the many Indians in our area used to obtain illicit liquor and run wild in their intoxication. Occasionally an Indian would knock at our door for a handout, frightening my mother half to death. She never lost her fear of them although most were quite harmless.

But Indians weren't her only cause for anxiety. Deadly diseases were running rampant; diseases that we seldom hear about these days: diptheria, membranous croup, quinsy, typhoid fever, a very dangerous type of measles, scarlet fever, whooping cough of a variety that killed thousands of children, tuberculosis. A fast-acting type of tuberculosis was dubbed "quick consumption." My Grandmother Elmore contracted this illness rather suddenly. One cold winter day after bathing, she discovered that a needed article of clothing was still hanging on an outside clothesline. Hurriedly donning a robe, she ran out into the snow with feet bare. That was enough to start the trouble. In three months she was dead.

So, you can understand my father's deep concern when it was discovered that my mother, then in her middle twenties, had also contracted tuberculosis. Would it be the fast-acting variety? Since Grandmother Elmore had died so quickly of this dread disease, would my mother follow in her footsteps, leaving a young husband with three small children? The church offered up earnest prayers in mother's behalf, as did my father, but her decline continued. Before long she weighed less than a hundred pounds.

Although mother was quite weak, my father decided to take us to the Oklahoma State Camp Meeting where there would be ministers to pray for her. Borrowing a covered wagon and team, he boxed up some food for the journey, and off we went for Oklahoma City, some seventy-five miles away. I was two years and four months old at the time, and the trip constitutes one of my earliest memories. As the sun dipped low in the west, my father unhitched the horses, tethered them by the trail, built a fireplace with stones gathered from here and there, and soon a crackling fire was underway. From the wagon he brought a large iron skillet, slicing potatoes and onions into it. Sometimes he would fry meat or eggs. I can still remember the aroma of the cooking food and the beauty of the sunsets along the trail. Surprisingly enough, there was a certain sense of security in sleeping inside a covered wagon. I remembered that covered wagon the other day while flying between Denver and Baltimore at 39,000 feet. The captain came on the intercom to say that, with a strong tail wind, our ground speed was 690 miles an hour.

In Oklahoma City we deserted the wagon to live in a tent on the campgrounds. One day an elderly minister came to say that he felt impressed of the Lord to pray for mother's healing. He prayed a simple, humble prayer and left. From that hour my mother began to improve and gain weight. She outlived my father by twenty years and finally passed away in 1965 at the age of eighty-four.

Such experiences leave an indelible impression upon growing children. After that it seemed a normal thing to pray when someone was sick. We expected healing and it came. Are you surprised that I still believe "the prayer of faith shall save the sick" and bring them to recovery?

During a visit to Ripley in 1970, I was told by an elderly minister that my father was the first pastor of the first congregation of the Church of God in the state of Oklahoma. He had received little scholastic training for the task. When Grandfather Oldham took my father to enroll in a good academy, only to discover that military training was a compulsory part of the curriculum, he refused to permit him to enroll. Grandfather Oldham was a Civil War veteran and hated war with a passion. So much for my father's secondary education. However, he had a good mind and an unusual amount of good common sense. He entered the ministry determined to do the best he could with what he had. That congregation of the Church of God is still the largest church in Ripley.

Chapter Three

We Move to Iowa

IN THE SUMMER of 1906 my father felt led to accept an invitation to move to Clinton, Iowa, where two or three families of the Church of God wished to establish a congregation. There was no salary, parsonage, or chapel, and yet Dad felt led of the Lord to make the change. The train trip took a couple of days. We children were all eyes, watching the passing scenery. Of course we couldn't afford sleeping coaches and so we arrived at Clinton weary and tired, but with the excitement that change always brings to children.

We moved into a bleak upstairs flat and held religious services first in private homes and then in a rented hall. As the little group began to grow, more money came in. Before too long a church building which had belonged to the Swedish Lutherans was purchased, and our congregation moved in with praise and thanksgiving. That was the beginning of better days for us and the church.

As already indicated, my father was a man of simple faith and believing prayer. I can still hear him saying, "Son, remember, it is always safe to trust the Lord." All his life he was a living example of that fact. Bless his memory!

After living in rented flats for a couple of years, Dad decided we ought to have a home of our own. We couldn't afford anything elaborate, but finally we found a five-room cottage on a quiet street which could be purchased for $1650.

The house wasn't large enough for our family, but we had always been crowded and nobody seemed to mind. The little cottage contained no modern conveniences. There was a pitcher pump at the sink from which we could draw rainwater from the cistern. An unfinished cellar under the house was reached by an outside stairway and was an excellent place in which to store apples, potatoes, and canned goods. The usual woodshed and outhouse, a fenced run for chickens, and space for a good garden just suited my father.

It was a great day for us when we moved into the cottage. Mother prettied up the place with curtains while dad painted woodwork and margins on the floor of each room. In the kitchen we had a "soft" coal burning range with a warming oven above and a hot water "reservoir" on the right end. How well I remember the loaves of hot bread which mother brought forth from that oven and the cold winter days when we ran in from school to find an iron pot filled with soup beans and ham "hock" simmering on the back of the stove! In the living room was a stove which burned "hard" coal. It would hold a fire all night if properly stoked. It had mica windows through which the red coals glowed with cheering warmth. By its glow I undressed before plunging into the icy bedroom at night, and by its friendly warmth I dressed again in the morning. Two bedrooms, six persons. No bathroom.

Generally, we took baths only on Saturday nights. We brought the big wooden laundry tub into the kitchen and mixed water from the reservoir into it until the right temperature had been reached. My oldest sister bathed first, then the second sister, and the third. I came last, with no change in the bath water! Next morning I put on the clean socks and underwear which would have to do for a full week. But everyone else operated that way.

We didn't know much about Louis Pasteur. Mr. Seymour owned and operated Seymour's Dairy all by himself. He would come to our back door periodically to sell my mother milk tickets, pints and quarts. Each morning his horse-drawn cart would come down our alley, the horse stopping of its own accord at our back gate. Mr. Seymour would run up the path to the house, a two-gallon container in one hand, a quart measuring tin in the other. He would knock briefly at the door, call out, "Milkman!" then enter. Mother would have placed a crock on the kitchen table with a milk stamp beside it. Seymour would measure out the proper amount, pour it into the crock, take his stamp, then cross our lawn to a gate into the next yard. His horse would obediently move on to the next stop. Mother would pour the fresh milk into a pan, bring it to a boil, let it cool, and then place it in our ice box. Next day, if the weather happened to be warm, any milk that was left generally turned "blinky." These were the "good old days" of which some people still speak so fondly. Thus we lived for several years in our little cottage on Olney Avenue. Here my youngest sister Hazel was born.

Iowa winters were cold and there was generally a considerable amount of snow. While in the eighth grade, I made a pair of skis in manual training class so I could enjoy the white hillsides with my friends. One day I got the skis crossed up when about halfway down the hill and took a header into a deep ditch filled with snow. I thought I would suffocate before finally managing to extricate myself.

Few of Clinton's streets were paved, just those in the business district. In midsummer when there hadn't been rain for several days, our street was velvet dust three or four inches deep. When a delivery wagon went by, clouds of that dust drifted across our yard and into the house. This was a constant worry to my cleanly mother. Summer was play time. Across the street was a large vacant lot overgrown with six-foot ironweeds. We boys made paths through this jungle and played hide-and-seek. We climbed trees and also played in a big sand pit a few blocks away.

Fruit and vegetable hucksters came along regularly in their wagons, shouting their wares. One of them used to cry, "Sweetcorn, honey, and plums." Only he made it "plombs." I used to follow his cart, feeling the warmth of the velvety dust between my toes. Afternoons, the ice-cream wagon came along. Sometimes—just once in a long while—my mother would send one of us out with a bowl and fifteen cents which would buy just enough for each of us to have a small dip. There never seemed to be enough.

In fact, there never seemed to be enough of any kind of food at our house except potatoes. Every year, Farmer Rummel crossed the Mississippi bridge from his Illinois farm to dump fifteen bushels of potatoes into a large bin in our cellar. So we always had potatoes. We ate them fried, boiled, and baked. Sometimes Rummel would also bring a barrel or two of good red apples: Roman Beauties or Northern Spies.

In Iowa our Churches of God were few and far between, but we managed to have a state camp meeting every summer, once at Hedrick, and later at Madrid. I liked Madrid better because several Church of God farmers lived nearby. They would allow us boys to play in their barns and sometimes ride or drive their horses. I enjoyed Frank Bengtson's farm best because he allowed me to drive his big team. At this writing, Brother Frank is in the Lutheran Home in Madrid and his children are planning to celebrate his one-hundredth birthday with him. The last time I saw this saintly man he laughed and said, "I used to call you my little fast driver." Frank Bengtson's son Paul and I became good friends, and he later named his son after me.

At the campgrounds we boys attended children's meetings in the big tent and afterward teased the girls. Meals were served in the basement of the church next door and were prepared, for the most part, by the preachers' wives.

People came for miles to attend the ten-day camp meeting, riding in wagons, sometimes with a milk cow tied to the endgate. They would pitch tents, and, in some cases, prepare their own meals over campfires. One family with several children brought a large crate of soda crackers with them. The crackers became damp because of too much rainy weather. Since the family could not afford to throw them away, they built a fire and dried the crackers out in pans. I ate one or two of those redeemed crackers but didn't ask for more.

The Hedrick meetings were held at the edge of a small town. My friend, Silas Tyler, also a P.K., became bored with too much church, as had I, so we teamed up to see if something of greater interest could be found to do. There wasn't very much to stimulate us. Finally we found ourselves out by the railroad tracks where we threw stones at the engine wheels when trains came by. I don't think we were damaging anything, but one engineer must not have been too sure of our intentions. Next time, as we were in the act of throwing, he opened an exhaust valve and sprayed us but good with hot water. We weren't seriously burned, but somewhere in the process we lost our enthusiasm for throwing stones at engines.

You will understand that I can't describe what the Ladies' Room was like at that camp meeting, but I do remember something of the men's accommodations. A hand-painted sign reading MEN had an arrow pointing into the adjacent woods. There a path led to a remote place where the low horizontal limb of a squat tree made a convenient perch. Beneath that limb was a shallow trench. A nearby sack of lime and a small shovel completed the facilities. Simple, but economical. No water bills. Our only defense against mosquitos was to swat them; so we did with our might what our hands found to do. To take a bath during camp meeting, we men and boys went to a creek in the woods.

The camp meeting preaching was fairly interesting, as I remember it, even if the sermons were too long. The singing was something else. People drove for miles to hear our people sing. That was the most enjoyable part of all for me.

Since the little church at Clinton could not adequately support my father during the early years, he supplemented his income by conducting evangelistic meetings in various places. But these did not pay very well either. Sometimes he was forced to do a bit of secular work in order to keep our bills paid. When I was about ten years old, dad surprised me with the gift of a red coaster wagon. I say "surprised" because I well knew we could not afford such a luxury. However, with an attitude of "the Lord will provide," I coasted up and down the street, enjoying every minute of it. But my understanding of dad's course in economics was clarified one morning when he loaded his paper-hanging board and ladders onto my precious wagon, and then gave me an address where he wished them to be delivered. This was why he had spent four precious dollars on a coaster wagon! By doing some occasional painting and paper-hanging the grocery bills were paid and father's credit rating was kept intact. "Slow, but sure," the Credit Bureau rated him, but they would have done just as well to have put it, "Poor, but honest."

For honest he was! Nobody ever lost a penny because of my dad. I can still hear him saying, "Son, during his lifetime every man must now and then borrow money. When the time comes that you must borrow money, go to a bank. That's the place to borrow it—from a bank. They are in the business for that purpose. Don't borrow from your friends because if you can't pay when the loan is due it may bring a strain to your relationship. Go to the bank when your note is due with the interest and whatever you can pay on the principal. Tell them your circumstances and explain what you mean to do about your obligation." It was good advice which I practiced and later handed on to my own son.

Again dad used to say, "Son, it is better to get a whipping for telling the truth than to tell a lie and escape punishment." He'd say, "Keep your shoes shined, son. It protects the leather and they will last longer. Shoes cost money. You are a better steward for the Lord when you make your shoes last longer." Of course, it was also easier on dad's purse.

My father once said, "Son, get this one thing straight. If you receive a whipping at school, another will be waiting for you when you get home." So I never received a whipping in school. And whippings by our teachers were an everyday occurrence. I did cut it pretty close one afternoon. I don't remember what I had done wrong, but the teacher told me to stay after school, and I knew a whipping was in the offing. The anxious look on my face may have caused her to change her mind because when school was dismissed she disappeared. After what I hoped was a properly long wait, I went home. But that was too close for comfort, and the next day I was a very, very good boy in school.

When I was eight, my father took me along on one of his evangelistic excursions, this time to Horton, Missouri. There Grandfather Oldham owned a good farm and made money by raising alfalfa and threshing out the seed which brought a good price among the farmers. Horton was but a whistle-stop on the railroad, and grandpa's farm was miles from town. We were to hold the evangelistic services wherever possible, but no schoolhouse or church was made available. So the men went into the woods and cut down small trees out of which they sawed eight-foot uprights, setting them up in rows and bracing them at the top. Long poles joined sides and ends together. Then the men brought loads of leafy branches which they laid over the rafters to serve as a roof, and we had a "brush arbor." A pulpit platform was built of rough planks and seats were of planks set across sections of logs. Light was furnished by kerosene flares of the old "banjo" type. One or two hung on posts at each side and one on the platform to give the preacher light. It served well as a chapel except when it rained.

I don't remember much about the meetings except the singing; but I do remember that Dr. J. T. Wilson, who was later to establish the Anderson Bible Training School, was a pretty good shot with a .22 rifle. We used to go down to the creek together and shoot turtles, snakes, and bullfrogs. There always seemed to be plenty of them. We were staying at grandfather's. One day the cattle got into a patch of wild onions. The taste of the milk and butter was spoiled for sometime afterward.

My father took me into central Iowa that same year for a series of meetings in a rural schoolhouse. I gave out hymn books and took an active part in the singing. Following my first boyish soprano, I sang alto until my voice began to change. Dad used to ask me to sing a solo in church once in awhile, but that sort of thing was ordinarily frowned on. Folks were afraid you'd become "puffed up."

During this meeting I enjoyed going out each morning to watch for the rural mail carrier. He did not come in a buggy or spring wagon. He rode a motorcycle. I think it was the first motorcycle I had ever seen, and I thought it a most interesting vehicle. It was a very primitive machine compared with today's Harley-Davidsons and Hondas. It had no battery, only a magneto. I don't think it had even a clutch. It did have a self-starter, the postman. When *he* stopped, the *motor* stopped. He would deliver the mail to the rural box, say "Good morning," and then, giving his cycle a push, would run down the road by its side until it fired. Then he would give a running leap into the saddle and disappear down the road in a cloud of dust. To me it was all very exciting. His letter bag took quite a swinging in the process. I have often wondered if every letter arrived at its scheduled destination.

27

During that meeting my father gave me quite a fright. He had eaten part of a Bermuda onion for supper one evening and during the night he was so ill and in such pain that he woke me to ask for prayer. It frightened me very much, but next morning to my great relief he was much improved. Somehow, I had never thought of the possibility of my father being ill. He always seemed to me to be different from ordinary people. When I was about four, I once took a switch to my father's legs. When he said, "Don't, son; it hurts," I was surprised. It had never entered my mind that I could possibly hurt my father.

A successful farmer attended this series of meetings in Iowa, driving ten miles each way in a buggy pulled by a fast pair of broncos. They were tough animals. We went home with him one night after church. I remember how reluctantly I anticipated that long ten-mile drive because I was tired and sleepy. But in half an hour or so we were pulling into the farmer's barnyard. Those ponies had just one gait and that was a fast trot. They kept it up for the full ten miles which pleased me very much.

That same year dad took me to a third meeting with him, held this time in Kansas City, Missouri. This was what we used to call an Assembly Meeting. Today it might be termed an indoor camp meeting since services were held morning, afternoon, and evening. In Kansas City I met people who were to become lifelong friends, among them Lewis Spaw, who was a few years my senior. Lewis had built a railed track clear around the edges of his backyard. He could get in his small flanged-wheeled cart, give himself a slight push, and travel the entire circumference of the yard without stopping. I thought it surely must be one of the seven wonders of the world.

In Kansas City I heard preaching of high calibre and was impressed, even as a child. Some of those preachers were inspired, and their inspiration thrilled me, even though I did not understand all they were saying. It gave me a new attitude toward preachers and preaching in general. For years I thought some of those preachers were but slightly lower than the angels.

Preachers' children have the privilege of meeting many talented and unusual persons, which contributes considerably to their general information and education. In my childhood home, whenever a visiting evangelist or missionary was with us, the table talk was always interesting. A. E. Rather, missionary to the West Indies, talked about far places and projected picture postcards on a screen by means of a "magic lantern." John A. D. Khan, from India, came to our house when I was seven and told us of his country and the strange ways of her people. Khan made a deep impression upon me. Tall, medium dark, he had fine features and was very dignified. He did a great work in India which still stands as a monument to his dedication and intelligence. I've considered going to South India on a preaching mission before long to do what I can to further the work which he began well over half a century ago.

Of course, not all of our visiting ministers and missionaries were this interesting. Some ate too much, slept too much, and talked too much. And not all were saints. Fifty years ago in the Church of God we had no uniform procedure in the church for ordaining ministers. Any preacher could ordain anyone he thought worthy, and at any time. One day, in Clinton, two men I had never seen before came to our home for the explicit purpose of having my father ordain them. Apparently, however, dad knew them better than they thought and softly but firmly declined to do so. This made the two quite unhappy. They stayed on and were persistent, but so was dad, who was also calm and relaxed. Mother was not, for she had to prepare dinner for these strangers and resented it. The men sat, talked, ate dinner, and talked some more. But dad finally got his message across and they left.

Most of our preachers carried small leather cases with them, just large enough to hold their Bible and hymnal. Many churches did not furnish hymn books; the people carried their own copies to and from church for each service. As a small boy, the preachers' book bags were always of interest to me. Some were black, with a snap, but strapless. Some were natural leather with a shoulder carrying strap. Occasionally I would see one with a fancy catch on it made of silver or gold colored metal. I used to carry the visiting preacher's book bag with as much pride as an armor bearer ever felt in carrying a sword for his master. I felt like a preacher when carrying the preacher's equipment.

29

Most traveling preachers also brought to their meetings a large wooden chest full of books which they offered for sale. First, they wished to indoctrinate the people; second, they badly needed a little profit for themselves. These were good-sized boxes measuring three to three and a half feet in length and fifteen to eighteen inches square at the ends. A hasp and padlock secured the contents during shipping. Every preacher hoped by means of such literature to "spread the truth," and *truth* to them was a very important word.

It would be said of a man that "He would not accept the truth." Or, "He is a truth-fighter." We used to talk about people "seeing the truth" or "walking in the light." We would say, "He doesn't see the church," meaning he did not discern the body of Christ or the true nature of the New Testament church. Books were an important help in spreading the truth. People had time to read since there were no radios or television sets and it was a long way to town when you had to go by horse and buggy. Most church people were more seriously concerned with doctrinal matters than they are now. Religious debates between outstanding clergymen were common. My father had books in his library titled *The Riggle-Kessler Debate,* and *The Riggle-Helbling Discussion.* The preacher who lost conclusively in such a debate generally had to relocate, for he would have seriously lost his standing in his community.

When I was still quite young, my father made the trip from Clinton to Anderson, Indiana, to attend our international camp meeting. It must have been about 1912. On his return he brought me the first Bible I ever owned, and I cherished it as one of my most prized possessions. It had my name in gold on the cover. I read the New Testament through within the next few months. The Old Testament took longer, but I kept at it until I had finished the entire Bible. I still have that Book and wouldn't trade it for the most expensive Bible you might offer me. The gift of any Bible is an offer of special knowledge, but that Bible, coming from my father, was to me more precious than gold. He is gone now, but the Bible he gave me has endured for a good sixty years.

Long ago when a certain amount of extremism was in evidence in many religious groups, I always admired my father for his center-of-the-road common sense. He was never a fanatic and never a liberal. There was a time in our movement and others when it was decided by the powers that be that all dress, both for men and women, should be very simple. There were several "hook and eye" denominations who would not tolerate buttons on clothing. Some of our own brethren were affected by this trend and finally decreed that "saved and sanctified" people should not wear neckties. Ties were not necessary, they insisted. They were of no utilitarian good and so were evidently worn for adornment only. And such adornment was worldly. So off came the ties. When the agitation came, dad took off his tie in order not to break with the brethren. When the flurry was over, he put his tie back on, and that was that. I don't think he ever said a word about it from the pulpit, one way or the other.

Although the necktie issue may not have affected him, it certainly affected me. At school the boys would kid me unmercifully. Personally, I couldn't see how a necktie could be a "superfluity of naughtiness," as some claimed, but I didn't want to cause trouble for my father. So I decided on a compromise. I put a tie in my pocket, and then donned it down the alley on my way to school. On the way home I took it off. That solved the problem for me so far as the boys' taunts were concerned.

Many of our preachers, like my dad, never made an issue of the necktie business. A. T. Rowe was one of them. Rowe, who later would serve for years as general manager of our publishing house, was brought up in a conservative area of western Pennsylvania. There, of course, none of the accepted brethren wore ties. But A. T. was young, ambitious, and had a talent for business. One day he answered an ad for a job in a Pittsburgh bank. He was accepted for the position, but there was one catch—they would not hire him unless he put on a tie. After weighing the matter pro and con, Rowe bought a tie and took the job. It caused a small flurry in the area, but the matter soon blew over and was forgotten. Such trifles seem downright silly to us, but in those uneducated, unenlightened times a man could be unfrocked or disfellowshiped just for the "sin" of going against the prevailing opinions of the group.

It seems to me that matters such as this necktie business are often hardest on the children. I was a sensitive child and found it most embarrassing to have to appear different from the rest of the boys. I resented hearing, "Too bad your father is so poor he can't buy you a tie." Or, "Go back home, Dale, you forgot to dress."

Another disputed matter had to do with the use of musical instruments in the church. They simply weren't used in our fellowship. It just wasn't the thing. However, one day as dad was rummaging around in the Swedish Lutheran church we had purchased in Clinton, he came across a well-preserved parlor organ; the kind you pump with your feet. Since Faith, my oldest sister, had been taking piano lessons and was already quite proficient in playing the hymns and gospel songs, my father got a daring idea. It was one thing to say to a congregation, "I want us to raise money to buy an organ for use in our services," but quite another to announce, "I have found a good organ in the back room of our church. If you don't mind, we will put it to good use during our services today." What would happen if he should bring the organ into the sanctuary next Sunday and have Faith accompany our singing?

I don't know of any of our churches where such an innovation had been dared at the time. Always in our church services my father sat up in front facing the congregation. He might announce the page number for a hymn, or more probably he would say, "Does anyone have a selection?" (Worship bulletins were totally unknown.) Someone would call out a number. The song chosen, dad would determine the key (most preachers were forced to take at least a few lessons in the sight reading of music in those days), adjust the slide on his tuning fork, tap the fork on his shoe heel, and lift it to his ear. Giving the congregation the benefit of his information by singing softly from the top down, "Do, sol, mi, do," he would then take off on the melody with the congregation gradually joining in. Nearly all would be singing by the end of the first phrase.

I still remember the saintly old sister who had a favorite song she couldn't hear often enough. When the invitation to suggest a number was extended, she generally beat the whole congregation to the draw by calling out, "Let's sing sixty." So we sang sixty! About sixty times a year it seemed to me.

My father pushed the little parlor organ out into the sanctuary, went over it carefully to be sure the bellows had not been damaged (seemingly quite a tidbit for church mice), repaired a couple of minor items, and gave the instrument a good dusting and oiling. Next Sunday morning Faith took her place, turned to the first song selected, played an introduction, and the congregation sang. Strange to say, I can't remember that one word of criticism followed. Actually, everyone seemed pleased. Dad put his tuning fork away as it was no longer needed. I wonder how many more of our religious "shibboleths" might go down like a set of ten pins if we weren't so afraid of someone's criticism?

Thus encouraged, dad even began to use a choir number now and then. Not that we put the choir on the rostrum! They just sat together down near the organ. Remember, we hadn't used soloists or choirs at all back in the "superfluity of naughtiness" days. It was assumed to be presumtuous for a person to stand up and sing alone. Folk were apt to whisper, sometimes loudly enough for you to hear, "Just who does he think he is?" My father broke that taboo also. We were a singing family and sometimes we would sing a special song before the whole congregation. The ceiling didn't fall. This new musical freedom added to the interest of our services. In fact, the people asked for more. So after a time we were hearing solos, duets, trios, and quartets. "Specials," we called them. Occasionally I still hear a preacher announcing, "John will now bring us a special."

We owned no automobile before 1918; in fact, that year as we left Clinton for Indianapolis, automobiles were just coming into use by our preachers. Most of them had been too poor to own one but World War I lifted the economy. Then, thanks largely to Henry Ford, even the working man could own a car. I well remember the first automobile in which we ever rode. It was a new Regal purchased by Farmer Rummel. I thought it really marvelous as it went chugging off down the country road.

I also remember the old chain-driven Brush which chugged down the street with every dog in the neighborhood barking after it. That Regal had cost Farmer Rummel a good $2,000, which was a great deal of money in 1910. We made a date to meet him at the

Illinois end of the Mississippi bridge, and from the moment the date was made we could think and talk of little else than the coming ride in an automobile.

The Clinton bridge was about a mile long, and it seemed to me we would never get to the other side. Walking was so slow. But finally we arrived and there, to our happiness, stood the gleaming, shining Regal. Farmer Rummel gave the bulb horn a resounding toot. The carbide headlights presented a glassy, brassy stare. A rubber tube led from the lights to a carbide tank securely fastened to a running board. The folding top of the car was down to give us the full benefit of the fresh air. O, happy day! (Remember the fellow who looked at the first train he ever saw and sagely said, "A man couldn't live traveling at thirty miles an hour. It would take away his breath.")

The brass-plated gas and "spark" levers on the Regal were located just under the right side of the steering wheel. Foot-operated accelerators had not yet been invented. A crank projected from the car just in front of the radiator. The handle, when not in use, was housed in a snug leather sleeve fastened by a strap to keep it from swinging back and forth when the car was in motion. In some automobiles, such as the Model T Ford, a choke wire protruded from the lower left front near the radiator, so that as you cranked with your right hand, you could manipulate the choke wire with your left. This combination of cranking and choking was a fine art which differed with every automobile. You had to know just where to set the "spark." You had to know just how far to pull out the choke and how long to hold it there. Hold it too long and you had a flooded carburetor. Hold it too short a time and the motor would cough and die.

And watch that crank! Half of the broken right arms came from cranking automobiles whose spark levers had not been sufficiently retarded. You would grasp the crank firmly, pull out the choke, and give the crank a strong turn. But if the engine backfired, it would reverse the direction of the crank too quickly for you to get your arm out of the way. The crank handle would strike the middle of your forearm and force you to take an unscheduled vacation with your right arm in a sling.

34

One of the first self-starters for automobiles was invented by a Clinton man who replaced the crank with a wheel set in front and just below the radiator. The rim of the wheel was slotted to accept a quarter-inch rope. The end of the rope was knotted through a hole in the wheel; the rope was then run around the circumference of the wheel, through a metal ring, and thence, to the dashboard, where it was fastened through a piece of wood about three inches long. To start the car you sat in the driver's seat, pulled the rope while at the same time tugging on the choke wire, now located on the dash. If you were lucky, the car fired and started. If the car didn't start, you were in trouble since there was no longer any place to put a crank. Of course, you could always have someone give you a push or start you down a hill. In the "good old days" automobiles were quite a problem. One cold winter morning I watched a frustrated neighbor take the crank of his recalcitrant car and beat the fenders into bent tin. But even that didn't start the cold motor. Finally we gave up and rode a streetcar.

Iowa was lovely country with its trees, pasture land, and record-breaking corn crops. As already mentioned, we generally had plenty of snow for skiing and there were ponds, rivers, and creeks frozen over for skating. I thoroughly enjoyed the ice skating. Once when there had been a heavy snow followed by a freezing rain, we awoke in the morning to find an icy crust so thick that we boys could skate on it. Hallelujah! We skated all over town until the crust finally weakened and we began breaking through.

My mother had warned me pointedly never to skate on the Mississippi River. I still don't know why because I had never even asked to skate there. It was a mile from home and there were creeks and ponds much closer. But like the child who is told never to look in the brown box on the top shelf of the closet, I now had to skate on the Mississippi! It really was dangerous. Although the ice was four to six feet thick, a hidden spring or a warmer current might cause a hole to appear. Or the ice might be dangerously thin at that point.

In a contrary mood a friend and I made our way to the frozen Father of Waters one cold morning and skated to our hearts' content. A farmer came along driving a heavy team hitched to a load of hay and crossed on the ice to save the bridge toll. I remember thinking that if a team and load of hay could cross without breaking through we boys were not in any danger. Yet my mother's warning was in the back of my mind. A school chum came walking across the ice, a twelve-gauge shotgun in the crook of his arm. He had seen no rabbits and said he had to hurry home. As he turned to leave he shifted the gun, the trigger caught in his coat sleeve, and the weapon discharged with the sound of a cannon. It frightened me half to death. I was even more frightened when I saw where the shot had gouged out a neat cup in the ice squarely between my feet. I came that close to having a foot shot off! I never told my mother about it, but neither did I skate on the Mississippi again. How come mothers have such long antennae?

At fifteen many boys are enduring a period of perplexity, problems, and difficulties. I was no exception. My high school crowd was a fairly decent lot, but there were a few rebels and also a couple of rascals among them. Students were often sent by the teacher to the high school principal for correction when they misbehaved. Our principal had been a football star in his college days and still had the shoulders to prove it.

One day while perhaps 150 of us were at our books in the large study hall, where old-fashioned seat desks were set up in rows across the room, the door opened suddenly and the principal stepped in. Pausing, he searched for one particular boy who happened to be occupying one of the front seats. He was one of the biggest, orneriest lads in our school. Profane, lewd, and vulgar, he was shunned by many of the boys and most of the girls. I don't know what he had done to deserve the principal's wrath that day, but as we watched, Mr. Yourd located his victim, lifted him bodily out of his seat, up and over the desk, and then gave him a hard shove toward the door. That is the last I ever saw of the boy. The principal hadn't said a word, and no word of explanation ever followed, but the offense must have been quite serious to deserve such violent action.

I am sure there were several good resolutions made by us students that afternoon. Today that kind of disciplinary action would probably result in a lawsuit. But haven't we gone to the opposite extreme in making it illegal for a teacher or a principal to chastise a student who deliberately disobeys the rules?

To make acceptable grades in the Clinton schools was not too difficult. I especially liked mathematics and used to work out unassigned problems in algebra and geometry just for the fun of it. The manual training class was also a weekly pleasure, for there I could work with tools and machinery to make small articles for our home. I also learned to read blue prints, and all through the years in my various pastorates this knowledge has come in handy.

Music was always important to me. Faith had sung in the school choirs, Etha had also done her share and now it was my turn. During our childhood years my father studied harmony and composed gospel songs, some of which were published. "Draw Me Close to Thee," which is still found in our church hymnals, was written while we lived in the little cottage on Olney Avenue. Dad had also studied sight reading and used to go about singing our gospel songs by note. I can still hear his "sol, sol, la, sol, me, do, do, la," as he had in mind, "What a Friend We Have in Jesus." So it was easy for me to pick up the do re mi at an early age, just by listening to him. Long before I could read a book I could sing any tune I knew by note. Someone stood me on a table at age five to sing one of our church songs by note. Whoever it was had given me a nickel to do it. My mother rebuked him, saying this should not be done as I might come to the place where I would refuse to sing without being paid for it!

Our whole family liked to sing. Faith would sit at the old parlor organ (later that brand-new piano) and play hymns and gospel songs by the hour. Sometimes in the evening we would all gather round and sing together. This I always enjoyed. Dad was a tenor, mother a soprano, Etha a soprano, and Faith a good alto. Fred Kleeberger, whom Faith later married, sang a fair bass. Hazel was still too small to sing very much. I generally sang alto just because I loved the "feel" of its harmony. We spent many such evenings singing together and the memory still warms my heart. Why don't families do more of this kind of thing today? It would be far better for them than watching the average television program.

In our school music classes I quickly learned to relate my do re mi with the A B C. But the do re mi had been with me so long that it took priority over the A B C. This caused serious difficulties when I began to take piano lessons. I could not read new music fast enough by the A-B-C method to play it well. The do re mi was too deeply engrained. I encountered the same difficulty in studying the violin, tuba, and slide trombone. However, my sight-reading ability stood me in good stead when I joined vocal groups or was handed a new solo. In any case, I have been grateful to the good Lord for my musical heritage, for it added many satisfactions to my life. All three of my sisters, as well as my wife, play both the piano and organ which has always pleased ne.

My father, born and reared on a farm, never lost his love for gardening. Whenever possible he also had some kind of livestock to care for. Every year dad planted a garden. He generally kept some chickens and sometimes added ducks, pigeons, rabbits, and even guinea pigs. Every spring he planted potatoes on Good Friday, even if it happened to be snowing. Just as regularly he planted hollyhocks along the back fences. To this day I never see hollyhocks in bloom without thinking of my father and how he enjoyed them.

Dad finally retired from the pastorate and purchased a twenty-seven-acre farm down along Big Flat Rock Creek, not far from Rushville, Indiana. Every chicken, duck, sheep, and calf on the place became his devoted pet and followed him all over the farm. It always seemed to me that the corn yield was better when dad planted the seed. The cabbages were larger, the green beans more tender and succulent. He loved the soil. I know it must have hurt him deeply when physical disabilities forced him to sell the farm and move into an apartment.

In Clinton, dad raised a few game chickens, some with spurs so long and sharp that they had to be clipped. He also had Rhode Island Red chickens and New Zealand white rabbits which grew to an enormous size. At one time we even had some pet white rats, but mother made dad get rid of them after one or two got loose and went we didn't know where.

All of which reminds me of the night my youngest sister Hazel was born. We children had been sent off to the neighbors to sleep, as Hazel would be born—not in a hospital—right there at home with the aid of a midwife. Next morning my father came for us. As we walked toward home he said that a surprise awaited our arrival. Curious, we asked, "What is it, papa? What is it?" He smiled and replied, "Something better than a white rat." Hazel, honey, he was absolutely right! Although I'll have to admit you were pretty wrinkled for a day or two.

At thirteen I obtained my first after-school-and-Saturday job at a downtown bookstore in Clinton. The salary was two dollars a week. I swept the place out in the morning, ran errands, took packages to the post office, delivered purchases, and dusted. My next job, paying a bit more money, was with J. R. Bather, a florist, where I learned to transplant flowers and other plants. The Bather delivery man taught me to drive the Model T Ford truck, which I immediately *almost* wrecked, bringing it to a chattering stop within a few inches of another car. At Bather's I also delivered flowers, riding the brand-new-second-hand sixteen dollar bicycle which I paid for at the rate of a dollar a week.

No boy, and I mean *no* boy, ever enjoyed a bicycle more! I *loved* it! Don't tell me you cannot love inanimate objects because I really loved that bicycle! It was the most wonderful object I had ever owned. I washed, polished, and tinkered with it, made my own repairs, and rode it lickety-split with the wind caressing my face. The mile to school was nothing now although I really hadn't minded it before. I had usually run all the way home just for the joy of running. My mother once said that she couldn't remember a time when I walked if it were possible for me to run. I used to go to the YMCA and run two or three miles just for the pleasure of running. I used to dream of running. I outran horses, automobiles, and boys on bicycles. I suppose a psychiatrist might hazard a reason for such dreams, but really, I don't ask for a reason. I simply enjoyed running, and at fourteen outran nearly every lad in the community, once winning a croquet set at a Larkin picnic. Remember the Larkin products? They used to be as common as the Sears-Roebuck catalogs.

Chapter Four

Indiana, Here We Come

LATE IN 1917 my father made a trip to Indianapolis "to see about the work," which meant that he went to look a church over with the idea of moving there as pastor. He discovered, somewhat to his dismay, that the northside church wasn't doing too well.

In fact, the pastor was being forced to abdicate. He was a likeable fellow, an excellent preacher and a good singer, but apparently he had made mistakes in judgment which were now catching up with him. My father was present one day when the pastor answered the phone only to discover that one of his critics was on the line. The former Sunday's sermon had been quite pointed, and the inquirer demanded, "What do you mean by clubbing the Lord's lambs?" To which the pastor wittily replied, "I'm not clubbing the Lord's lambs; I'm dehorning goats."

My father stayed in Indianapolis three months, serving almost without salary, striving to promote tranquility in the church. Meanwhile, I dropped out of school and took a job so the bills at home would not go unpaid. In March of 1918 we moved to Indianapolis. There my father did some of his finest work.

We moved shortly before my fifteenth birthday. Since I could not reenter school until fall, I applied for a job at the Nordyke and Marmon Company, manufacturers of Nordyke flour milling machines and plush Marmon automobiles. Because I was not quite fifteen, it was necessary to obtain a work permit from the Board of Education before Marmon's would hire me. Since Oklahoma could provide me with no birth certificate to prove my age, I had

41

to take our big family Bible downtown to the Board office. It contained clear records of all the births, marriages, and deaths in our family.

I was a bit embarrassed riding the streetcar with the big book on my lap, but it served its purpose. I was given the work permit, and, with the job promised, the next streetcar took me out to Marmon's. World War I was on and the Marmon Company was manufacturing Liberty motors for our fighting airplanes. The factory was heavily guarded. Captain Pope, head of plant security, happened to be at his desk at the office entrance when I arrived. When I explained why I was carrying the big Bible, he suggested with a smile that I wouldn't need it while at work; so I left it in his care. He certainly must have been the most religious guard in the entire plant that day because he sat and read our Bible all afternoon.

Since Indianapolis was booming with war production and the church owned no parsonage, we were hard put to find a suitable place to live. We moved in with the William Feldman family for two weeks and thus began a warm friendship. How kind and hospitable they were, even though we crowded them uncomfortably. William Feldman was a union bricklayer and made good money. Russell and Dorothy were about my age, and during the following summer we enjoyed swimming together at White River beach. There was no serious pollution problem then, but certainly no one would care to swim in White River today. Finally dad located a suitable house, made a down payment, and promised to pay twenty-eight dollars a month on it. We cleaned the pleasant bungalow thoroughly and moved in.

Before very long the old Roach Street church was packed to capacity. Sunday school attendance boomed, running well over the three hundred mark, and offerings were good. The church gave my father his first automobile, a 490 Chevrolet, to help on his pastoral calls. There was a good youth organization in the church and it was well led. There was a better than average choir and I enjoyed singing in it. Four of us fellows formed a quartet and frequently sang in the Sunday evening services. The Sunday school continued to grow until we were crowded out, forcing the trustees to consider plans for relocating.

In 1918 Spanish influenza struck the United States and people died by the thousands. Those were frightening days; fear was everywhere. People wore gauze masks to keep from breathing in the death-dealing germs. Thirty-two funerals entered one gate of Crown Hill cemetery, located a block from our house, in a single day. A person could be in robust health one day and dead the next. It was like the black plague I had read about in my history books. Public meetings were forbidden. My father conducted funerals from front porches with the people standing on sidewalks and lawns. He buried many but never contracted the disease. I did and for ten days was very ill. During the period of my recovery I went for a walk in the spring sunshine, over-tired myself, and went back to bed for another two weeks. This time I barely made it. I was delirious with fever. But through the mercy of the Lord I finally recovered.

Spy scares were everywhere during the war. Anyone of German extraction who spoke English brokenly feared constantly that he would be hailed into the police station for interrogation. I rode to town one day in a "jitney bus" with such a fellow. He had been summoned by the police for a hearing. He kept saying over and over, "I haven't done anything. I haven't done anything." Mass hysteria unbalanced some of the people.

They quit calling sauerkraut by its proper name and dubbed it liberty cabbage. Pastors damned the Kaiser from their pulpits and prayed God to destroy all the Germans. Some of the young men from our church went marching off to war and a few didn't come back. So dad was faced with serious problems, many having to do with the grief, loneliness, and heartaches of his people. When military men did return, serious readjustments often had to be made in their family relationships. My father worked hard, kept his poise, never complained, and was never ill. His energy always seemed sufficient for the hour. His sermons were simple, but helpful, and the people felt the warmth of his love and the depth of his concern. He was a good shepherd of the sheep.

Then the war was over. "The Armistice" they called it. Whistles blew and sirens sounded. Factories closed and the workers rode inside, outside, and topside of the streetcars in order to get to town to celebrate. The Indianapolis business district was bedlam. The people laughed and cried. Strangers hugged and kissed each other. Some beat on drums or tin pans and danced in the streets. Sighs of relief went up from the hearts of those whose sons, brothers, or husbands were still in Europe. The war was over and all of us gave fervent thanks to God.

In spite of the restricted wartime economy, the Church of God had been able to build a large frame auditorium on our international convention grounds in Anderson, Indiana. It had cost $25,000, which seemed an enormous sum at the time, and would seat 6,000 persons. In June we traveled the forty miles from Indianapolis to enjoy the ten-day camp meeting. I slept in a small tent along what is now Third Street, but which was then the right of way for the interurban trolley line running between Anderson and Muncie.

My tent was equipped with a wooden bedstead made of two-by-fours and one-by-sixes. A set of somebody's discarded bedsprings was topped with a straw tick which had drawn dampness from the rains. Bed linens and quilts had been brought from home. Of course, a fifteen-year-old boy can generally sleep just about anywhere, and I would have done quite well had it not been for the motormen who operated the interurban cars. Just as they were racing past our tent area they would blow those deafening electric horns, which were almost enough to raise the dead in nearby East Maplewood Cemetery. At two o'clock in the morning it was a shattering experience.

The camp meeting was a very interesting affair for me. I had never seen such large crowds at a church gathering. Five or six thousand would stream into the big new tabernacle for services. How they sang! With no organ and no public address system, the singing was still wonderful. Professor H. C. Clausen of the Bible Training School was in charge of the music. I never dreamed that two years later I would be leading that same audience in congregational singing.

Sermons were often an hour long—sometimes an hour and a half. When a person tired or became bored with some uninspired preacher's message, he generally got up and walked out. Many

44

preachers had voices which were too weak to be clearly heard in such a large building. Hundreds walked out on them. In those "good old days" I once saw about two-thirds of the audience walk out on a speaker whose terminal facilities were faulty. No wonder many a preacher trembled as he waited to enter that pulpit. Three strikes and you were out!

Years later when I was frequently invited to speak to this great gathering, I often wondered if the people would always stay with me. Would I ever experience the sinking sensation which comes to a man when his listeners walk out on him? Then came that never-to-be-forgotten Sunday morning when it happened! The auditorium was full. Following a good song service, I was perhaps ten minutes into my message when the people began walking out. By the dozens! Down every aisle in the place! I was shocked and puzzled. Was my sermon that bad? I had thought I was getting along fairly well. But facts are facts and the people were walking out on me!

So, you can imagine my great relief when the chairman, Dr. W. E. Reed, interrupted to announce that one of the nearby dormitories was on fire. Honestly, *I* didn't set that camp meeting on fire! It was done by an electrical heating gadget which someone had forgotten to turn off in one of the rooms. After the situation had been explained, the audience settled down and heard me out. But for those few awful minutes I experienced what it feels like to have people walk out on you. Dear Lord, please don't ever let it happen to me again!

Early in June of 1919, when I was sixteen, Carl Struckman, a young married man with whom I had swum, fished, and sung, invited me out to his house one evening to help work on his anti-quated roadster. He wished to get it in condition for the trip over to the Anderson meetings. I hadn't been living as I should and went to Struckman's not only with a guilty conscience, but also with a desire to do something about it. After finishing our work Carl and I went for a long walk during which I purposely switched the conversation to religion. My heart was hungry for peace. I had carried the burden of condemnation too long. Carl finally took the hint. When we returned to his garage it was to get down on our knees and pray. Very simply I asked the Lord to forgive my sins and make me his child. Then, because I knew the Bible promised, "If we confess our sins, he is faithful and just to forgive us our sins, and to cleanse us from all unrighteousness" (1 John 1:9), I accepted that word as being valid, exercised faith for salvation, and arose from my knees a new person. It was just that simple. I felt no particular emotion in this new experience. I just knew that if I would repent and believe, God would, for his beloved Son's sake, forgive me. And he did! That night my life was changed and I have been serving the Lord ever since.

The following September, having had only two years of high school, I entered Anderson Bible Training School, which was beginning its third year. Although I was really too young for such serious theological training, I managed finally to graduate from their two-year course of study.

Chapter Five

Cutting
The Apron Strings

THAT SAME FALL of 1919 as I entered school at Anderson, a young teacher from Missouri arrived to become principal of ABTS. I was sixteen; he was twenty-six. John Arch Morrison was a handsome young fellow with a beautiful head of black wavy hair. He carried himself with the dignity he felt his position required. Little did either of us realize that Dr. John would serve as president of Anderson College for thirty-nine years, teaming up with Dean Russell Olt to lead that institution to full North Central Accreditation and also to establish a graduate school of religion. Dr. Morrison made a tremendous contribution to youth and to the Church of God in general down through the years.

As a Bible school student I found myself living away from home for the first time. This is a crucial period in the life of any young person. Even when home ties are strong, it is difficult for a youth fully to appreciate the value of his earlier training until he has been removed from the immediate area of parental control.

However, I enjoyed my newfound freedom and the privilege of being more of a person in my own right. Preachers' sons are so often apt to be judged by their fathers' accomplishments rather than by their own abilities. Much of the rebellion among young people today stems from their desire to be persons, not just shadows of their parents. They want to be more than a name or a number. Each of us was born with an inherent urge to find a meaningful existence. We all wish, down deep inside, to make some significant contribution to life. We want to feel that we make a difference in the sum total of things. We want to be loved and we want someone upon whom we can bestow affection.

In these days of exploding populations, more and more young people are striking out at life in an effort to achieve a personality which is truly and distinctly their own. No young man wants to be known chiefly as "Tom's son," or a young girl as "Mary's daughter." Yet, in the midst of its youthful inexperience and its impatience with "the institution," the younger generation sometimes discards values of proven worth. It is one thing to aspire to be a person; everyone has the inherent right to live his own life, but to intrude on the rights of others in order to achieve that end is wrong.

I was the youngest member of the ABTS student body and understandably immature. But the group accepted me, for the most part, and I was soon caught up in a full round of curricular and extracurricular activities. There was the Literary Society, where we met monthly in what was really a talent contest. Participants sang, played musical instruments, and recited humorous or serious readings. Sometimes the performances went well but often they were not particularly commendable. I was scheduled to appear in one of the sessions as a soloist but from the moment I accepted the invitation I worried about it. Soloing before that critical group would be a new and risky adventure. The prospect filled me with anxiety. I finally chose a song, learned it well, and then awaited the crucial evening.

The night before the meeting of the Literary Society brought with it a full moon, and this, combined with the warm evening breezes did something to me, and also to my good friend, Laude Clark. Weren't such spring evenings created for strolling? Laude and I decided to take advantage of the occasion. After walking slowly north to the edge of Anderson, we kept right on going. It was simply too glorious a night to think of returning to dormitory rooms. The farther the night advanced the more brightly the moon shone, so on we walked and talked.

The hour for returning to the dormitory passed and we joked about being locked out for the night. It really didn't worry us. In fact it didn't worry us as much as it should have. Finally, we returned to the campus at five o'clock in the morning. We sat on a bench until the doors were unlocked at six, then washed up, ate breakfast, and went to our classes where I immediately became very, very drowsy.

At long last classes were over for the day and there was time for rest, but I dared not sleep because afternoon naps invariably roughed up my singing voice. I doubt very much if that or any other Literary Society ever listened to a solo from a sleepier singer. However, fifty years later as I type this I can still feel the warm softness of the night breezes and see the brilliant moonlight flooding the road which runs from Anderson north toward Alexandria.

Not every student who stayed out after hours was content to spend the remainder of the night on a campus bench. There was a way by which late entrance could be gained, but the night watchman making his hourly rounds had to be circumvented. Our four-story dormitory was equipped with iron fire escapes, whose lowest ladders dropped to within about eight feet of the ground. An athletic (or frightened) student found it not too difficult to leap up, lay hold on the lower rung of the ladder, and pull himself up to the first landing. After that he could climb the steps to his particular floor, and, with luck or by prior arrangement with his roommate, enter the unlocked fire-escape window and stealthily make his way to his room.

But you had to have things timed out just right, or "Scotty," the night watchman would catch you. You couldn't always trust Scotty to be where he was supposed to be as he made his rounds. He seemed to draw genuine pleasure from outsmarting the boys. This peculiarity made late entrances a form of gambling and, as I remember it, Scotty's win-and-loss average was considerably in his favor. He would turn your name in to the office and next day you would be standing on the president's green carpet trying to explain why you had been so brash as to violate such good, solid, sensible rules. Three strikes and you were out. I mean, three times on that carpet and you would be sent home!

In those days of "bitter herbs and unleavened bread," the rules governing contacts between young men and women students were very strict. They would seem unbelievably so to the youth of this generation. You were not permitted to stroll down the street with a girl for ice cream at the drugstore. In fact, you couldn't walk anywhere with a girl at any time or for any reason except possibly through the halls to classes.

If you met a girl student by chance on the street during a downpour, you didn't dare ask her to share your umbrella. To date a girl you asked permission of the matron, then met your date in one of the dormitory parlors while the matron sat in the adjoining room with large, open double doors between. Large, open eyes and ears, also. You may be sure that this setup had a definite tendency to inhibit the flow of any meaningful conversation between boy and girl. The matron could hear even the most softly whispered word. In addition, on beautiful Sunday afternoons made by the good Lord for young couples to stroll together, this matron seemed not at all embarrassed to sit on the front porch, binoculars in hand, in an effort to identify and apprehend those who dared to meet and walk together in the adjacent cemetery.

At the ripe old age of sixteen I came to the conclusion that rules of this nature were downright silly and manifestly unfair to young people in general. So I began to break them frequently, regularly, and without, I fear, a proper feeling of guilt. In fact the girl who lived just across the street from the campus was so cooperative that we managed to spend an hour or so together about five evenings a week. It was inevitable that we should be found out but I had not expected it to happen as it did.

Fifty years ago every city of any size had its lecture or concert series during the winter months. This time the series was being presented in the large First Methodist church downtown. My date and I cautiously made our way up a side stairway to the comparative privacy of a far balcony and were thus shielded from being seen by most of the audience below. We expected to find other students in the balcony, but it never occurred to us that any of the faculty would choose to sit there. After being seated my friend and I sat in animated conversation for some minutes. Then she became strangely silent and I noticed a peculiar expression on her face. As she pointed, I saw that sitting directly in front of us was the matron and her husband. No doubt they had been listening with extreme interest to every word we had said.

So next day, to the president's office I went again, a place which was taking on a more and more familiar appearance. I can still see him sitting behind his desk looking at me, at the floor, and then out the window. He allowed me to wait for some time before speaking. Then he said, "Dale, you are a disappointment to me. Since you have stood here before to answer for similar misdemeanors, I must warn you that if there is a next time I will have no choice but to send you home." "Yes, sir!" I replied and was dismissed. Inside of two weeks I was standing on that same spot again.

Let me explain. Again there had been a beautiful moonlit evening with its invitation to stroll the countryside. What else was there to do, except study? And only bookworms would be caught studying on such an evening. We fellows had no automobiles, not even bicycles. All types of "worldly" amusements were out of bounds. But who could forbid seven young men the delight of strolling together under such a brilliant night sky?

Everything would have gone along properly and well had not two of our seven been endowed with extremely active imaginations. After strolling out East Tenth Street we were in open country with a pasture to our right and a large cornfield to the left. Next to the cornfield was a wooded area deeply shadowed. It was here that our two more-imaginative classmates broke the monotony of mere strolling. They discovered how to liven things up a bit. When I saw what they were about, I climbed the fence and disappeared into the woods. I turned to watch just as one of the lads lay down by the side of the highway as if he had been injured. His companion immediately stepped forward to flag down a passing car. When the motorist had slowed almost to a stop, the lad on the ground jumped up; then both boys shouted and waved their arms. The startled driver stepped on the gas and left in a hurry.

The boys thought their prank to be very funny. Frankly, so did I. We all laughed hilariously, yet warned the two that they were asking for trouble. It was such fun, however, that they repeated

51

their performance two or three times. But, when headlights were seen approaching from town at high speed, we all hid in the cornfield. The car stopped; then turned slowly about as its lights searched us out. At long last it went back to town. Even so, we fellows cut north through the cornfield into another wooded area where we frightened a very surprised young man and woman who quickly ran. We returned to school before lockup time and in all innocence made our way to our rooms. It had been good fun!

Next morning all seven of us were summoned to the office. Dr. J. T. Wilson, acting head of the school, sat behind his desk, an ominous expression on his face. At the end of the desk was J. A. Morrison, his new assistant. Dr. Wilson was slender and about six feet and two inches tall. In very serious tones he declaimed on how unbecoming it was for ministerial students to conduct themselves in such a brash manner. Among other things, he said, "Now, I am a minister and you are ministers. (I don't think any of the seven had ever delivered a sermon.) What would you think of me if I had been seen out there on the road frightening drivers as you did last night?"

Well, I got tickled. I could just see this tall, dignified man lying by the roadside, then jumping up and yelling his head off at some startled motorist. It was too much, and I nearly broke up the meeting with a snicker, which didn't help our cause any. We were all campused, but later in the day I received a note requesting that I come to Dr. Morrison's office. As I stood before his desk, exactly where I had stood before, he said sternly, "Dale, I do hate to send you home. It would break your father's heart and hurt your mother deeply. I declare, I don't know what to do with you. What would you suggest?"

Frankly, I was willing to call the whole thing off and go back to class, but he seemed to have other plans. Yet, when he said "What do you suggest?" I felt he was taking a new approach to an old problem. It was more like man to man conversation instead of teacher to boy. I grew up a bit during that moment and finally said, "If you will not send me home, I solemnly promise not to get into any kind of trouble again as long as I am a student here." My ears could scarcely believe what my mouth was saying.

After this ordeal with the powers that be, the "Lucky Seven" (we should have changed the name right there) got together for a bull session. We had to know how the president found out about our mischief. At long last someone reported that one of the cars the boys had flagged down had been driven by Dr. Morrison.

It has often concerned me to think what might have resulted had Dr. John sent me home that day. Certainly it would have hurt my parents deeply, but it might also have sidetracked my entire career. I was standing that day on the crest of a great divide. Had I been sent to the left instead of to the right I might, in bitterness, have turned forever from the work of the church. For this and other reasons I still hold in my heart warm memories of Dr. John and thank God for the patience, good sense, and mercy he manifested in dealing with a sixteen-year-old boy.

To me, music was an important part of the curriculum at Anderson Bible Training School. First of all, we had a fairly good choral group sparked by soprano Mona Moors, who later served years in India as a missionary. Burd Barwick, later to become Mrs. B. E. Warren number three following the death of Lottie Charles Warren, was one of our best altos. John H. Kane and John Settlemyre were anchor men in the bass section. I helped to form a male quartet which consisted of Charles Smith, first tenor; I sang second tenor; Homer Byers (son of songwriter A. L. Byers) baritone; and John Settlemyre, bass. We didn't set the world on fire but did receive many calls to sing in church services.

One day the quartet was asked to sing at a funeral to be conducted in Elwood, Indiana, twenty miles from Anderson. Herman Borgers volunteered to transport us in his trusty Model T Ford sedan. North from Anderson, in Alexandria, a railroad cuts across the highway obliquely. As we approached the crossing, Herman looked back, or southwest—the hard way—but I looked northeast just in time to see a train bearing down on us at full speed. I cried, "Look out!" and Herman turned the wheels of the car to the right into the curb. The train tore by at great speed, missing us by not more than three feet. My heart was beating like a triphammer. This was probably the closest brush I have ever had with death.

53

We arrived at the church to discover that the imported minister for the occasion was a gray-haired man in his seventies. He was sitting on one of the large clergy chairs, his equally aged wife by his side. The service began, we sang, the Scriptures were read, we sang again, and the preacher preached. And preached. And preached some more. On and on he went in evangelistic style for an hour and a half! This was bad enough, but when he sat down his wife arose and exhorted the congregation for another forty-five minutes. I thought she was going to give an altar call before she sat down. It was winter and the days were short. When we finally emerged from the church to go to the cemetery it was already getting dark. Most funeral directors have learned to be calm and collected, but this one nearly had a stroke. Never have I seen such an angry mortician. But, as I remember it, the blood-pressure of Herman Borgers was also considerably above normal.

On our international convention grounds which bordered the campus was a large dining hall used only during our summer meetings. The interior was unfinished, the ceilings high, and the building was unheated. On the second floor was a dormitory for the use of convention visitors. Our school officials obtained permission to use the dining hall as a gymnasium. This pleased me very much as I have always enjoyed participation in competitive sports. Soon we were playing basketball a couple of evenings a week. I was a forward on the first team our school ever organized.

Our "gym" was used chiefly by the students, but on one or two nights a week any man from the school or Warner Press could come for exercise. From Warner Press came the longtime treasurer, N. H. Byrum. He was then in middle life and certainly not an athlete, but he played for exercise and recreation. However, a captain, choosing up sides for a game of basketball, would not have chosen Byrum first.

Since the gym was unheated and N. H. Byrum was completely bald, his wife made him a blue calico cap fitted with an elastic band to hold it in place. Byrum wore it unself-consciously, joking about his "turban." We had just five players on our team, which meant there were no substitutes. Aden Guilder, H. G. (Grady) Montague, Lawrence Hatch, and John Settlemyre (my roommate) were the other members of the team. We often played the Warner Press team, some of the members of which were Clarence Patterson, Myrl Byrum, Bill Bowser, Everett Boyer, and I think, Clarence Peyton.

Martin Odell also played with them, and it was my job to guard him. I hated to be pitted against Martin, not only because he was a good player but because more than once Martin's foot managed to trip me up. He was clever at it and seldom had fouls called on him. One night he caused me to fall hard and it hurt. As I rose to my feet I told him to be on guard because I was going to return the favor. A few minutes later Martin was charging down the floor dribbling the ball at full speed. I was after him. I managed to touch his heel with my toe just enough to cause his foot to hook behind the other. Down he went, all six feet of him, hitting the floor with a thud. Martin had a temper in those days and was bigger than I. I wasn't sure just how he would react. But he got up smiling and said, "Well, you did!" and that was that! But it bothered my conscience and I later apologized to him. I don't think he ever tripped me again. We are still good friends. Martin retired from Warner Press recently, having served two or three years beyond the usual retirement age of sixty-five because he was a good pressman and his services were needed. After retirement he went out to Bay Ridge Christian College in Texas to teach young black boys the art of printing.

Psychology was an infant area of study in 1920. It was not considered to be a subject of very great importance in our school. Dr. Morrison taught the first class in psychology ever offered there and I was in it. I doubt if he had ever taken a course in the subject, but he was intelligent and always managed to keep a chapter or two ahead of the class. The course stirred our curiosity and we all developed a desire to understand ourselves and the workings of the human mind.

About this time a phrenologist named Hanson appeared on campus. Students by the dozen flocked to have the bumps on their heads interpreted in terms of their personalities at a dollar a head. The phrenologist was blunt and spoke in plain language. After letting us in on our good points, he informed us just as glibly of our shortcomings. His frankness left some of us in a state of discouragement because we took everything he said as being the gospel truth. He didn't stay around very long, but he left a group of young people more determined to improve themselves. For this I suppose we all should be thankful. In the months that followed I would look in the mirror and examine the contour of my head to see if any radical changes in conformation had taken place. Finally I gave the whole thing up as a bad job and forgot it. So far as I know, all the original bumps and hollows are still there today.

I wonder what happened to that phrenologist? and to phrenology? Isn't it strange how much hocus-pocus can be presented as a science to trap the gullible? I suppose there have always been witch doctors, and probably always will be. Along the highway not too many miles from where I live a nice new brick home is being constructed to replace a ramshackle cottage which was about to fall down. Do you know who lives there? A palm reader. In front is a big sign showing the palm of a hand and underneath in big letters is the word *Adviser*. Business must be good or the advisor couldn't afford that nice new brick house. P. T. Barnum is credited with once saying: "Never give a sucker an even break."

One of the music classes at school was given over to a study of evangelistic music: how to plan the program and lead a large congregation in singing. Professor H. C. Clausen was quite well qualified to teach this class, which I attended with interest and profit. Sometime during the semester each student had to get up before the class, announce a hymn, nod to the pianist, and attempt to get all the group to begin and end at the same time. I enjoyed the whole adventure very much, probably because there was a bit of show-off in my nature. There may still be. Anyhow, when my time came to direct I was not afraid although I had seen some of the others shake with nervousness as their turn came.

The end of the school year arrived just a few days before the beginning of our big international camp meeting. To me it still is a camp meeting in spite of all the efforts that have been made to turn it into a convention. Hundreds of people still camp on the grounds in tents, campers, and trailers.

One day as Professor Clausen was giving me a voice lesson he stopped to say, "Dale, I think you have advanced in song leading enough to help me during the big camp meeting. As you know, it is a ten-day affair, and with three general services a day it is too much of a job for one person to undertake. I'd like for you to alternate with me and take every other service."

It was quite an assignment for a seventeen-year-old boy. I may not have been afraid to lead singing before a music class but this was a different matter. Although it challenged me, it also frightened me to a certain degree. I had seen one or two men make a mess of the job. With no public-address system you had to command the audience or soon that vast congregation would begin to seesaw and the situation would get hopelessly out of hand. I had seen Professor Clausen, on more than one occasion, rap loudly on the pulpit with his baton right in the middle of a stanza, stop the whole congregation of five thousand persons or more, admonish them to watch more closely, and then start the stanza over again. I didn't want that to happen to me. So, it was with a certain amount of apprehension that I consented to assist the professor, asking only that he would appoint for me a pianist who was heavy on the keys and had a good sense of rhythm. This he agreed to do.

Thus I began my major work as a song leader. What a thrill it was to lead those thousands of people in singing the great hymns and gospel songs which are our Christian heritage! I am still deeply grateful to Professor Clausen for his training and for the opportunity he gave me to serve at such an early age.

In the meantime my father was beginning to feel that his work in Indianapolis was just about done. Since we had come from Oklahoma, where he still felt much at home, he decided to make a trip out there to investigate a pastorate which happened to be open. Perhaps he would also conduct a week or two of evangelistic meetings before returning. Because of the latter possibility he decided to take me along.

In 1920 it was a two-day trip by train. We sat up all the way to save money and I was tired when we arrived at our destination. After being assigned to our room I slept soundly all night. I took a nap the next morning and another in the afternoon but still was drowsy in church during the evening. The dry Oklahoma breezes were refreshing and restful. When things did not open up for dad in Oklahoma, he returned to Indianapolis.

I stayed on in Oklahoma City and worked for an oil refinery the rest of the summer. I hired in on the labor gang. The work was hot and dirty. We dug ditches, cleaned crude oil out of tanks that had been emptied, and did pipe fitting. At the end of eight hours my coveralls were oily and grimy. I would swish them up and down in a five-gallon can of gasoline to rid them of the sludge. At noon a neat little restaurant across the street, where lunch cost forty-five cents, served a wonderful Irish stew. My straw boss was a six-foot Irishman named Kelly, who had spent seven years in the penitentiary for killing a man. Since he still retained an obstinate disposition and fiery temper, I never crossed him. However, as he was not unreasonable in his work demands, we got along quite well.

One day we turned off the master valve on a four-inch pipeline in order to change a connection. This pipe came straight up out of the ground. After we removed the cap, someone, not realizing the pipe was open, set the pump to running. Immediately there gushed forth a geyser of their most highly refined oil. It began to spread a golden flow all over the ground. We called for the pump to be stopped but no one heard except the boss, who came running. He commanded the Irishman, "Cap that pipe!" Since to do so meant being deluged with oil, Kelly shot back, "Cap it yourself!" The foreman closed his eyes, stooped over that golden spouting stream and finally managed to screw the cap into place. He was a sight. His hat had been knocked off and oil was streaming from his hair and face. Gruffly he called, "Give me a rag!" Maliciously the Irishman handed him a cloth black with oil with which he mopped his head and face. You should have seen him then! Mad as a wet hen. When he could see, he reached down, picked up his soggy, oil-soaked hat, and without a word headed for the bathhouse. To my surprise he never mentioned the incident, but I can still see his grimy face and matted hair dripping with oil and black-slimy sludge. Such are the joys of being foreman in an oil refinery!

Because wages were low and room, board, and transportation costly, I had saved little money with which to begin the new school year; nevertheless, the summer had been educational. I learned enough about pipe fitting to be of help at home tasks all through the intervening years.

Our Oklahoma State camp meeting was held in Oklahoma City that summer of 1920 in a big tent on Capitol Hill. The imported speaker was Dr. H. M. Riggle, one of our most successful evangelists. The song leader was big, rotund G. E. Wright, a preacher, singer, and composer. Both men were popular and the meetings drew large crowds. Wright asked me to assist in the music and I was happy to do so. I had been taught to use a baton in directing congregational singing. The one I owned was of aluminum and had been made for me by a friend. One day as I was leading, the baton struck a low-hanging light bulb which exploded with a bang. It was an unscheduled sound effect which amused the people, embarrassed me, but did not cause a pause in the singing. For years afterward, some chairman in introducing me would suggest that for the safety of the people perhaps the light fixtures ought to be elevated another foot or two.

Among the young people with whom I associated that summer was a personable young man whose company I enjoyed very much. Red-haired, with a quick smile, he made friends easily. But he was not a Christian and I very much wanted him to become one. During an evening service while the invitation was being given, I put a hand on his shoulder and pled with him to surrender his life to Christ. He was under deep conviction and almost made the step. At last, however, he drew back saying, "I know I ought to but I just can't make it tonight." Next day his mother reproved me for bothering her son saying, "Let him alone. Every young man has to sow a few wild oats. He'll come to Christ later on." Fifty years rolled by but her boy never made the surrender. He died a few years ago. It came to me that had his mother been a wiser Christian her son's life might have been vastly different. He made a great deal of money during that half-century. But what shall it profit a man if he gains the whole world and loses his own soul?

59

When school opened in Anderson that fall, one of the new students was Steele C. Smith, from Vandergrift, Pennsylvania, with whom I was to establish a lifelong friendship. Steele was an affable, good-looking young fellow, and a perceptive student. Although he didn't appear to be particularly ambitious at the time, this certainly corrected itself during the years that followed. Steele's popularity was enhanced by his bright red Oldsmobile roadster. One other student had a Model T Ford, but as I remember it, the rest of us ordinary folk either walked or rode bicycles.

Steele further ingratiated himself by inviting me to drive when out with him. Steele C. Smith went on to Harvard, served a few years as pastor of our Capitol Hill church in Oklahoma City, and then moved back to Anderson to join forces with our Board of Church Extension and Home Missions. Afterward he transferred to Warner Press, where for many years before his retirement in 1967 he served as president and general manager of our publishing house. Incidentally, during a visit he and his wife made to our Florida home a few years ago, on all our side trips I had. to drive his Cadillac. So, he is still the executive; getting other people to do things for him.

The chief delight during my second year at ABTS was the production of "Ruth, The Gleaner." It was my first cantata and I enjoyed every minute of it. The fortissimo climaxes with the choir at full volume gave me a tremendous thrill. I was given a baritone solo part at which I worked for weeks. A few days before we were to present the cantata something happened to our bass soloist. Professor Clausen asked me to assume his part, also. I can still sing many passages of "Ruth, The Gleaner" from memory.

Chapter Six

My Ministry Begins

IN JUNE of 1921, with my schooling behind me, I made known my availability as an evangelistic singer. Moving my few belongings to Huntington, Indiana, where my father was then pastor, I more or less patiently waited for the world to beat a path to my door. But the path threatened to grow up in weeds for lack of use. I took a job in the country with a threshing crew and stayed with the Earlywine family.

Our crew first harvested the neighborhood wheat, rye, and then the oats. The work was hard on an eighteen-year-old, fresh from school, even though athletics had kept me in good physical condition. My job was to pitch bundles of grain from the ground to the wagon. The modern combine had not yet been invented. On that first day I found muscles I had never known existed, and that night I slept very little. The sore muscles and sunburn combined to make me utterly miserable. But in a day or two my screaming muscles firmed up, and I began to enjoy the work and the fellowship with the men. Always hungry, I also relished the huge dinners which the farm women were forced by custom to serve to threshing crews. The Earlywines and their farm will always have a fond place in my book of memories.

About the first of August I received a penny postal card (you wouldn't believe that postal cards ever sold for a penny, would you?) inviting me to participate in an evangelistic series to be held in Hinton, West Virginia. The card was from R. C. Caudill, of whom we had never heard, but in my situation that made little difference. I wanted to go. However, I had no money with which to purchase a railroad ticket. When I wrote my acceptance, I was forced to add that money would be needed for train fare. A few days later a letter arrived containing a check for twelve dollars and I was on my way. But since twelve dollars wouldn't take me all the way to Hinton, I bought a ticket only to Huntington, West Virginia.

Alighting from the train there, suitcase in hand, I stood wondering what to do. Finally, I called the pastor of our Huntington church and R. B. Roan took me to his home for the night. I was happy with his hospitality and happier still to learn that he was treasurer of the West Virginia Evangelistic Association, although, as I would discover later its name was much more impressive than its treasury. The Roans gave me supper, lodging, and breakfast, and then furnished me with a ticket to Hinton.

Since the Church of God had no congregation in Hinton, we were being brought in to establish one. A forty-by-sixty-foot tent had been erected on a nearly level lot in that very unlevel country, just a couple of blocks above the New River which ran parallel to the Cheasapeake and Ohio railroad yards. Those were the days of coal-burning locomotives. The black smoke used to roll up the hillside and fill the house in which we were lodged. To add to our problem, the lady of the house had died some months previously and housekeeping was being done by a relative who came in once or twice a week. It was quite a trying experience for me. My bed was furnished with just one sheet. I remember turning that sheet over every few days, saying to myself that it couldn't possibly be that sooty on the other side. My only cover on those August nights was a wool blanket.

To add to my discomfort, we seldom ate except when invited out, which to my way of thinking wasn't nearly often enough. In addition to all this, R. C. Caudill didn't show up until a week after services were under way. He said he was delayed by the birth of a child.

In any case, Ronceverte's pastor, I. P. Hamrick, filled the pulpit during that first week. I thought him to be quite an interesting person. He was six feet seven inches tall and invariably wore a long-tailed preacher's coat. In the two months we worked together

I never saw him without that long-tailed coat, even in his own home. He had an older one which he wore when doing stable chores, such as milking his cow. Brother Hamrick was a sincere, godly man, and had done untold good while traversing the West Virginia mountains holding meetings in schoolhouses, churches, and private homes. Many were won to Christ through his ministry. Born and reared in the mountains, he possessed a native intelligence and a pleasing sense of humor. If I remember correctly, his ancestors had lived in the area for one hundred fifty years or more. His background and experiences were of a nature so in contrast to my own that his conversation was especially interesting.

I. P. Hamrick married under rather unusual circumstances. One day while walking past a small farm, he saw a girl working in a garden. It was toward evening and he stopped at the house and asked if they would put him up for the night. Hospitality was cordially extended and soon he and the family were partaking of a good meal together. Afterward in the living room, young Hamrick said to the man of the house, "I have something to discuss with you. Today, as I passed by the garden and saw your daughter, I was impressed that she is to be my wife. I believe the impression is from the Lord and would like your approval to marry her."

His host thought the matter over for a minute or two and then replied, "Well, if the Lord is leading in that direction, you have my permission if it is all right with my daughter." The daughter seemed pleased with the turn of events and with little hesitation gave her consent. They were wedded soon afterward and, strangely enough, the marriage worked out very well.

Shortly afterward young Hamrick opened a small country store which turned out to be one of those nonprofit business enterprises, although he hadn't planned it that way. Hamrick had insured the building for $1500. Now, with business so poor he found himself dreaming of what could be done with that amount of money if something should "happen" to the store. Psychologists say that "whatever gets your attention finally gets you." So one night, without disturbing his wife, Hamrick crept from the house, set fire to the store, and then stealthily crept back into bed. Sometime later, when neighbors came beating upon his door to tell him of the fire, he seemed appropriately sleepy and surprised. After accepting neighborly sympathy over the "disaster," he wrote out a claim and mailed it to the insurance company. In a week or two he was patting his billfold wherein nestled a check for $1500.

However, my friend Hamrick did not live happily ever after. It became increasingly difficult for him to sleep at night. His slumbers were often interrupted by anxiety dreams in which burning buildings played a prominent part. So the $1500 gave him scant comfort. Hamrick's wife blamed his sleeplessness on the loss of his business and sought to redirect his thoughts and energies, but peace still evaded him.

I. P. Hamrick had always been somewhat of a religious person. Certainly he knew right from wrong, and now his conscience was giving him an enormous amount of trouble. Memory of how he had defrauded the insurance company made him especially uncomfortable in church. The preacher's every word now seemed directed individually to him. Finally, Hamrick realized that his only hope for peace was in confession. But to confess would lead to arrest and probably to a heavy fine, even imprisonment. What could he do? The pressure was really on. At last he could stand it no longer. Surrendering his life to Christ, he wrote a letter to the insurance company confessing what he had done. He concluded by saying that the good Lord had forgiven and saved him and he had decided "it would be better to go through the penitentiary to heaven than around it to hell."

To his vast relief he was told that if he would refund the $1500 the insurance company would not prosecute. This transformed him into a very happy man. This experience of forgiveness, as he told about it in his sermons, gave him rapport with many whose consciences were also bothersome, enabling him to lead them to Christ.

R. C. Caudill finally arrived at Hinton to take over the preaching responsibilities. There was something striking in the man's appearance. He had sandy hair and his deep-set eyes were piercingly sharp. Born in the bluegrass region of Kentucky, he was a typical product of his environment. During World War I he worked for the government in Washington as a telegrapher, sending and receiving messages eight hours a day. When the war ended, he settled down with his wife and the first of their children on a little farm near Indian Fields, Kentucky, and took employment as a telegrapher for the Louisville and Nashville Railroad Company. An excellent operator, he nevertheless jeopardized his job by drinking a quart or so of whiskey a day. R. C. hunted and fished, put out a few crops on his small acreage, and worried his wife with his conduct.

But again a godly heritage proved its value. At long last R. C. Caudill bowed at an old-fashioned altar of prayer, repented of his sins, and was born again. It was a miracle. His conversion was a great loss to Satan but a sizeable gain for the kingdom of God. Later he became "Doctor" Caudill, through the courtesy of Anderson College and served for many years on their Board of Trustees. He also became one of the most gifted pulpiteers our fellowship has ever known. Endowed with a good voice, he was a compelling speaker, a successful evangelist who mastered the fine art of story telling. Thousands were converted to Christ during his fruitful years of ministry.

The meetings at Hinton were well attended and many were converted. At the end of three weeks forty-five persons "took their stand for the truth," and we had the beginnings of a congregation. But, sad to relate, the West Virginia brethren fumbled the ball by failing to send in a good pastor to consolidate our gains. The church ultimately lost the whole venture. It was poor business. We had put forth sacrificial efforts to raise up a work and it was disappointing to see everything lost. But that sort of thing used to happen all too often through lack of organization.

In addition to I. P. Hamrick and R. C. Caudill, H. M. VanHoose also came to Hinton to help in the meetings. He was not an oratorical preacher but had a fair education. He had taught school before entering the ministry. Watchful of our grammar, he sometimes reminded us of our mistakes and R. C. didn't take correction too easily. I remember once calling his attention to the pronunciation of the word *hotel,* which he called ho'tel. I said, "It isn't ho'tel, its hotel'." When he disputed this I showed it to him in the dictionary. "That doesn't mean a thing to me," he replied. "I have as much right to my opinion as Webster had to his." Just for orneriness I set him up on another word one day. I said, "R. C., I have a word here I can't identify. I don't know whether it is German or French. Maybe you can help me." He indicated his willingness to bring light into my darkness. "What is the word?" he asked. So I spelled it for him. "It is *bac kache*." His identification was instantaneous. He said, "It is a German word, pronounced *bakatchee*." I said, "Thank you, R. C., but back home we always called it just plain *backache*." He could have killed me but mercy prevailed.

One evening while R. C. was preaching at Hinton, H. M. Van-Hoose made a note once in awhile on the back of an envelope. He was listing the grammatical errors being made. There weren't many. When the service was over he showed the list to R. C., who thanked him. I felt that down deep inside he was probably a bit lacking in appreciation. A day or two later VanHoose spoke in one of our daytime services. He had no more than entered the pulpit when R. C., sitting right down in front, took out a piece of paper, and poised his pen for action. VanHoose noticed, and it upset him. After the benediction he rushed to R. C. and asked to see the paper. R. C. laughed and handed him a blank sheet. He thoroughly enjoyed turning a trick on his critic.

We went from Hinton to Ronceverte where I. P. Hamrick was pastor, pitched the tent, and had a very well-attended and fruitful series of meetings. One day I was invited out into the mountains for dinner. I found the family living in a well-preserved log house, the inside of which was paneled on walls and ceiling with tongue and groove lumber. This had been stained and varnished and made a very good appearance. The man of the house knew R. C. but he and I had never met. When I told him my name was Oldham, he laughed fit to kill; thinking it to be the funniest name he had ever heard. He enjoyed putting the emphasis on *ham* which didn't particularly bother me as it had happened many times before. When he had finished laughing I asked his name and he replied "Loudermilk." I could have made something out of that to turn the tables, but, since I was his guest, I passed it off without a smile.

Out from Ronceverte about fifteen miles I visited a most unique farm. It was a perfect example of American inventiveness, pioneer ingenuity, and self-sufficiency. The family needed almost nothing from town except salt and pepper. There were sheep from which they sheared, carded, and spun wool. A weaving machine transformed the thread into cloth. A big steam tractor was used for powering a sawmill, threshing out grain, and extricating wagons from the mud. Maple trees enabled them to make their own syrup and sugar. They grew all their own grain, fruits, and vegetables. The cattle gave milk, which in turn produced butter and cheese. These were kept cool and fresh in a spring house down under the hill, where cold water came issuing forth in a considerable stream. There were dead trees which they cut up for firewood and great live trees from which they sawed boards and beams for their building needs. At a smithy's forge they fitted shoes for their horses and fashioned other articles from metal. I was reminded of our pioneer fathers and their need to be self-sufficient while living miles from the nearest settlement. These good West Virginia mountain folk had that hard-working, independent spirit which built America. All of us would be better persons if we had more of it today.

It was my privilege and pleasure to accompany Dr. Caudill in several evangelistic meetings. How he could preach! The people came from far and wide to fill the largest available church buildings. R. C. had an engaging smile and a great, if sometimes pain-giving, sense of humor. He took his Bible seriously, reading the New Testament through about once a month. He studied hard, did a fairly good job with his sermon outlining, and preached with authority and power. He was blessed with a phenomenal memory for texts, facts, faces, and people.

While in the Ronceverte, West Virginia meetings, R. C. and I. P. Hamrick used to sit up till a late hour swapping stories about people and happenings. I never ceased to be entranced by their conversations. I had never known men of their kind during my childhood. It was as if they had been brought up in a different world, and they had. Their stories of hunting and fishing, fighting and shooting, feuds and court trials were of unending interest to me. At an early age their eyes had been sharpened to see a rabbit crouched in a clump of grass. Their ears had been tuned to tell which hound was ahead as the pack trailed a fox or raccoon.

It seemed to me as if R. C. knew everybody—senators, governors, well-to-do farmers, cattlemen, and horse breeders. But with it all, he was as independent as any person I have ever known. Once while we were in Louisville, Kentucky, President Franklin D. Roosevelt visited the city. Thousands thronged the railroad station to catch a glimpse of him. But not R. C. He stayed home saying, "If the President wishes to meet me, he will have no trouble finding out where I am staying." Some of this may have been humor but not all of it. Anyhow, R. C. was a great fellow and I learned much from him.

Dr. Caudill was at his best in a big camp meeting. His favorite sermon subjects had to do with the church and the Holy Spirit. He was a genuine master in the pulpit, and after the first ten or fifteen minutes generally had the entire audience with him. I worked with him in many meetings between 1921 and 1924, and after my marriage my wife traveled along as pianist. Hundreds were converted in our meetings.

Many years later Dr. Caudill was pastor of the large Church of God in Middletown, Ohio, and I was serving at Dayton, just twenty miles distant. We continued our friendship until a strange twist of circumstances bought an alienation on his part which continued for several years. It hurt me deeply and I did everything possible to erase it, but R. C. was a proud man and did not bend easily. Our relationship was never again quite the same, although I preached for him at Middletown and he for me at Dayton, and we managed again to find pleasure in each other's company.

Dr. Caudill attracted large crowds as pastor, conducted hundreds of funerals, officiated at hundreds of weddings, and unostentatiously gave a great deal of money to men who were down on their luck or in trouble. His passing a few years ago brought genuine sorrow to my heart, for there has not been another pulpiteer like him in two generations.

During the first years of my evangelistic work I traveled with several evangelists and also held meetings where local pastors did the preaching. The passing months brought many deep satisfactions, a few thrills, and one or two rather sobering disillusionments. The halos disappeared from the heads of two or three preachers with whom I labored. The rosy glow which had surrounded my initiation as a young evangelistic singer began to fade a bit. There were boards of trustees in churches we served who seemed totally unaware of our financial needs. Total income during the first fifteen months of my evangelistic work was $495, about half of which went to the railroads for transportation. I owned one suit, which was well-worn; three shirts, all of which were patched, and had but one pair of shoes. Then came a month when no meetings were scheduled. I had a dollar and a half in my pocket and my parents lived too far away for me to join them.

Frustrated and perplexed, I began to ask myself whether I was in the right business. It would have been so easy to quit and take a job where the income was assured. I happened to be in Anderson at the time and some of the Bible School students and I were out on the lawn tossing a ball. I leaped into the air for a high one and when I came down my right shoe broke completely across at the bead. This was *really* trouble! If a call for a meeting did come— what would I do for shoes? I couldn't stand before hundreds of people wearing *those* shoes. Just then a girl came out on the porch of the Bible Training School and said, "Dale, did you get your letter?" I replied, "Letter? Who would write to me here? Nobody knew I was going to be here?"

The letter was from a young couple I had met during meetings in Fort Wayne a few months previously. Hastily I read, "While we were in family devotions, the Lord impressed us to send you ten dollars. We want to obey him and here is our check. God bless you." Isn't it strange how the Lord knows *today* what our needs are going to be *tomorrow?* Two days before my shoe broke the Lord had impressed George Guysinger and his wife to send money for a new pair. With a lighter heart I purchased a new pair of Bostonians and praised God from whom all blessings flow. Then, with a vacant month before me I went to Indianapolis, found welcome at the Feldmans, worked for four weeks for Marmon's, bought new clothes, and was ready for my next meeting. The shadows passed and the sun shone again. I have always been glad that I stayed with my calling.

Those were the days of mass evangelism in America. In 1922 my first three meetings were with pastor-evangelist E. L. Bragg, of Marion, Indiana. A portly man of forty years or so, he was not well-educated, but he had a good mind, a resonant voice, and a pleasing personality. His sermons were logical, forceful, and effective. The Fort Wayne, Indiana, Church of God was in its beginnings in January of 1922 when E. L. Bragg and I went there for meetings. J. E. Sheefel was pastor. The little flock had rented a hall for a meeting place. Sheefel helped to support his family by operating a haybaler during the summer.

My records show that we were in Fort Wayne two weeks, about twenty were converted, and I received twelve dollars for my labors. Our February meeting was in Payne, Ohio, twenty miles east of Fort Wayne. It also ran for two weeks and I was given twenty dollars. Ira Kilpatrick was pastor and supplemented his income by operating a small grocery store. In March, Brother Bragg and I went to Muncie, Indiana, where Herschel Allen was pastor. I think there were thirty-three conversions. For this three weeks I received thirty dollars. Three months, sixty-two dollars, out of which I paid train fare and laundry bills. However, I was neither unhappy or discontented. There was always the feeling that as long as I was doing what the Lord wanted me to do he would somehow take care of me. The details were his business not mine.

In May of 1922 I joined W. F. Chappel, his son John, and R. C. Caudill for a tent meeting in Middletown, Ohio. B. F. Lawson was pastor of a good-sized congregation there. An unlearned but loving man, Lawson was doing a very good piece of work. I had been present for the dedication of the Young Street church the previous October when Sunday morning attendance was above four hundred.

Lawson had a tender heart and compassion unlimited. Tears trickled down his cheeks as he stood by the bed of a seriously ill child or was forced to conduct the funeral of a young mother. He was not a pulpit orator; in fact, he found it difficult to express himself in ordinary conversation, but the people loved him and would not trade him for the most gifted orator.

70

In Middletown I learned the importance of loving people; that love is far more important than pulpit oratory. That fact stayed with me. There was never a sermon flowery enough to supplant the pastor's need to love people.

I had never sung in a campaign where the preaching was shared, but in the big tent W. F. Chappel and R. C. Caudill were alternating from night to night. I wondered how such an arrangement would work out because people are apt to play favorites when it comes to preachers. However, Chappel and Caudill were fond of each other and there seemed to be no jealousy between them. Both were preachers of such ability that I can't remember hearing a single partisan word concerning their sermons during the entire four weeks.

Attendance was excellent. Folks drove in from Dayton, Hamilton, Springfield, and other neighboring churches. I had an acceptable choir of untrained but enthusiastic singers, plus a few who were good enough for solo, duet, or quartet work. So the special music helped to popularize the meetings. About this time W. F. Chappel, his son John, Mildred Neff, and I began presenting a song titled "The Sunny Side of Life." It was a simple song, but it caught the people and was requested again and again. Since about three-fourths of those attending the Middletown meetings were originally from Kentucky, it may help to explain why they enjoyed these words:

> *There's a sunny side where no ills betide,*
> *On the road that we must go;*
> *There are pleasant vales, verdant hills and dales,*
> *Where sweet flowers ever grow.*

Brother Chappel took the melody, Mildred the alto, John the tenor, and I the rolling bass. The big tent meeting brought substantial growth to the church at Middletown.

Fifty years ago people used to "get happy" in church. Occasionally, some of the more emotional might even jump and shout a bit. During the Middletown tent meeting, one of the older brethren became blessed, strode up to the platform, and began to jump and shout. He was a bit overweight and couldn't jump very well.

71

At any rate, his performance was brought to a sudden halt when his rather valuable pocket watch jumped from his vest and fell to the floor. Ruefully, he retrieved his wrecked timepiece and resumed his seat, where he sat for some time holding the watch, occasionally shaking it and listening to see if it had resumed operating. But it had not.

I can remember only one black person attending that particular meeting. He seemed a good old brother for whom the Middletown people had genuine affection, although age was beginning to cloud his mind a bit. One evening, while Brother Chappel was preaching in a big way, our black brother sat in the first row to the right of the platform mumbling to himself. I was close enough to hear him mumble, "Praise the Lord, I'm going straight to heaven," when Brother Chappel just happened to declare in his sermon, while looking in the colored brother's direction, "You are going straight to hell!" The poor old man must have thought the preacher had overheard and was answering him, for he was silent the rest of the evening.

One day Tom Steenbergen and I decided to go fishing. When this became known, well-driller O. O. Pegg and Pastor Lawson decided to join us. When behind the wheel of an automobile, Tom was quite a chariot driver, particularly on his way to fish. Pegg and Lawson were in the back seat. We hit an elevated railroad crossing altogether too fast and they were pretty well shaken up. Tom slowed down, but at a request from Pastor Lawson brought the car to a stop along the road. Then Lawson in his characteristic drawl said, "Brother Tom, I can't get up." When we hit the crossing the two men plus the back seat went up into the air. When things settled down, Pastor Lawson's feet were both *under* the back seat. His weight on the seat made it impossible to free himself. We had a high and hilarious time getting him out of his predicament. Both of his legs were skinned and showed black and blue the next day and for several days afterward.

O. O. Pegg was a well-driller for whom Tom worked in the twenties. Pegg had formerly been employed by ARMCO, the American Rolling Mill Company, which has huge steel mills at its parent Middletown plant. He must have been quite a character

72

before his conversion. As he arose from his knees on the momentous night of his rebirth and thanked the Lord for forgiveness, about all he could think of was that one whole wall of his garage was hung with tools he had taken over the years from ARMCO.

His newfound joy was understandably somewhat dampened by the seriousness of the problem now confronting him. It is one thing to be gloriously forgiven and redeemed; it is something else to have to confess to thefts which could send you to the penitentiary. Pegg's job with ARMCO was a good one and he didn't want to lose it. But stealing was a crime and, as a new Christian, he felt it was absolutely necessary to make both confession and restitution. Hadn't the evangelist quoted Ezekiel 33:15 which reads, "If the wicked restore the pledge, give again that he had robbed, walk in the statutes of life, . . . he shall not die?"

Well! Now, what to do? When Pegg made his surrender to Christ, it was with the determination to go all the way with him. Now his duty became crystal clear: he must confess his thefts to his boss and do it soon. It was already well into December. Pegg waited until Christmas morning, a time when he thought the mill superintendent might be in a benevolent frame of mind. Timidly he rang his doorbell, in response to which the superintendent appeared in robe and slippers to say rather gruffly, "Yes, what do you want?" Pegg *wanted* to run but instead answered, "May I come in?" Reluctantly he was admitted, "Now what can I do for you?" came the direct question. Since Pegg was but newly converted and didn't know much about the evangelical vocabulary, he just blurted out, "I got saved the other night down at the Church of God and I've got to straighten some things out." Then, calling the superintendent by name, he continued, "I've got the whole side of my garage hung with tools taken from ARMCO during the years I've worked for you. What shall I do with them?"

"Take them back," came the blunt reply. The words and their tone didn't assure Pegg very much, but he had gone this far and had to finish the job. "And what are you going to do with me?" he inquired.

"Hmmm," mused the superintendent, as the trace of a smile came to the corners of his eyes, "What am I going to do about you?

All I'm going to do is pray that whatever happened to you will happen to a lot more of our ARMCO employees. Boy! If it would, we'd sure get back a passel of tools."

Brother Pegg thanked him profusely, drove his pickup truck to his garage, loaded up the stolen tools, and pulled up to the ARMCO gate where a guard inquired, "What do you have there?" and Pegg responded, "A load of tools to deliver to my department." The guard waved him on and, as he unloaded, friend Pegg found a joy and a testimony which stayed with him to the end of his long and fruitful life. It was always a delight to hear him relate how both the Lord and ARMCO had forgiven him. I still think the forgiven Christian will straighten up his past.

While conducting an evangelistic campaign in Bradenton, Florida, with my son Doug a few years ago, I was relating publicly the story just told to you when I happened to see in the audience the very man of whom I was speaking. I said, "Why should I relate this story when the man to whom it happened is sitting right here in the congregation. Brother Pegg, stand up and tell us about it."

And he did as tears of praise and thanksgiving rolled down his cheeks. It was the last time I ever saw him. Shortly afterward our heavenly Father called him on to a better country. But he was a good man and full of the spirit of Christ.

Another elderly brother in the Middletown church was named Byrd. He had been quite a rounder in his B.C. days. He had run with cronies who met regularly at a place down on the corner to drink and gamble and tell off-color stories. Then the Lord came into his life and Byrd was soundly converted. Isn't it a miracle what Christ can do by way of transforming human personality? Now he no longer spent his evenings with the old crowd. Old things had passed away; everything was new. One day he met one of his old buddies on the street and they paused to pass the time of day.

"Haven't seen much of you lately, Byrd. What's happened to you?" It took a moment for Byrd to get his emotions under control. Finally he replied with tears in his eyes, "I've changed my hitching post."

My good friend Tom Steenbergen, now in his seventies and retired, was quite a man at twenty-five. He stood nearly six feet four inches tall and was all bone and muscle at one hundred eighty pounds as the result of his heavy work in the steel mill. In his preconversion days Tom was frequently in trouble of one kind or another. Sometimes he was broke the day after payday because of an all-night crap game.

One day as he took a shortcut down a railroad track on his way to the afternoon shift at ARMCO, Tom looked up and saw six men approaching. On closer examination he realized that at one time or another he had beat up all six of them. I imagine that a couple of quotations may have flitted through his mind, like, "He who fights and runs away, lives to fight another day." "Discretion is the better part of valor." He wanted to turn and run, but, having been brought up in the Kentucky mountains, it had been instilled into him that a real man never backs down from a fight.

All six men jumped Tom at once and began hammering away at him with their fists. Tom's advantage was that he had no one to look out for but himself. So he waded in. When the smoke of the battle cleared away, all six of his attackers were strewn over the tracks. As Tom started on for work he met a black man who had witnessed the whole scrimmage. "Boss, I don't see how you done it," the fellow said admiringly. "This is how I done it," Tom replied, and laid him alongside the rest.

After Tom was converted, he turned all that energy into serving the Lord and became a fruitful worker in the church. A few years later he began preaching. During the intervening half-century he raised up several churches and pastored growing congregations. He had exceptional ability in building programs. Several church edifices stand today as memorials to his leadership and skill. Tom and I preached together, golfed, bowled, hunted, and fished together, and one time nearly drowned together. I count him as one of my dearest friends.

In the Middletown church was another fine young man whom I shall call Johnny, although that was not his name. He had been gloriously converted shortly before I met him. He was personable and before long became a leader in the youth group. I have never heard a young man who could pray more movingly than Johnny.

He married one of the finest girls in the church, established a home, and settled down to married life. Johnny was a good husband and provided well for his wife. However, misfortune lay in wait for the young couple. Their first child died when but a few months old and Johnny was inconsolable. I was in Middletown at the time and sang at the funeral which was held in the church. It was a difficult assignment.

Johnny's theological education was scant and his philosophy of life immature. All during the service he sat with a tense expression on his face. He couldn't understand how God can love us and at the same time allow grief to come our way. Frustrated and angry he left the service muttering, "If this is God's love, I want nothing more to do with him." To my knowledge Johnny has never darkened the door of a church from that day to this. Sometimes we need to find a forgiving attitude toward God, especially if we have been carrying a grudge against him.

In September of 1922 (I was still nineteen), a call came to assist in an evangelistic meeting which had as its object the establishing of a congregation near Crown City, Ohio. We pitched a large tent miles out in the country, on a ridge, in the corner of a pasture. A vacant church building was just across the road. I wondered why we didn't use it. Why this spot had been chosen for the tent I still have no idea. No Church of God families lived in the immediate neighborhood. The two preachers, D. T. Koch, Laban Hauck, and I slept in a small tent near the large one. There wasn't a restaurant within ten miles. This fact didn't exactly thrill me because at nineteen I was always hungry. I was informed that we would eat whenever someone happened to bring us food.

The meeting opened with good attendance, but the method of supplying board and room for the evangelists did not suit me at all. Sometimes we ate but once a day. I put my mind to work to see if a better way might be found. I was not long in working out a plan.

The pasture where our tent was pitched belonged to a widow and her grown son, Vernor Adkins. Every day Vernor was in the adjoining field with his machette, cutting corn. He and his mother had been attending our meetings. Next morning I climbed the fence and struck up a conversation with Vernor. After speaking of the meetings and the weather, I told him I was bored and time was hanging heavy on my hands with nothing to do all day long. I said that if he would supply me with a knife and a pair of overalls I would be glad to help him out. He was soon back from the house with the requested articles. Thus I went to work and enjoyed every minute of it.

Of course, at noon Vernor took me up to the house for lunch. Doesn't the Bible say something about the laborer being worthy of his hire? Mother Adkins had prepared a beautiful lunch of fried chicken, mashed potatoes, cream gravy, and green beans. She also had baked a delicious pie. There was plenty of cold milk to drink with extra cream to mix with it if I so desired.

At their insistence, when evening came I moved into an upstairs bedroom. When rain fell a day or two later Koch and Hauck had to abandon their little tent and move into the empty church house. From a word or two they dropped later on, I received the distinct impression that they felt I had somehow betrayed them. But after all, *they* could have asked for corn knives too, couldn't they?

Forty years later, Vernor Adkins attended services we were conducting not too many miles from his home. We recalled those days when he had owned a Model T Ford roadster which he had purchased new (without a self-starter) for three hundred sixty-five dollars.

D. T. Koch was a specialist in doctrinal preaching, and, although not a great pulpit orator, was a sensible preacher and able to communicate the truth. As our tent was in hill country, hill people attended our meetings. Many were too poor to afford transportation of any kind. They walked as much as seven miles to be with us. Money was scarce, but the people were friendly and the meetings went fairly well. Before long we were being invited into the homes of the people and Koch and Hauck were better fed. Some of the farmers gave us bottles of fresh cider they were making from a plenteous supply of ripe apples.

Brother Koch had one fault, common in his time; he generally preached too long, sometimes an hour and a half. Afterward some of the people still had that seven-mile walk back home. I noticed that some of them were not attending every night. When I inquired as to the reason, they replied, "We live so far away and have to walk. It takes nearly two hours each way and it is nearly eleven-thirty when we get home. Then we have to be up early the next morning to do the chores. We decided we'd stay home every other evening to catch up on our sleep."

"Fools rush in where angels fear to tread." I hinted to Brother Koch that perhaps he ought to put a little shortening into his sermons and thus increase attendance. He said, "Well, I thought about shortening my sermons. But after hearing how far some of these people have to walk to get here, I felt I ought to make their coming worthwhile." We were at Crown City three weeks but failed to establish a church there. My train fare was twenty-two dollars and my honorarium sixteen dollars. I wonder sometimes if the people simply paid me what they thought I was worth!

Following the Anderson camp meeting in 1922, Brother Chappel, John, and I were called to Stanford, Illinois, by a retired farmer who hoped to establish a congregation of the Church of God there. Stanford had a population of about five hundred and was located in the midst of championship corn-growing country.

We stayed in the home of the widowed Henry Kauffman, with his sister as housekeeper. We pitched a large tent on the centrally located school grounds and advertised services. The meetings caught on and soon the tent, seating some three hundred, was full. People were parking their automobiles in a circle around it to provide for overflow seating.

As the meetings progressed, forty or fifty gave their hearts to the Lord and prospects for establishing a church were bright. Things were going too well to suit Satan and so he began to intensify his opposition. A group of teen-aged boys began riding their horses around and around the tent during services, which caused considerable disturbance. However, the boys' pranks were harmless until the night they sent word that they planned to cut the tent ropes. This could put us out of business.

Since Henry Kauffman had been to considerable expense in setting up the tent and bringing us to Stanford, he was understandably upset at the boys' threats. At home that night he declared emphatically, "I'm going to Bloomington tomorrow and get deputized. Then I'm coming back here to see that we have order." There was static in the air as he spoke, and the Chappels and I felt that what he had in mind might cause more trouble than it would cure.

After a moment Brother Chappel said, "Brother Kauffman, this is the Lord's meeting. I don't think you ought to go up to the county seat to be deputized. Instead I suggest that we get down on our knees and ask the Lord to patrol this meeting." So, down on our knees we went and this man of God, this man of prayer, began to talk to the Father about our problem. In his typical way of expressing himself Brother Chappel asked the Lord to "deputize" our meetings. That man's prayers always seemed to bring results. He prayed as if God were standing at his right hand, intently listening. There never seemed to be any doubt that the Lord would hear and answer. On this particular night I felt as if my friend had a hot line straight to the Throne. When he said amen and we arose from our knees, it was with the assurance that everything was well in hand. The prayer relaxed Henry Kauffman, too, and we all went to our beds.

Next day, the ring leader of that group of obstreperous young men was riding a horse when it reared up with him, overbalanced, and came back on him, ramming the pommel of the saddle into his middle. They rushed him to a Bloomington hospital. About the first thing he did was to call for Brother Chappel to come pray for him. After that we had perfect order in our services and successfully established a church in Stanford.

When Brother Chappel was really inspired in his preaching, he had the habit of batting his eyes and running his fingers back through his hair. But I saw him bat his eyes one time when he was something less than inspired. Following a Sunday morning service in Stanford, most of the people left before we were through praying with several who had responded to the invitation and were kneeling at the altar. By twelve-thirty these had all prayed through with the exception of a woman from Tennessee who had trouble believing the Lord would forgive her sins. So we waited, prayed, and instructed her as best we could. Kneeling near were perhaps half a dozen good Christian women, all of whom were in earnest agreement in her behalf.

Suddenly this dear woman "prayed through" and came up shouting and praising the Lord! Her tears were now tears of joy. She grabbed the woman standing next to her, hugged and kissed her, then did the same with the next woman in line, and the next. Brother Chappel was standing at the end of the line and had a premonition of what was coming. By the time this deliriously happy convert had hugged and kissed the last woman in line the preacher had retreated to the platform where she followed him. When she finally came to herself, the two were playing a little dodge game, back and forth on opposite sides of the pulpit.

Not everyone in Stanford was happy to have us there. When John and I walked uptown we sometimes inspired catcalls or slurring remarks from occupants of benches in front of the barbershop or post office. But I can't recall that it even irritated us. We joked about it. Several years later my father served a term as pastor of the Stanford church.

After Stanford, Brother Chappel and I went on to a camp meeting at Grand Junction, Michigan. During the 1880s our publishing house had been located there and so the camp meeting was old and well-established. It was also ultraconservative. No piano or organ accompanied the singing. The program committee had not invited me to the meeting; I was there only as Brother Chappel's associate. But since I was on the grounds they began to use me. For years the music had been in the charge of a good brother from Illinois, and my presence irked him considerably. A large, enthusiastic group of young people was in attendance, and before long I had a first-class choir in rehearsal and singing beautifully. We were also helped considerably by the Green Brothers, an excellent male quartet from Kalamazoo. The Chappels and I sang "The Sunny Side of Life," seemingly to everyone's delight. Everyone, that is, except the good brother in charge of the music. We weren't halfway through the week when he became ill and had to return home. I felt sincerely sorry for him.

At the conclusion of the Grand Junction meeting we went on to Springfield, Ohio, where one of our largest state camp meetings was held. Here I rendered similar service. Springfield was to become a dear and familiar place during the years to come as I preached and sang for those excellent pastors, C. E. Byers and F. L. Blevins. Grand Junction gave me $30.00 and Springfield $15.00, so my total for August was $45.00, less train fare. During the year of 1922 my total income was $488.50.

Chapter Seven

Diversity

ONE RUNS INTO some peculiar situations in evangelistic work. At least that's the way I found it fifty years ago. December of 1922 took the Chappels and me to Louisville, Kentucky. W. E. Monk, former mayor of a suburb of Houston, Texas, had led his congregation to purchase a large church building located at the corner of 19th and Jefferson Streets. Years later Dr. Monk became a highly esteemed worker with our national Board of Church Extension and Home Missions. But in 1922 he was struggling to make a success not only as a pastor, but as a Christian, at least this is what he later told me.

The seating capacity of the newly purchased sanctuary was much larger than the congregation. There was a considerable debt with payments to be made monthly. So Pastor Monk called the Chappels and me for a three-week evangelistic meeting. Brother Chappel was very popular in Kentucky and his presence was enough to assure a good attendance.

The series was launched and immediately friends began to attend from a radius of fifty miles or so. I felt we were off to a good start. However, there was a marked contrast between Brother Chappel and Dr. Monk. Monk had a dignified appearance, portly, with a sandy moustache and goatee. Although not a college graduate, his political and other experiences had broadened his outlook and given him a rather interesting personality. His sermons were short and to the point, generally from fifteen to eighteen minutes in duration.

Brother Chappel was equipped with a different kind of timer and habitually spoke from an hour to an hour and a half. I may have already mentioned that it was characteristic of him to spend twenty or thirty minutes "generalizing," after which he would read his text and preach for an hour. I didn't mind because he was an interesting speaker and I had such affection and admiration for the man that I could have listened even longer. But the long sermons and many days we had without a break in the meetings irked Pastor Monk. He had hoped we would bring considerable growth to his congregation.

Dr. Monk had a rather low boiling point in those days. One morning he called the Chappels and me into his study to explain to us the facts of life. John, he said, needed considerably more practice before he would ever become a very accomplished pianist. Dale, he continued, never sang a really good solo unless before a larger than normal crowd. As for Brother Chappel, his sermons were interminably long and that fact was undoubtably keeping people away by the dozens, perhaps hundreds. Dr. Monk said considerably more than this but it was all in the same mood and the three of us got the message: the pastor was not pleased with us or the meetings.

Brother Chappel was a calm man, not easily provoked, but Monk's words were so pointed, direct, and emphatic that they could not be ignored. After concluding his speech, there was a rather pregnant silence for some time. Finally, Brother Chappel said softly and slowly, "Well, Brother Monk, I see that the boys and I are not pleasing you at all. In fact, we seem to be displeasing you, and for this we are sorry. Under the circumstances I don't see how we can go forward with the meetings. It seems best for us to pack our suitcases and leave."

With that the three of us arose to go, but suddenly Monk saw the handwriting on the wall. He hadn't been in politics for nothing. He knew that if it got out over Kentucky that his attitude had forced the Chappel team to pack up and leave, his name would be mud. So he began to backtrack, saying he didn't want us to leave, just to change. Brother Chappel answered that he was too old to change, that his way of doing things had proved fruitful over

84

the years, and that he probably would continue to be a long-winded preacher. But we stayed on.

The Louisville church had experienced inner troubles in years past, and Evangelist Chappel had sought to resolve some of them in his nightly sermons. There was no visible sign that he was succeeding as there had been few, if any, conversions.

I have already told you of my complete confidence in Brother Chappel's prayers. But may I add that he was the only one whose *dreams* ever received my full attention. When W. F. Chappel had what he termed a significant dream, I waited eagerly for his interpretation of it. Now, don't laugh, for if you had known him, you would have paid attention, too.

One morning, shortly after our run-in with Pastor Monk, Brother Chappel told John and me he had dreamed an important dream the night before. "I dreamed that I was out there in the pulpit preaching a woman's funeral." (Of course all of us know that in the New Testament prophetic writings a woman represents the church.) "She was lying in her casket right in front of the pulpit," Brother Chappel continued, "and a sizable audience was present. Suddenly, as I was speaking, this dead woman spoke. 'Let me out of here,' she said. I looked down at her and admonished, 'Be quiet; don't you see that I'm preaching your funeral?' However, a minute or two later the woman sat up in her casket to say rather strongly, 'Help me out of here.' Her unusual attitude irked me, for it was spoiling the occasion. So, when she continued to interrupt, I went down out of the pulpit, put my hands on her shoulders and tried to press her back into the casket, whispering, 'Sister, you're dead. I am preaching your funeral.' This really roused her and she said, 'Now you listen to me, Brother Chappel, I am *not* dead. If I were dead would I be sitting up in this casket talking to you?'

"Well, that sounded reasonable enough, so instead of returning to the pulpit, I gave the good sister my hand and helped her out of the casket, whereupon, there was great rejoicing among all the people. You see, boys, in my preaching I have been trying to bury this church. Instead, the Lord wants me to cooperate with him in resurrecting it. I am changing the direction of my preaching, beginning tonight."

As he did, attendance in our meetings immediately increased. Two or three mornings later Brother Chappel told of another dream which had come to him the preceding night. He said, "Boys, the break is coming. We are going to have a great revival. Last night I dreamed I was fishing, pulling them in as fast as I could bait the hook." That night thirty-three persons bowed at the church altars to yield their lives to Christ. I pay little attention to my own dreams and probably wouldn't think yours to be of any particular significance, but when Brother Chappel dreamed I gave heed to his interpretation. The Louisville meetings ended well and brought growth to the church. After paying the Monks $18.00 for three weeks board and room I went on to my next meeting with $42.00 in my pocket, less railroad fare.

W. F. Chappel was one of the finest friends I ever had. His understanding and wise counsel helped me considerably during our months of association together. He knew the problems of the teen-age boy seeking to grow into full manhood. He knew all about a lad's frustrations, temptations, hungers, and thirsts, and cared enough to take time to help me over some very rough places.

Never will I forget the day during the meetings in Paris, Kentucky, when he came to my assistance. We were staying at the farm home of Joe Bodkins a few miles from the city. That day I was enduring a rare case of the indigo blues. Lonely and discouraged, I had just gone through a rather humiliating experience after which I wanted to be alone to feel sorry for myself. In this mood I walked out through a field and over a hill until I was some distance from the house. There I threw myself on the grass in the shade of a tree and gave myself to moody meditation and self-pity. I hadn't been there very long, however, until I heard footsteps approaching. There was my friend Chappel, understanding, caring, wanting to help.

After a good talk together, he offered up a helpful prayer in my behalf. I felt better and returned with him to the house. Not too many preachers with whom I worked in those early years were either this observant or this understanding. Some were critical and faultfinding. Some were attention seekers or filled with a sense of self-importance. Some didn't care whether I existed or not. After

86

I had filled the pulpit for an older evangelist on a hot summer morning, a young girl asked what he thought of my message. "Hmph!" was his only reply. That may have been a true estimate of its worth, but certainly I have no feeling of indebtedness to *him*. But I *am* in debt to W. F. Chappel and trust that down through the intervening years I have been able to help, bless, and encourage at least a few young preachers as he helped, blessed, and encouraged me.

In Paris, the Chappels and I were again holding meetings with the hope of establishing a congregation of the Church of God there. That summer of 1923 the Ku Klux Klan was quite active in Kentucky. One day the local chapter sent word that a delegation of Kluxers would attend our services on a given night. Since they did not say why they were coming, the announcement made me a bit nervous.

It is one thing to see a man face to face but quite another to look at a white mask and not know who is behind it. At the appointed time three or four automobiles drove up in front of the tent and unloaded their passengers. The white-sheeted procession marched silently down the center aisle. Arriving at the platform their spokesman made a short speech saying that he and his masked brothers appreciated what we were trying to do to make Paris a better city. Before turning to leave they gave Brother Chappel an offering of ten dollars. My musings were that had I been one of their number I would have tried to make the offering more than ten dollars and would also have stayed for the church service.

Somehow I've always classified masked men with anonymous letters. Neither gives you much of a chance to talk back. Both hide behind the safety of anonymity; afraid to reveal their identity. One can be very brave when he doesn't have to show his face or give his name. That ten-dollar KKK offering still titillates me. It reminds me of a Christmas in Iowa about sixty years ago when we gave poor little Ruby Mae a gift, probably from the ten-cent store. After looking at it thoughtfully for a moment, she remarked, "Well, it ain't much, but it's better than nuthin.' "

Another pastor-evangelist with whom I worked before my marriage was A. Q. Bridwell of Harrisburg, Illinois. Most of those early preachers were self-made men with limited education, but several had keen minds which they had sharpened through hard study. It is my observation that they knew their Bibles far better than does the average preacher today. They were men of one Book and knew that Book from cover to cover. Bridwell was no exception. His was a homespun type of preaching mixed with considerable humor. He was an excellent doctrinal preacher and could establish new congregations and educate them in scriptural truth. But there was one area in which the man simply could not be trusted. Let me tell you about it.

Fifty years ago many ministers used the proof-text method of preaching. Some had the habit of asking the chairman or another preacher to read various passages of Scripture for them as they were needed in the sermon. It seemed easier to give a list of scriptures to someone ahead of time than for the preacher to have to find and read each one as needed. I had thus read texts for C. E. Byers and now was giving A. Q. Birdwell the same assistance.

But Birdwell pulled a trick on me while we were evangelizing the tough little river town of Golconda, Illinois. I had been with him in Muncie, Indiana, and Clinton, Iowa, and thought I knew him quite well. But not well enough. One night at Golconda, in his usual manner Bridwell asked that I read for him as he preached. This time, however, he did not furnish me in advance with a list of the texts he intended to use. This did not particularly surprise me, for in those days many men preached rather extemporaneously, calling for the reading of scriptures as they needed them.

Bridwell was an excellent student of the Bible and I am sure could have quoted every verse he needed from memory, but he liked the people to see the open Bible being read instead of merely listening to quotations. This evening he was preaching on "The Church." I knew I would be doing a considerable amount of reading for him. He opened with certain familiar verses and then rather smoothly transferred to the Song of Solomon. Suddenly I became uneasy. I knew that book and remembered that there are a few passages in it which are not altogether appropriate for public reading, especially if a nineteen-year-old boy happens to be the reader.

Bridwell's sense of humor got out of hand that evening and he was merciless. I know my ears were red as he called for Chapter 4, verses 1 to 7; and Chapter 7, verses 1 to 9. You can be sure that I read without lifting my eyes from the book. Bridwell stood behind the pulpit, with a cherubic smile of innocence on his face as he (vainly I hope!) tried to tie all this in with a vision of the New Testament church. I declare, I could have strangled the man that night! Afterward, he enjoyed cornering me at someone's supper table, and then asking me how the Song of Solomon can be used to explain the church. Personally, I was never of the opinion that the writer of the Song of Solomon was thinking about the church, *any* church, as he penned those chapters. But A. Q. Bridwell was a fine, likeable fellow and we had some excellent meetings together. He was a deeply consecrated man with a warm love for the truth. I am sure that hundreds will be in heaven because of his ministry.

As previously mentioned, every June about 20,000 of us journey to Anderson, Indiana, to attend our international convention—called for more than half a century the Anderson camp meeting. The program opens on a Monday night with the Anderson College and Theological Seminary Commencement. Tuesday morning a big, complicated convention program gets underway, featuring in addition to three daily, general preaching services, conferences on Christian education, Home and Foreign Missions, pastors' wives, youth, church building, and evangelism. You name it, we have it. A great choir sings in the evening services, and some of the nation's best soloists and singing groups are on hand.

For fifty years I did not miss one of these meetings. Originally it was a ten-day affair, beginning on Friday and ending on the second Sunday night. Later, it was shortened to run from Sunday to Sunday and finally from Tuesday through Sunday. I remember when there was a large barn on the campus of Anderson College, which joins the convention grounds and used to be a part of it. Cows and a team were quartered there. A huge garden was cultivated to help feed the employees of our publishing house, who in the early years served without salaries. In 1918, a farmer might ride to camp meeting with his family in a spring wagon with a cow tied to the tail gate to furnish milk for the family. The people stayed in tents, wagons, and private homes until crowds became too large to be thus accommodated. Later, several large dormitories were built, but during the years these wooden structures have surrendered to the general decay which is the end of most wooden things. Only one remains standing at present.

Some years after Anderson College was founded, dormitories used for students during the school year were made available to the summer convention crowd. This considerably eased the housing problem. However, hundreds of people still find lodging in private homes and motels and hundreds more in trailers, and tents.

In the early '20s the Anderson meetings were somewhat different from what they are today. We had a few missionary conferences and ministerial business sessions but preaching was the big thing. All the big evening services were evangelistic in nature. The music was very enjoyable. The preaching ranged all the way from excellent to mediocre. Yet hundreds were converted as men like W. F. Chappel, J. W. Lykins, R. C. Caudill, J. D. Smoot, S. P. Dunn, H. M. Riggle, J. Lee Collins, F. G. Smith, E. A. Reardon, Paul Bennett, and others delivered their messages.

There were a few pulpit giants, men of a calibre not too common today. A bit on the crude side, some of them, but effective. Then there was the one who, running in high gear in his denunciation of worldliness, exclaimed, "Why, some women wear so little clothing today that if you wadded it up and threw it into hell there wouldn't be enough flame to scorch your eyebrows." I also remember the good brother who drew criticism by saying to a packed auditorium, "If you women want to know whether or not you are dressed modestly, go home and stand before a full-length mirror. Then bend forward as far as you can and see what you can see." If I remember correctly that was the last time he ever appeared on that platform.

I said crude, but effective! Sometimes just crude. One chap was preaching in a great way about eternal punishment. In a moment of high inspiration he spoke of the "thunder-scarred walls of eternity." Did you ever see a scar left by thunder? Then there was the novice (not in Anderson) who in the early years of his ministry was much too loud and demonstrative. During one of his more erratic moments, while gesturing rather wildly, he hit himself in the nose and it began to bleed profusely. He got out his handkerchief and soaked up the blood fairly well but kept right on preaching. Other handkerchiefs were contributed from here and there as his nose continued to bleed and he continued to preach. Finally in an aside from his sermon he confided, "The devil is trying to stop this sermon but I'm going to finish if I have to wade in blood up to my ears." It looked for awhile as if he might be headed in that direction.

Sixty years ago we didn't have program committees for our camp meetings. They were thought to be a hindrance to the free working of the Holy Spirit. I'm not sure but what I've seen one or two programs that *were* a hindrance, if the truth were known. In those days when you attended a camp meeting service, you were never sure who was going to preach. During the song service you'd see half a dozen preachers sitting in a row along the back wall. When it came time for the sermon the people would anxiously peer to see which preacher would rise to the occasion. Sometimes there was quite a pause. On other occasions there was a footrace to the pulpit, with two or three runners. Folk criticized men with the "preach spirit," which I always thought generally referred to the fellow who won the last race but shouldn't have. Then somebody fostered the idea that perhaps, just maybe, the Holy Spirit *might* be able to work through a program committee—even weeks before the meetings. So one was formed, and for better or worse, that is the way it has been ever since.

About twenty years ago, when I came to Anderson to meet with the program committee for the Anderson convention, J. A. Morrison was absent because of the flu. It was during a time when there had been a bit of a squabble in the church. Anyhow, when I learned that Morrison could not be with us, I said facetiously, "Well! It looks like we'll have a smooth meeting." Dr. John got well right away and met with us the next day. The first thing he said was, "Hello, Dale. You know, we might have had a good smooth meeting if you had just stayed home." Do chickens *always* have to come home to roost?

In what we nostalgically refer to as "the good old days" someone was always getting his ears knocked down or his head cut off in private sessions during the big Anderson meetings. Figuratively! Preachers loved to declaim on texts like, "Let judgment begin at the house of the Lord." Brother! When a preacher read one of these texts it paid to slip down low in your seat; because soon the arrows would begin to fly. I know! I did a little of that kind of preaching myself. That is, before the days when the study of psychology became common. Then we preachers began to learn with some embarrassment that a man preaches what he is and sometimes takes out his own personal hostilities on the congregation. Many a preacher who early on Sunday had an argument with his wife made it hot for his church that morning about eleven-fifteen. His "inspiration" stemmed from irritation and frustration.

Every church group has had its fusses and ours is no exception. I've seen good men leave council meetings with tears running down their cheeks, never to return to the fellowship. I'm afraid I use that word *fellowship* loosely. Very loosely. It was all done in the name of truth, you understand, and with the excuse that there has to be judgment in the house of the Lord. God forgive us!

I have seen men who happened to differ on some rather insignificant point of doctrine grow red in the face as they sought to discredit each other. I've seen them angrily leave a committee meeting never to return. Life always seems to be trying to find out what we are made of, doesn't it? Can you take it? *Is* God's grace sufficient? It all depends upon whether we have our eyes on men or on God.

Nearly forty years ago I received a scorching letter from an older preacher whom I admired very much. However, he was a bit spoiled and accustomed to being the bell sheep in his area. I hadn't seen fit to join his retinue of lackeys, and the letter was for the purpose of whipping me into line. It was also intended to intimidate me. Its accusations were unjust, unfair, and uncalled for. I suppose that most young preachers have similar experiences. This letter disappointed me deeply because it was from a man of stature and intelligence. I wrote back saying how much I loved and respected him. I said that I valued the sizable contribution he had made to the church, but I couldn't understand why he should write such a scathing letter to me. I closed by saying, "Please, if you ever have anything like this to say to me again, come to see me or call me to your office, so I can see the expression on your face as you say it." Gradually, over the years, our churches and preachers grew up and tolerance largely replaced the bigotry of former days.

In January of 1923, Sidney L. Wingert and I conducted a four-week meeting in Praise Chapel, located in the country outside Union City, Indiana. I was nearly twenty at the time and appreciated the opportunity to live among farmers for a month. The weather was bitter cold that January and there was quite a bit of snow, but the church, which seated about three hundred, was packed to capacity night after night and dozens were converted. On one or two occasions the crowd made it necessary to seat children on the platform. They were packed so closely that the preacher could scarcely move about. And preachers did move about during their sermons in those days. It was a great meeting.

Sid Wingert was a big man with wide-set eyes and a booming bass voice which was even better at singing than speaking. He made a solid contribution in a male quartet, and I sang with him in various places. His personality would have made him a great success as a salesman or in politics, but he chose to use his talents for Christ and in this he was wise. The Lord used him in a thrilling way as the church in Lima, Ohio, developed under his leadership.

Toward the close of the Praise Chapel meetings, Sid instigated a drive to buy the pastor, Mary Murray, a new automobile. The necessary money was raised almost effortlessly. This benevolent gesture gave the meeting an extra spark and did not affect revival offerings to speak of. Well, maybe it did. My records show that I received $40.00 for the four weeks, but my train fare didn't amount to much since I lived in Indiana.

It hurt me deeply when a cloud came over Sid Wingert's ministry shortly afterward, for our association had been very enjoyable. He left the ministry and was under the "juniper tree" for awhile. Later he emerged victoriously, moved to California, and died beloved by thousands, many of whom called him dad. I was proud to call him my friend. His son Bert, a football star at Ohio State, became a pastor of a fine church in California thus following in his beloved father's footsteps. It would be interesting to know just how many preachers are preachers' sons. Isn't it a compliment to their fathers?

How the complexion of America has changed during the last sixty years! And what problems have arisen out of the shift from country to city! We moved from gas lights and wooden sidewalks and muddy streets to their more modern counterparts. We evacuated the little one-room country schoolhouses in favor of buses and consolidated schools. We exchanged one-man-operated shops for gigantic manufacturing concerns with their assembly line methods of production. We traded the streetcar for Fords, Oldsmobiles, and Cadillacs. We exchanged the sixty-hour workweek for the forty-hour workweek, and the one-week vacation for a three-week vacation with pay.

With all this came a change in the clergy, also. Sixty years ago although few of our clergymen were college graduates, they were highly esteemed in the community and their counsel was sought out by most of their flock. Preachers left the plow to begin preaching. Some came from machine shops, foundries, factories, and offices to preach the Word. Some had no training except that which they received by studying their Bibles and listening to other preachers. You might say of a young man who felt he was called to preach, "He's studying with Reverend Smith." Evangelists used to take young preachers along in their meetings to teach them and help break them in on the job. The late, revered J. Grant Anderson took this kind of interest in young preachers. When I was twenty, I assisted him in meetings at the old City Rescue Mission in Toledo, Ohio, managed at the time by song writer W. J. Henry.

J. Grant Anderson was not an imposing figure. He had keen brown eyes and unusually quick perception. In the days when it was thought to be worldly for the preacher to take notes into the pulpit, J. Grant Anderson was a systematic sermonizer, with a considerable amount of homiletic skill. He was the first preacher to say anything to me about sermon styles and methods of outlining.

In those early days few preachers knew how to build a detailed sermon outline even if they had desired to do so. My beloved father had no study and not much of a library. When thinking about next Sunday's message, he would take his Bible and a small writing tablet, seat himself in the living room among playing children, and rock. While he rocked he "meditated." Once in awhile he would leaf through his Bible to refresh his memory of passages of Scripture. Occasionally he would write one statement on the paper, following this by jotting down half a dozen texts to support it. That was his sermon outline. In the pulpit he was guided by scriptures and inspired of the Lord for his sermon. W. F. Chappel and R. C. Caudill were more thorough in their outlining. E. L. Bragg used an outline which was in reality about half a manuscript. But it was single-spaced on large loose-leaf notebook paper, crowded at the margins, and, I thought, would be very hard to follow in the pulpit, especially for a man with bifocals.

But J. Grant Anderson knew how to construct a sermon outline as it ought to be constructed and was not only willing but eager, to share his knowledge with me. He knew the value of brevity in an introduction; knew how to lead from point number one to point number two. He knew how to tell a story and which story would best illustrate each section of his message. I shall forever be indebted to J. Grant Anderson for the few days we spent dissecting some of his sermon outlines.

George Lorton was another of the old timers with whom it was a pleasure to associate. George had perhaps a fifth-grade education. He had been converted while working in a foundry in Springfield, Ohio, about the time when my good friend, E. E. Caldwell, also found the Lord. Lorton was "different." The Lord made just one of him and threw away the mold. He had been quite a rounder. But when the good Lord saved him all this changed, and he could not be content until the whole world heard how it had taken place. Brother George had springs in his heels. When he was preaching and "got blessed" like as not he would jump into the air, sometimes clearing the floor by a good eighteen inches. Then he might take off and shout a bit. He was short and bald, but his testimony was effective. He made you know that if God could do so much for him he could do the same for you, also. No wonder so many were converted under his simple labors.

Brother Lorton studied doctrine under the tutelage of C. E. Byers, who for thirty-five years was pastor of the Maiden Lane Church of God in Springfield, Ohio. So he knew "the truth." At the Ohio State camp meeting he would lead "ring" meetings at six o'clock in the evening, and over the grounds you could hear him shouting and praising the Lord. He seemed totally uninhibited and never met a stranger. Because he had been of the rougher element he was especially successful in winning many of that kind to Christ. The young people loved him also, and although they laughed at his stories and antics they had genuine respect for him.

In October of 1922 Lorton and I were called to Milledgeville, Ohio, where a vacant Methodist church building had been secured for revival services. Lorton laughed, cried, preached, jumped, shouted, and told his choicest stories. I sang my best, but Milledgeville was a tough little town, and we were not successful in seeing a congregation established there. It was one of the few failures in which I participated. However, the meeting was not a total loss, as there were several converts.

Although it was October, a nearby field still contained dozens of small-to-medium-sized watermelons, and George Lorton loved watermelons. When the owner discovered this, he invited Brother George to help himself to all he wanted. From that time on if you wanted Brother Lorton you would probably find him out by the barn. He had taken his car to the field and filled the entire trunk with watermelons. George Lorton was a product of his times. Today, nearly his entire generation has moved on into eternity.

Camargo, Kentucky, is only a wide place in the road, but interesting memories center there. I preached my first sermon in Camargo and did my first hunting there. Until I was eighteen I probably had never held a shotgun in my hands, and so in this bluegrass region where game was plentiful I was a greenhorn— but willing to learn. The Chappels had a single-shot .12 gauge gun which they placed at my disposal. In my walks across the fields of bluegrass I began carrying it with me.

I had no success as a hunter. Most of the rabbits were sitting tight and I wasn't trained to see them. One day as I was walking through a pasture a young man approached and stopped for conversation. He asked if I'd seen any game. He seemed interested in my gun which had a ring for a trigger. When he asked to see it, I handed it over. He sighted down the barrel, pulled the trigger, and a rabbit which had been snugly hiding in a clump of tall grass not more than a yard from my feet gave up the ghost. The shot nearly scared the daylights out of me. But I can still hear the young man laugh as he handed me the gun and said, "Pick up your game, man." I wonder how many times he told that story the following week? I don't blame him. I would have told it, too.

You couldn't always trust those Kentuckians. They were tricky, just like that fellow. Some of the church men heard about my rabbit hunting, kidded me a bit, and then said that because my education had been sadly neglected they were forming a hunting party for next day and I was invited. At the appointed time half a dozen men set out crossing roads and fences, a dog or two leading the procession. The day was bright, the November air crisp, and I was excited about our prospects. These were experienced hunters and with the dogs along we were sure to get game. I was last in the procession as we crossed a field to follow a path paralleling a fence.

We hadn't gone far before a controversy broke out up ahead. Two men were arguing. Maybe three. One said, "I saw him first. He's my rabbit." The other remonstrated, "I know you did. But you've killed hundreds of rabbits, and Dale, not a one. Let him shoot it." They went on and on and finally the first fellow reluctantly gave in. "Okay, Dale, shoot him." I couldn't see any rabbit and I asked, "Where is it?" "Right there in the fence row." Then I saw him. I aimed and fired and nothing happened. I mean nothing. That pesky rabbit just sat there. I went over to pick him up and found he had been dead for about a week. He smelled to high heaven. Someone had found and planted it just to get a laugh on me. I was embarrassed but tried to enjoy the joke along with the rest.

I wish I could report this ended my distress for the day, but in all good truth, it didn't. Crestfallen and letdown, I trudged along, still at the rear of the procession. We walked down a hill, crossed a creek, and entered timbered land with the fellows shooting a rabbit now and then. All kiddingly urged me to keep my eyes open for game. I did keep looking and finally, after all the men had crossed a creek, I saw a squirrel crouching on a limb high above me. "Ah," I said to myself, "all those smart hunters and none of them spotted him." With great satisfaction I pointed my gun skyward and pulled the trigger. The procession of hunters came to a sudden halt. One or two walked toward me as my squirrel plummeted to earth. The trouble was, when I walked over to pick him up, he, too, had been dead for a week. They couldn't have planted the squirrel! But from the laughter which erupted you would have sworn they had. I haven't lived that day down and doubt that I ever shall. So, don't ever bet on me.

I had one good friend at Camargo who defended me at every turn. He probably felt sorry for me. Al Richards was poor, had a large family, and never made much money; yet, there was always food for his children and a roof over their heads. I liked him. Al enjoyed hunting and owned two of the best rabbit dogs I have ever seen in action. He offered to show me how to hunt and so at the appointed time we set out with the dogs. I had a shotgun, but Al just filled his coat pocket with medium-sized rocks.

This seemed a bit strange to me, but in the back of my mind some story about a boy named David and a man named Goliath kept going round and round. Al said, "Really, I'm not very good with a gun, so I use rocks. I can throw pretty well." Later, I found this to be the understatement of the year. Al continued, "I have only one rule. When we see a rabbit, I get first shot. If I miss and he runs, its your turn." You won't believe that I almost came home without any game. Never have I seen a man who could throw as well as Al threw that day. It made me think of Dizzy Dean, the baseball pitcher, who was "discovered" by someone who saw him throwing rocks at birds on his father's farm—and hitting them. In the first place, Al could see a rabbit where I could see none at all. He'd point and say, "There he is right back of that root on the bank." Or "Right there in that clump of grass." Most of the time I couldn't see him even then until Al's rock had killed him or set

98

him running. He'd see a rabbit, aim, let go his rock, and we would have a dead rabbit.

You'll want to call me a liar, and I really don't blame you. If you had told the story, I doubt if I would have believed it. This tale stretches the credulity of my good friend Everett Hartung, but I declare it is true. W. F. Chappel and R. C. Caudill went out with Al and me one day. Al again claimed first shot with his rocks. He got so many rabbits that Chappel and Caudill began shooting first. This so disgusted Al that he took his dogs and trudged off home. I've always been glad that Al named one of his sons after me.

Speaking of throwing rocks, Polly and I were in North Carolina in a meeting back in the mountains, a place called Pores Knob, about 1926. In the home where we stayed was a fourteen-year-old named Byrum Propes who had a skill similar to Al's. As he and I stood at the gate to the barnyard one day Byrum saw a bird on a post some fifty feet away. Picking up a stone he said, "See that bird over there?" He let go the rock and the bird fell dead. "You don't see him now, do you?" Byrum exulted and laughed as he walked away. I suppose you have to see it to believe it. I was properly impressed with the lad's skill and couldn't help but notice the scarcity of smooth, small stones about the place. The other day I tried to hit a three-foot rattlesnake in the head with a four-inch piece of broken concrete but missed him by six inches. Finally, a piece about eight inches square did the job properly. That gives you a pretty good idea of the kind of baseball pitcher I would have made.

In July of 1923 I traveled to Maryland to lead singing in their Eastern Shore camp meeting. I had never been in Maryland but accepted the invitation with pleasure as my good friend R. C. Caudill was to do the preaching. Emma Coburn had been my correspondent. I found her to be a capable person who seemed to know her job well. A large group of young people was in attendance and we soon had a good choir organized. Services were well attended, especially on weekends, but when Sunday evening came we might as well have canceled out.

The Maryland young set formed a habit which made listening to a sermon well-nigh impossible. I have never seen anything like it. The big crowd was on the grounds all day, of course, but when the evening service started those not seated in the open-sided tabernacle began to walk, circling it again and again. Most of them talked as they walked. Announcements and pleadings to halt the parade were of no effect; they just kept on walking. In desperation the trustees finally set up a fence to block passage at each side. But when the walkers came to the fence, they simply turned and walked the other way, repeating the performance until the benediction was pronounced. I wonder if this thoughtless habit was responsible in any way for the closing down of the Eastern Shore meeting a few years later.

I returned to the Eastern Shore in 1924 and again R. C. Caudill was the evangelist. This time, however, he had brought W. H. Hunt along and made him do half the preaching. I had always considered Hunt a good preacher, but at Eastern Shore, with a big crowd and R. C. to back him up with a great deal of genuine encouragement and a considerable amount of blarney, he outdid himself. The man blossomed like a rose and did the finest preaching I had ever heard from him. Even after returning home his improved style and presentation stayed with him. It is strange how such times of challenge now and then seem to act as a special "baptism."

R. C. also took his son Herschel with him on that second trip to Maryland. About seven at the time, the lad was full of ginger. With an engaging personality, he was soon receiving a great deal of attention, especially at the lunch stand. The clerks seemed to think that the evangelist's young son ought to be served both frequently and free. Herschel adjusted rapidly to this ice-cream-on-the-house philosophy and became one of the stand's most frequent patrons. But alas, the lad overdid it. One day he ate so much ice cream and so many hamburgers that he became ill and was completely out of circulation for a day or two. But, since the illness was not serious, R. C. seemed more amused than concerned by it. But had his mother been there Herschel might have been in for a bit of schooling. How often liberty has a price tag attached to it!

R. C. was not only an indulgent father; he was also a bit tricky at times. The Caudills, W. H. Hunt, and I were sleeping on the second floor of what was fondly referred to as "the evangelists' cottage." It was more like the haymow of a small barn. Access was by a rear, outside stairway. Inside the door was a wide shelf whereon sat an old-fashioned washbasin and a bucket of water. Here we washed, bathed, and shaved. (The good old days!) There was no waste bucket for used wash water, so we dumped it out the back window. But R. C. threw more than wash water out the window. One day when the ever-immaculate Hunt was standing down below, R. C. showered him with the remains of a watermelon feast. If I remember the incident correctly, and I'm sure that I do, Hunt had a bit of difficulty in demonstrating the proper amount of appreciation for this kindly deed. Knowing Hunt, I'd guess that he probably got even with R. C. eventually, but if he did I failed to hear of it.

Some of those Kentucky preachers seemed perennially uneven with each other; always trying to settle a score. Their sense of humor did not always coincide with mine, but I had to live with it. Naturally, I enjoyed their humor most when tricks were played on the other fellow. Tom Steenbergen held a revival for Roger White in Piqua, Ohio years ago. On the last night of the meeting someone brought in a couple of dressed chickens for Tom to take home with him. Tom was properly appreciative and expressed his thanks to the donor. When he arrived home late that night, he told Margaret about the gift. But both were somewhat taken aback when they opened the package to find, not chickens, but rocks. And not Plymouth Rocks! Roger had deftly made the exchange while Tom was saying good-bye to his Piqua friends. Next day he and his family enjoyed two good roasted chickens.

Roger was like that. While holding him a meeting one time, my father was admiring White's little pet dog who was soon to have offspring. Seeing father's delight in the dog, Roger promised that dad could have one of the pups. Months later my father learned that four pups had been born. Not having received one, he asked Roger about it. White laughed and replied, "Sorry, Brother Oldham, but *your* pup died." *Which* pup?

In one of the Maryland camp meetings a group took off one hot afternoon for a beach on nearby Chesapeake Bay. I went along, anticipating my first swim in salt water. G. Q. Pye, minister and former missionary to the West Indies, was in the group. When we arrived at the beach, he and I decided to swim out into the Bay together. Remember, I was totally inexperienced in ocean swimming and had no thought of how tidal action might affect our fun. Pye should have known better. He had spent many years near ocean beaches. I had been told of the buoyancy of ocean water and soon found that everything I had heard was true. We were swimming along at a good rate, and with ease. Too much ease! When perhaps 500 feet from shore, we agreed that we should turn back.

When we did, to our dismay, we found a strong tide running against us. Quickly I realized that unless we really exerted ourselves we would be carried out to sea. Never have I put so much into swimming as I did that day. We fought every inch of the way. I suppose we could have cried out for help and someone might have launched a boat and come for us, but the young are too proud for that. So we battled away. At long, long last I reached a post supporting a pier. There I clung for quite some time gasping for breath. It was a hard way to learn a lesson but I learned it, and learned it well. Pye was embarrassed after having led us into such a potentially dangerous predicament.

The Maryland camp had one or two major disadvantages. There was no public-address system. Since the tabernacle had a corrugated iron roof, whenever it rained the preacher (or singer) was in trouble. The sound was deafening. Even without the rain, a preacher had to have a voice which could be heard and vocal cords that would stand up under a program in which he preached twice a day for ten days in the open air. A preacher would get hot and perspire. The cool breezes of evening would blow in upon him and next day he would be hoarse. It was even worse for singers; and nothing is more calculated to give you the blues than to be a singer in a meeting where you can't sing as you should.

Chapter Eight

The Early Composers

B. E. (BARNEY) WARREN attended the 1924 Eastern Shore camp meeting, chiefly, I think, because he was at the time courting Miss Lottie Charles, pastor of the First Church of God in Baltimore. Warren's first wife, the former Nanny Kiger, had traveled with him in the early '90s as a member of the D. S. Warner gospel team, but she had passed away about 1922. B. E. Warren was one of the most prolific of our Church of God songwriters, composing more than 7,000 gospel songs. During his work with D. S. Warner he suffered a considerable amount of persecution. After Warner had been forced to flee into a Mississippi thicket to escape from a mob bent on violence, Warner wrote these words:

> *Who will suffer with the Savior,*
> *Take the little that remains*
> *Of the cup of tribulation*
> *Jesus drank in dying pains?*
>
> *Who will offer soul and body*
> *On the altar of our God?*
> *Leaving self and worldly mammon,*
> *Take the path that Jesus trod?*
>
> *Soon the conflict will be over,*
> *Crowns await the firm and pure;*

Forward, brethren, work and suffer,
Faithful to the end endure.

Chorus:

Lord, we fellowship thy passion,
Gladly suffer shame and loss;
With thy blessing pain is pleasure,
We will glory in thy cross.

I have never been too strong for women preachers, but nevertheless have always thought that Lottie Charles and Esther Kirkpatrick Bauer were two of the best. Lottie had done a good work in Baltimore and had the confidence and respect of the people. Her judgment was sound. She could organize her work well and get it done. Now, however, she had consented to become B. E. Warren's bride. The wedding date had been set to follow the close of the camp meeting by a day or two. Although I was much younger than either of them, B. E. Warren had asked me to be his best man. This I was happy to do, but the sad truth was, I didn't own a suit of clothes fit for the occasion. So the day before the wedding, Brother Warren took me to town and outfitted me in a very presentable black mohair suit which made both of us feel better. Thus B. E. Warren and Lottie Charles were happily united in marriage. We joyously saw them off on their honeymoon and I went on to another camp meeting.

I shall always be glad that I came into the ministry early enough to know some of our most prolific music composers. Besides B. E. Warren, I met and came to appreciate deeply A. L. Byers, D. O. Teasley, and folk who wrote some of the poetry to which their music was set, C. W. Naylor and Clara M. Brooks. D. S. Warner passed away in 1895. Although I had no opportunity to meet him, I have always respected his literary and poetic ability. B. E. Warren set most of Warner's poetry to music since they traveled together for several years.

B. E. Warren's songs had a lilt to them and were always singable. He also managed to give a considerable variety to his melodies. Since he was a tenor, I thought he sometimes put his compositions in a key about one step too high for the average singer, such as one of his most popular numbers titled "Beautiful." However, he must have been inspired of the Lord while composing many of his songs, for the singing of them still lends inspiration to our churches. Warren had studied harmony and composition as a young man. By the time I met him he had forgotten most of the rules but still followed them out of force of habit.

A. L. Byers was a totally different personality. A precise man and a stickler for details, he was a hard worker. When he composed a song, you could be sure that there would be no consecutive fifths or octaves and that every chord would be resolved as correctly as if he had been doing it for an examination paper. Yet his compositions were singable and not stiff or objectionable in any way. Byers had an excellent bass voice. It was to be expected that some of his compositions would give bass singers an opportunity to carry a lead part now and then.

There was a solidness about his work which always merited my admiration. His manuscripts were precise and legible, which was quite a contrast to some of the hen scratches made by some composers. As music editor for the Gospel Trumpet Company for many years, it was Byers' duty to scrutinize new music manuscripts, many of them from budding songwriters and would-be song writers. There were few of the first, but many of the second.

Isn't it strange how at some time during his life nearly everyone considers himself a poet? How many letters have I received from folks who have enclosed a "poem" and added, "Go ahead and publish this. Use it any way you think best. I am not interested in making money from my songs. I just want them to be sung worldwide." Generally the "poetry" was not worth printing and the music consisted of melody only. They expected literary correction on the poetry, and someone to harmonize the music for them and have it printed. Almost none seemed to have any idea as to what makes a song poem valuable or what it costs to print a song. Rarely did a manuscript come to my desk that I considered worthwhile.

Bill Gaither has used one or two of my song poems, but he has "filed" dozens of others which *I* am sure are "inspired" and "wonderful."

Byers received countless compositions in the mail and, since most were of little merit, it was his job to return them to the author. He often accompanied the returned poem or manuscript with a blunt note, "This song really has nothing to justify its being printed." Or, "If I were you, I would enroll somewhere for a course in harmony and composition." If a submitted song did happen to have merit, but was weak at one or two points, Byers was not past giving it the benefit of his surgical skill, making out of it something worthwhile. Since he generally did this without asking permission of the author, some were rather surprised, I am sure, at how their composition finally emerged from the printshop. I am one of them.

A. L. Byers' orderliness could be seen not only in the correctness of his compositions but also in the preciseness with which he wrote. Long months of research preceded the writing of his *The Birth of a Reformation*. His personal library was an example of neatness, with every book exactly catalogued and in place. He did not lend his books readily, as his son Homer discovered after we had formed a male quartet and wished to raid the section of his father's library in which male quartet songs were to be found. Homer sneaked one or two books out of the house without his father's knowledge. When A. L. found out about it he was a bit unhappy.

Byers' handwriting reflected his demand for orderliness and preciseness as personal, handwritten letters in my files attest. He rendered a much-needed service to the church as editor for several of our hymnals. He was a hard worker and faithful to his task.

Although Warren and Byers were talented men, they were also rather average human beings, subject to times of elation and discouragement just as we are. As B. E. Warren got up in years he lost a bit of his magic touch and nearly every composition had a peculiarity or quirk somewhere, either in words or music. The better songs became fewer and the poorer ones more numerous.

In 1935 a group of music men met for a week or two in Bessemer, Alabama, to select songs for a hymnal which was to contain nothing but new compositions. The book was to be titled *His Praise Anew*. When final selections had been made, several of the new songs B. E. Warren had submitted were not included. In his aging judgment he surmised that A. L. Byers and I had joined forces against him which, of course, was not the case at all. A few weeks later I received a letter from Warren asking that I return any poems or manuscripts of his. This I did with a letter which I hoped would be pacifying. The matter ended there and for the rest of his life we were again warm friends.

When I entered Anderson Bible Training School in the fall of 1919, D. O. Teasley, another of our talented songwriters, had already gained quite a reputation as a multitalented man. He was very versatile and whatever he chose to do he did well. He had served as manager of our publishing house and was the author of two or three books. He was an interesting speaker whose humor and personality made it a pleasure to listen to him. He had a good bass voice for singing and speaking. I think he was probably the best all-round songwriter among us. Teasley not only knew the rules of harmony and used them correctly and creatively, he also was able to teach and communicate those basics to others. I learned more from him in a ten-day course in harmony than I had learned in a year in the Training School. He did not generally write the words for his compositions.

I well remember the night, more than fifty years ago, when Teasley honored me with an invitation to go with him to the home of C. W. Naylor, where we would sing some of his new compositions for the aging invalid. Mona Moors would be there to sing soprano, and an alto, Hope Nelson, I believe, would also help out. I would sing tenor and Teasley bass. Teasley held Naylor's judgment in high respect, particularly when it came to sizing up the appropriateness of the poetry, or its wedding to the music.

I can see Naylor yet, lying there on his cot, an eye-shade pulled down over his forehead, listening intently as we sang one after another of Teasley's compositions. Between songs there would be blunt conversation regarding the merits or demerits of words and music. As I remember it, Naylor made several helpful suggestions which Teasley was quick to adopt. Altogether it was a pleasant and thrilling evening for me, a boy of seventeen, and I shall never forget it. I was even more pleased when several of the songs we sang for the first time that evening, appeared in our next hymnal.

One of them was the song, "We'll Praise the Lord," which our churches still sing.

D. O. Teasley disappeared from the scene not long afterward because of a time of discouragement which came out of his relationships with some of our executive group. I don't know much of the story or who was at fault, but I have always thought it a shame that a man so talented was not given better understanding from his brethren. We are so quick to censure and so slow to encourage. Be that as it may, Teasley dropped out of church work for a number of years, making a living through the use of yet another talent, commercial art.

We lost track of him for awhile but finally heard that he had again found a satisfactory relationship with the Lord. It hurt me deeply to hear later that only four persons attended his funeral which had been conducted by a minister from the Church of the Nazarene. However, the good men do lives after them, and D. O. Teasley will live in our hearts so long as his songs continue to bless and inspire us. My boyhood memories take in the singing of his remarkable gospel song, "Eternity," which produced a solemnity and soberness in any congregation where it was sung. I consider it one of his most inspired compositions and have been sorry that just one apparent inconsistency in the words caused it to be dropped from our hymnals.

C. W. Naylor's name will also remain in our history books for a good many years to come. I first met him on the occasion mentioned above, but later I became well-acquainted with him and served as his pastor during the closing years of his life. Naylor had entered the ministry as a young man and had seriously injured a kidney while helping either to raise or lower a big tent. He had been an invalid ever since. For years Brother Naylor conducted a helpful question and answer column in *The Gospel Trumpet.* He wrote several books, one of which, *The Secret of the Singing Heart,* it was my privilege to tape record for the Library for the Blind, at Louisville, Kentucky. His sane, wise counsel was given freely to hundreds whose problems were causing unhappiness or confusion. He had one of the first dictating machines I ever saw. He recorded his correspondence at home and had it transcribed by a secretary at the publishing house.

Naylor seemed bothered by eye trouble and always avoided bright lights. In fact, he lived his last years in a darkened room, which, I felt, was detrimental to his psychological well-being. Actually, he confessed sometime before he died that there was nothing particularly wrong with his eyes. He just liked to shut out the world when at work on his books or manuscripts. They used to bring him up to the Anderson campgrounds during a June meeting to speak to the ministers. I can still see him lying there on his cot, his white eyeshade shielding him from the lights. Naylor had a gravelly voice but it carried well and he had no difficulty being heard.

As he advanced in age, there were times when he felt neglected and forgotten. He may have had some cause for thinking so. His wife had died and he had been left alone too much. In advanced age, as death drew near, Brother Naylor seemed filled with anxiety and did not approach the end with the calm serenity he had displayed through his lifetime. I put it down to hardening of the arteries. In senility a person often undergoes a change of personality. Naylor lived a dedicated life and rendered much helpful service. He died as he had lived, and all who knew him testified to his worth and integrity.

It was during one of the Eastern Shore camp meetings in Maryland that I first met Paul Cook, who was sixteen or seventeen at the time. I shall never forget his quick broad smile and happy face. Everyone loved Paul! Bright appearing and intelligent, he had a talent for music and sang well. Paul was receiving an unusual amount of attention from the people of the area who held him in genuine affection.

Some of this attention stemmed from the fact that as a small boy Paul had lost his mother. Also, his somewhat alcoholic father was on the careless side. The two had been found living in a barn-like structure which, from what I was told, was scarcely fit for human habitation. When in his cups, Mr. Cook would mistreat Paul; so it was a good day for the lad when some people from the church found him and took him under their wing. Actually, the church became Paul's family. Welcome in any home, day or night, he became active in the youth organization and church music. It was a pleasure to hear the lad sing the kind of solos which brought tears to one's eyes, especially the eyes of mothers.

Some years later, Paul combined with George W. Blackwell to write a gospel song, "Trust in the Lord," which reflected what had become his philosophy of life. Paul married a fine girl, attended Anderson College, entered the ministry, and became one of our more successful young ministers, eventually pastoring our largest congregation in West Virginia. After his wife's tragic death, Paul went into a decline and was never quite the same again. But some of us still carry him in our hearts, write to him, and pray for him. How blessed are children whose thoroughly Christian parents bring them up in the nurture and admonition of the Lord. Paul had lacked this advantage.

Chapter Nine

I Come of Age

MY TWENTY-FIRST birthday found me in evangelistic meetings with the Bethany Church of God in Detroit, Michigan, pastored at the time by Dr. Charles E. Brown, who later became editor in chief of our church publications. John L. Williams was serving as evangelist. "Jumping Johnny" we called him, because when Brother John "got blessed" he could clear the floor by a good two feet. John was a Welshman, proud of it, and beloved by the people. He had a great sense of humor matched by an overflowing love for God and people.

As a birthday gift my parents sent money with which to buy a good pocket watch. I chose a twenty-one jeweled South Bend watch of white gold which still keeps good time. The trouble is we don't wear vests any more and so the watch lies unused in a drawer.

It was a pleasure to stay with the Lovett family while in Detroit. The older son, Hugo, had trained me on the addressograph machine at the Gospel Trumpet Company during my first year at ABTS. Loyd and Beulah added to the fun and fellowship and their widowed mother acted as a balance for all of us. One day, Hugo suggested that we ride the ferryboat across the river to Windsor, Canada. Since I had never set foot on foreign soil, I thought it a good idea. In Windsor we looked the downtown section over for half an hour or so, became bored, and headed back to the river. As we crossed on the ferry, an attendant asked to see my vaccination certificate. Surprised, I had to confess I had never been vaccinated.

Unknown to Hugo and me, there was a minor epidemic of small-pox in Windsor and health authorities were doing all they could to keep it from spreading. The attendant said, "You'll have to be vaccinated." I replied that I didn't want to be vaccinated. "That's all right with me," he countered, "but you'll be on the next boat back to Windsor." So that's how I was first vaccinated for small-pox, right there on the boat. During my childhood our teaching on divine healing was such that none of us was vaccinated, even when pressure was put on us by the public schools. I had never been vaccinated or inocculated against anything. The vaccination took effect, and in a day or two my arm swelled to about twice its normal size. I think the nurse must have given me an extra-large injection. It was forty-five years before another smallpox vaccina-tion "took."

During the Detroit meetings an industrial psychologist in the church took me aside for a personal interview. He was probably curious to see if I had anything besides a singing voice to offer the world. After giving me a series of aptitude tests, he told me I would make a good secretary, typist, or pianist. Since I had already flunked the piano bit, I discounted his judgment about fifty per-cent.

But one thing he revealed interested me. "You have an unusually fast eye," he told me. "You see things before others see them. Things register with you at a glance. A fast eye is gained during only one period in life; that is at the age of fifteen or sixteen. What were you doing at that age?" Well, as already related, at fifteen and sixteen I was working in the mailing department at Nordyke and Marmon's. They had flour milling machine dealers all over the world, and to each went several letters almost daily, mimeo-graphed information sheets for the most part. Our office girls folded these and placed them in envelopes which we sealed on a machine. Then it was my job to place these envelopes in their in-dividual cubbyholes for later mailing. I would glance at an en-velope, slip it into its box, and go on to the next. It could be that this work, done over a period of eighteen months, did quicken my eyes. In any case, I do know that quick eyes have been a great advantage over the years, helping me in the pulpit with my sermon notes. Also in reading 1160 Christian Brotherhood Hour sermon manuscripts before a microphone in our recording studios. We had a good meeting in Detroit and about thirty were converted.

A year earlier I had served in Detroit with another church pastored at the time by an elderly preacher named Sheldon. He was a saintly old fellow who reminded me of the patriarchs. I enjoyed his company. E. L. Bragg was the evangelist. The weather was cold, as only Detroit in its dampness can be cold.

One night after the evangelist had preached a convincing sermon, I was leading the invitation song when there was a commotion at the door. Soon a middle-aged woman entered assisting her stumbling husband who was very much under the influence of alcohol. He was having great difficulty staying on his feet. I can still see the anxious, pleading expression on his wife's face as she helped him down the aisle. I think we were singing "Just As I Am," but the alcoholic began loudly to sing "The Old Rugged Cross." He won, and we quit. There was something very pathetic about him as his wife brought him to kneel at the place of prayer. He was in no condition to carry on a sane conversation. The evangelist said, "Let us all pray earnestly for this man. He needs help. Let's pray first that the Lord will sober him up so we can talk to him." Earnest prayer was offered and answered almost immediately. That was the first miracle. One minute the alcoholic was incoherent; the next he was able to converse soberly.

The evangelist instructed him in how to pray, after which this needy brother got down to business, repenting of his sins and asking the Lord for forgiveness. Then the second miracle was performed. The Lord heard his prayer, had mercy, forgave his sins, and made a new person out of him. Within minutes the relieved man looked up, tears in his eyes, and humbly thanked the Lord for what he had received. It broke all of us up. He was genuinely converted.

Taking his weeping wife into his arms, he asked and received forgiveness for the mistreatment he had meted out through the years. Later on I was invited to their home for dinner, and we enjoyed a wonderful fellowship. He recalled, "Everything was going wrong for me. I was about to lose my job because of liquor. We

113

were about to lose our home because I had defaulted on the payments. My wife was fed up and about to divorce me. When I found the Lord, everything was changed. Our marriage was saved, my job was saved, and we saved our home. Best of all my soul was saved." Isn't it wonderful how a miracle-working God can take a man who is down and almost out, forgive his sins, change his nature, and make a completely new person out of him?

Ansonia, Ohio, is a small town located almost on the Ohio-Indiana line some sixty miles east of Anderson. In December of 1923 the pastor was a man named Ball. He had called in an Indianapolis evangelist and asked me to sing in a revival series. There had been a lot of rain and snow, and some of the roads were almost impassable. Few country roads were paved. I was staying with a farm family several miles from the church. Their home was located a quarter of a mile down a quagmire of a lane. Every time we left or arrived it was a gamble as to whether the old Model T Ford would make it. When we left for church, the driver would say, "Pray!" I still don't know how we made it so many times without getting stuck but those Model T Fords could negotiate some pretty deep ruts without hanging up. But there were several times when I wanted to suggest to my host that he wouldn't have to strain his faith in God so hard, if during better weather, he would spread about fifty loads of gravel down his lane.

The Indianapolis evangelist was an ordinary unskilled preacher of the old school. He did the best he could, but the meeting lagged until seventeen-year-old Walter Shriner came to spend a weekend with us. Walter was from Lima, Ohio, and while still in high school had begun to preach. He did unusually well, even by adult standards. His sermons were orderly, logical, and delivered intelligently and effectively. It was a pleasure to listen. We all enjoyed his messages and folk were converted. I felt sorry for the evangelist, who complained that the people preferred Walter, which was true. But we older men should prepare ourselves for the fact that younger, more vigorous lads are constantly coming on and will have their day. We need to pat them on the back and give them every possible encouragement. It might also help if we took a good honest look at ourselves occasionally.

In looking back over my early twenties, it seems that I was perennially in need of a new suit. My time at Ansonia was no exception. The folk looked at me, and then took up a collection which they bluntly said was for the purpose of buying me a new suit. $28.50. I was quite happy to have the new clothing, but when the three-weeks meeting was concluded, they paid me off with $23.00, adding, "Of course we bought you a new suit. Remember?" I remembered, but I would have been happier had they given me the money and allowed me to shop alone.

Thus I went from meeting to meeting, always poor, but always with a feeling of satisfaction in the work we were doing. In May of 1923, as winter faded and the warm spring breezes began to blow, oil man Claude Townsend shipped a large tent to Paintsville, Kentucky, and had it erected on a vacant corner lot near the center of town. Again I was teamed with the Chappels. Paintsville is located at the edge of the mountains in eastern Kentucky. At the time of our arrival, because of heavy rains, it was barely accessible by road. During the three weeks we were there, I saw only one automobile make it through town. The "highways" were quagmires. People coming to town either rode horseback down a path along the fences, or walked. One spring wagon came through with mud all over it, pulled by two mule teams. The mules were covered with mud halfway up their bodies.

Roads like that may be bad for business but they are good for revivals. When the people can't go anywhere else, they go to church. We had no Church of God in Paintsville. We roomed and took meals at a little one-story hotel. The charge was a dollar a day per person for room and fifty cents per meal. We had no money and that mounting bill for rooms and board caused me considerable concern. The meetings caught on almost at once and people filled the tent. Brother Chappel preached, batted his eyes, and ran his hand back through his hair. John played the piano from one end to the other, and I sang the best I could. "The Sunny Side of Life" became popular and was requested again and again. Best of all, the Holy Spirit moved with conviction in the hearts of the people to such a degree that things happened in Paintsville which I have never seen happen before or since.

As we stood singing an invitation song, someone back in the congregation would fall to his knees as if hit on the head. Then he would begin calling on the Lord to save him. I thought this phenomenon might be the result of suggestion, as was the case during the Shaker revival, but inquiry revealed that in no previous meetings in Paintsville had such things ever been witnessed. One thus stricken was a prominent business man in town. Another, a lovely young girl of about eighteen. My only explanation is that the Lord sent conviction for sin in such power that the people simply could not stand up under it and were forced to their knees. Anyhow, we had a great meeting, and a congregation of 50 or 60 persons was established.

Naturally, John and I looked upon his father as head of our little evangelistic team. But when we arrived in Paintsville, Brother Chappel said, "I've always made the decisions for the three of us; planning what we would do and how the offerings were to be divided. In this meeting I want you boys to run things. Take the offerings, pay the bills, and when the meetings are over and all financial obligations have been taken care of, divide the money between us as you think best." The offerings were good. After bills were paid, we gave Brother Chappel $200 and kept $100 apiece for ourselves. It was the most money I had ever received in my life and I was twenty years old. Brother Chappel was pleased with our stewardship and said to our delight, "I put you boys to the test and you came through with flying colors." I saved some of that money, for Polly and I were already talking about marriage.

Before saying more about the girl I was to marry, let me tell you about the 1924 camp meeting held at West Frankfort, Illinois. C. E. Byers of Springfield, Ohio, was the evangelist, and, for the first time, the program committee had also imported a singer. Had I fully understood the situation I probably would have turned down the invitation.

It was not difficult to organize a good choir and there was other special quartet music of fairly good quality. I was given a first-class pianist, which was very helpful. Southern Illinois churches were ultraconservative, but the people were warmhearted and friendly and so we enjoyed a fine fellowship together. Midway during the ten-day meeting one of the pastors informed me that the ministers had decided to ordain me to the ministry next day. I was shocked, for such a thing had never entered my mind. Why should the Illinois brethren ordain a person from Indiana? I had done much singing but little preaching and was thought of as a singer, not as a preacher. When I suggested this, the pastor smiled and said, "We mentioned all that, but decided that since you travel so widely you really belong to all of us. So unless you have some serious objection, we want to ordain you."

Next day the ordination took place in the ministers' meeting. I felt an indescribable solemnity in my heart as men of God laid hands upon me and the ordination prayer was offered. The date was July 27, 1924. My ordination certificate bears the signatures of C. E. Byers, S. J. Lane, and I. M. Heddin, all long since deceased. That worn and faded piece of paper is still one of my treasured possessions.

We Church of God people hold to the idea that the divisions in Christendom are unnecessary, uncalled for, and perhaps even un-Christian. We believe that spiritually speaking all followers of our Lord are one. Didn't Jesus pray in John 17 "that they all may be one"? We teach that you can't join the New Testament church; you must be born into it. As Jesus said to Nicodemus, "You must be born again." We believe that the New Testament church is composed only of the born again. We emphasize the verse in Acts 2:47 which reads, "The Lord added to the church daily such as should be (or, were being) saved." We also underscore verses five and six of the 87th Psalm, "And of Zion it shall be said, This and that man was born in her . . . The Lord shall count, when he writeth up the people, that this man was born there." I'll confess that our fathers probably made too much of a passage found in 2 Corinthians 6:17, "Wherefore come out from among them, and be ye separate, saith the Lord, and touch not the unclean thing; and I will receive you."

They applied this text to denominationalism, "sectism" they called it, and said that it called for all Christians to come out from all the denominations and stand together free and clear. Only thus would we experience true Christian unity. They had misap-

117

plied the text of course, since any student of the Bible realizes that it pointed, not to denominationalism, but to unbelieving pagans. However, I still feel that competitive divisions among Christians are a slap in the face to Christ and should be abolished.

Why are we Methodists, Baptists, Presbyterians, or Congregationalists? Why can't we just be Christians and leave it there? Years ago I told Dr. E. Stanley Jones that I didn't like it because he was a Methodist. When he asked why, I explained that I didn't think he had any right to live behind a Methodist wall because he belonged to all of us, not just to the Methodists. I do not like denominational walls. They tend to separate the sheep of God's pasture.

During the West Frankfort camp meeting evangelist C. E. Byers decided to preach a sermon on the origin of the New Testament church. He summarized certain facts of history and explained what happened to hide the original church from our view. He asked me to assist by reading selected scriptures for him as they were needed. The evangelist also decided to add some "visual aids" to clarify his message. So, ahead of the service, we set up a fairly large chalkboard where it could be plainly seen by the people. Then Byers drew upon it the outline of a church building large enough to cover the chalkboard. This was to represent the original church of the New Testament, the church of the morning time. When the song service ended, the preacher read his text and the message was under way. Everyone wondered what he planned to do about the church on the chalkboard.

As he went forward with his message, Brother Byers began to show how the first Protestant denomination appeared on the scene in Germany under the leadership of that valiant monk, Martin Luther. And how, although Luther had not intended to begin a new church when he tacked his 95 theses to the door of Wittenburg Chapel, a new denomination was started in spite of him. The speaker had provided me with perhaps fifteen smaller "churches" cut out of white tissue paper. When he mentioned the Lutherans, I took one of the tissue paper churches and pinned it over a corner section of the big church which had been drawn on the chalkboard. Then, as he came down through history and mentioned the emer-

118

gence of other denominations one by one, I pinned a tissue paper church over the chalk drawing to represent each of them. This continued until the original church was completely covered and could not be seen. The church of the New Testament had been obscured by "manmade" churches.

I had pinned these tissue paper churches in such a way that they stood out from the chalkboard by at least three-fourths of an inch, which left room for air to circulate beneath them. Brother Byers began to bring his message to a climax quoting Zechariah 14. He reminded us that we had been living in days clouded by a misapprehension of the nature of the true church. In these "latter days" God was rolling back the clouds to permit the light to shine in. I read verse 7 for him, "But it shall come to pass, that at evening time it shall be light." This meant that truth long hidden was about to break forth, that the true church was again being revealed in all her purity and glory.

At a signal from Byers, I touched a match to the tissue paper churches and they all disappeared in a few puffs of fire and smoke, leaving "the church of the morning time" revealed in all her glory. It was one of the most dramatic sermonic illustrations I have ever seen and certainly served to get the point across. Spontaneously, shouts of "Hallelujah!" and "Praise God!" broke forth from all over the tabernacle. Thank God for *his* church!

Chapter Ten

That Girl
In My Life

BUT NOW TO "POLLY." Pauline Edith Brown was born on Ogan Avenue in Huntington, Indiana, in 1905. During the summer of 1918, when I was fifteen and she thirteen, we met at the home of a mutual friend, Merton Merica, then pastoring the Church of God at North Webster, Indiana. Polly had come with her parents for a visit, and I had been brought from Indianapolis by the Carl Struckmans.

I was drawn to Polly the moment we met. Her hair was the color of corn silk, her smile gay and mischievous. But when she went to the piano and played the current World War I song "K-K-K-Katy," she stole my heart. We managed to spend several hours together during the next couple of days. And we still have snapshots taken together during this visit. Shortly, however, our ways parted. I returned to Indianapolis for the beginning of school, and it was two years before we met again.

In the meantime Polly had grown from girl to young woman and was quite a lady. She had continued with the piano and was much more proficient. By this time I had entered Anderson Bible Training School. One weekend I came from Anderson with my roommate, John Settlemyre, to Huntington, near which his parents owned a farm. I was both surprised and pleased to meet Polly in church on Sunday, as she had been living in Saint Louis for a year or more.

In 1921 my father moved to Huntington as pastor and the Brown family was in his congregation. I began my evangelistic travels that summer but returned home every several weeks to rest. On one of these occasions Polly brought over some things her mother had baked. I found that at sweet sixteen she was very easy on the eyes. As she left the parsonage, my father, in whose judgment of people I had the utmost confidence, said, "That girl will make some man a mighty good wife." I filed his remark away for future reference, and on July 4 I had my first date with her. The more I was with Polly the more I admired and respected her. She had unusual poise and dignity for a girl of sixteen.

When we were together, conversation was easy. We discovered that we had a community of mutual ideals and interests. She was playing the piano very well, and I began to think how convenient it would be to be married to such a first-class instrumentalist. In my evangelistic work I had been afflicted with a few very incompetent pianists. Church pianos are generally poor enough, but when you team up a poor player with a bad piano you have a lamentable duo! Polly could play! However, she had given herself exclusively to classical music and showed little interest in playing hymns and gospel songs. I felt it wouldn't take her long to make the transition. And it didn't.

We began to date whenever I was home from meetings and we corresponded when apart, which was most of the time. Monday through Friday we would see each other every evening and perhaps be separated for five to eight weeks. My chief solace was in the three letters which came regularly each week and the photo which I set up in every room I occupied.

Polly was converted in revival services held in the Huntington church in 1921. I well remember the night because I was there to sing in the meetings. In a conversation the day before when I had suggested that she should yield her heart to Christ she had laughed. This both distressed and confused me. My solo that evening was titled, "For You I am Praying" and I put my heart into it. I sang it at her as well as *for* her. To my delight she came forward in response to the invitation and has been a steady, faithful servant of the Lord ever since.

122

Pauline Brown was a shy, modest girl, so self-conscious she would avoid going to the ice-cream parlor with me. She didn't want me to sit watching her eat. Our courting was done chiefly without the benefit of money but this wasn't too much of a hardship. Neither of us had ever had money to spend freely. Anyhow, it was enough just to be together. We took many long walks during which we discussed our future. Most of our evenings together were spent in her parents' home where Polly often played the piano and we sang together.

Young people are amused when I tell them of the evenings when I read aloud to Polly by the hour. We attended a few concerts and basketball games but more often than not stayed at home. We made fudge. Sometimes we went on picnics with our folks or double-dated with Polly's cousin, Mildred Overmyer, and her boy friend, Dewy Cozad, who owned a car. All the while I was becoming more and more impressed by Polly's personality and the soundness of her character. I was head over heels in love with the girl, and it made me very happy when, after some hesitation, she consented to become my wife.

The previous April I had sung in revival services in Mount Sterling, Kentucky. J. W. Lykins ("Little Joe") was the evangelist. Brother Lykins was a capable, interesting preacher and a good man with a well-developed sense of humor. Having recently passed my twenty-first birthday and with plans to marry in August, I was becoming anxious as to whether or not I would be able to support a wife. My income in evangelistic work had been scarcely enough to support one person, much less two.

One day I asked Lykins what he thought of Polly and me getting married. I asked, "Do you think I will be able to support a wife in evangelistic work?" My total income during the previous year was $833.00. I'll never forget Brother Lykins' reply. "Is the girl you plan to marry a Christian?" he asked. I told him she was, and a good one. "Well," he continued, "God has promised to take care of his children. If you are a Christian and she is a Christian, I don't see why he can't take care of the two of you together." With this encouragement, I went ahead with my plans, but believe me I was having to mix a great deal of faith in with them.

The summer passed with its camp meetings: Anderson, West Frankfort, and Maryland, with a three-week tent meeting thrown in somewhere for good measure. Polly and I managed to purchase a few pieces of furniture, some of it secondhand, which we stored in a neighbor's vacant apartment. I tried desperately to save money but money was scarce, and this worried me. My final camp meeting for the summer was at Payne, Ohio. Polly came over on the last Sunday, and we were showered with a number of useful gifts.

We were to be married in Huntington on Tuesday, August 26. When I arrived on Monday, it was to find an anxious girl who wasn't entirely sure she wanted to marry me after all. She was frightened and who could blame her? After all, what security had I to offer? Could I provide her with the necessities of life? Would she have the clothes she needed? Besides, I was a somewhat tempestuous person. Her mother had warned that I would cause her tears with my quick words.

Polly must be a gambler at heart because when the hour for the wedding arrived she was there in all her glory. She was a beautiful bride. But aren't most brides beautiful? Church weddings weren't at all common among our people in 1926. They cost too much. So we were married in Polly's home and friends came in from as far away as Indianapolis. The home was modest. Everything in it was modest. But the ceremony my father read was sincere and serious.

Later, my smiling mother remarked that I would never be whiter even when dead than I was standing there before the minister. Oscar Wiles played appropriate music on his flute, my sixteen-year-old sister, Hazel, accompanying him at the piano. Polly's attendants were Maybelle and Clarabelle Whitinger, twins who had been good friends during Polly's employment at Gospel Trumpet Company as telephone operator and receptionist. Russell Feldman came up from Indianapolis to serve as my best man.

Russell brought his fiancée, Esther Miller, his mother, and his sister, Dorothy. Since Russell and Esther planned to be married in the near future, some of us began kidding them, suggesting that they ought to get a license and be married with us. We never dreamed they would take us seriously. But they did. So, after they returned from the courthouse, dad had *two* couples to marry instead of one.

This new turn of events precipitated several problems. First, Esther had brought no dress suitable for the occasion. Finally, Russell's sister, Dorothy, lent her a white dress in which she had recently been graduated from high school. Of course, when Russell decided to become a bridegroom, I lost my best man and so was married without one, as was he. The whole turn of events pushed all of us a bit, but finally the two couples lined up before my father who opened his little black book and began to read.

Standing before him, I was overcome by the seriousness of the situation. This girl by my side would not only be united to me in marriage, she would be *tied* to me for the rest of her life. She would wear only the clothes I could provide; live only as I could afford. Her destiny would be bound solidly to mine. From this hour on I would be responsible for any bills she might incur. It would be difficult for her to go much further in life than I would be able to take her.

I'll have to confess to a feeling of considerable anxiety as I stood by Polly's side waiting to make the proper responses to the questions being put by my father. I suppose all of us made the responses correctly, because in a few minutes everyone was laughing, shaking hands, kissing the brides, and moving on to the refreshments. The wedding was over. For better or for worse, I was a married man. We couldn't afford a photographer, but Bill Ramey (later the Reverend William Ramey) had a Brownie box camera and took a few snapshots. These were our only wedding pictures.

Yes, I was a married man, but so was Russell—unexpectedly! Polly and I had that $150 worth of new and used furniture. I had paid a $25 rental fee for a week at a cottage located on the south shore of Webster Lake, an ideal place for a honeymoon. Russell was broke. Nevertheless, he and Esther decided to take a day or two off from their jobs and honeymoon with us. I wasn't too keen about this turn of events. But having egged them on to marry, it seemed the sporting thing to help them enjoy a short honeymoon, even though I would have to foot the bills. My father offered us his Model T Ford for the trip. When the wedding guests began to thin out, I began packing our things in the car. North Webster was about a forty-five-mile trip, and we wished to arrive before nightfall.

At this point other developments were revealed to my further abashment; Polly and I were destined to have even more company on our honeymoon. I hadn't given dad a fee for performing the ceremony, so he and mother decided to enjoy the lake with us for a couple of days. Hazel would have to go with them, of course. And Russell's sister, Dorothy. Then Polly's father and mother got into the act. They hurriedly packed and joined the caravan. Brother!

So two cars, carrying ten persons and their luggage, arrived at our four-room lake cottage about sunset. There was a lot of fun and kidding and talking about where everyone would sleep. Of course, we also had to stock up on groceries. That first trip to the supermarket made an alarming dent on the $40 which had to run me all week. Strange, now that I think of it, nobody else seemed to have a dime.

With supper over and the dishes done, everyone was weary from the long day. Before ten o'clock our parents announced bedtime. There were two small bedrooms. Wouldn't you have expected that these would be occupied by the two newly married couples? Certainly! But it didn't turn out that way. My parents took one bedroom, Polly's parents the other. By the time other allotments had been made, involving a daybed and what we used to call a "sanitary couch," the two newly married couples discovered that they were to sleep on the dining room floor. Polly and I had one thin quilt to serve as our downy mattress! Russell and Esther had the same. Great! Just great!

Everyone was laughing and talking up a storm until my mother said, "Children, it's getting late. We need our rest," and everything quieted down. For a few minutes. Then someone snickered. This triggered a laugh and then everyone was talking again. But at long last things simmered down, and I began to realize how hard a dining room floor can be. With Polly's head resting on my arm, for some strange reason, I recalled an incident which had taken place about dawn one morning during the Maryland camp meeting.

A good preacher brother from Virginia was sleeping upstairs

126

with the rest of us in the ministers' large, open dormitory room. About four o'clock in the morning he rolled out of bed on his knees and began to pray audibly for the unsaved. Of course, it awakened the rest of us, but we all lay quietly, respecting our brother's right to pray out loud even at that hour. He started out in a low key, but as he became more inspired he raised his voice until I'm sure that some of those sleeping in adjoining cottages must have been aroused. When our good brother saw no one else roll out of bed to join him in prayer he seemed disgusted and said (I'm sure for our benefit), "O Lord, how can these men sleep with the world in its present condition?" Strange that I should think of this while lying under the edge of a dining room table by the side of my bride of a few hours!

About two in the morning, Russell went out to one of the automobiles and lugged in one of the back seats. He curled up hopefully on this, but it sloped too much and soon he was back on the floor. Man, what a night! About four-thirty it began to turn gray in the east and I was glad! We roused everyone out of bed, put on the coffee pot, and before long breakfast was ready and the day under way. I felt like I had been run over by a truck. I ached in every joint and muscle.

However, I can't remember any week in my entire life when I laughed more. The total situation was hilarious in spite of the ten-person honeymoon. The second evening as we sat at supper around the big dining room table, I asked my sweet bride if she would mind bringing me another cup of tea. She was happy to do so and refilled my cup in the kitchen. I added the customary cream and sugar, but when I put the cup to my lips and took a good swig of the stuff, I knew that a mistake had been made. Never had I tasted such a concoction! I said, "Is this tea?" Polly assured me it was; that it had been dipped from the large pan in which it had been prepared. Curious, I left the table to investigate for myself. I was forced to the conclusion that although Polly's mistake may (or may not) have been perfectly innocent, my blushing bride had poured from another pan the water in which our supper wieners had been boiled. Friend, if you cannot imagine how this mixture tasted, try it sometime! Just for a change.

Our honeymoon party was reduced from time to time until Polly and I were finally alone for the last couple of days. How quiet it seemed! All too soon we had to move on for our first evangelistic meetings together at Stanford, Illinois. But you may be sure of one thing: if I get married eighteen times more before I die, there will never be more than two persons on our honeymoon.

Chapter Eleven

Partners

BEFORE LEAVING for Stanford, Polly and I moved what furniture we had to Indianapolis and rented a little three-room apartment in a house owned by my father. Polly took delight in fixing up the place, doing the best she could with our limited resources. Then dad let us drive his Ford to Stanford, which was quite a treat.

However, in Stanford I was to preach as well as sing, and the prospect was frightening. I had perhaps half a dozen sermon outlines and that was all. To add to my anxiety this was to be a two-week meeting which meant that I would have to create a new sermon nearly every day. This would have been a big job for the most mature preacher, but I was *not* mature. Only the good Lord knows what I would have done during those two weeks had it not been for my copy of R. R. Byrum's *Scripture Readings and Sermon Outlines*. I didn't perspire those two weeks; it was sweat! I worked, prayed, and did the best I could. To my great relief a few persons were converted during the two weeks. The church gave us $135 for our efforts, which reflected Polly's being with me. It was the most I had ever received for a two-week meeting. In Stanford we stayed with our friends, the Miles Pantlen family.

Years later, while attending our big convention in Anderson, Lester Shields, who had brought us to Stanford, stood recalling old times. Rather whimsically he said, "Brother Dale, I suppose you wondered why we invited you to hold that meeting for us since we knew you had not had much preaching experience." "You can say that again," I replied. Laughing, he continued, "Well, when our leaders were discussing who should be invited as evangelist, your name was brought up and we decided to give you a call. We realized the risk involved but felt that the Lord had his hand on you for the preaching ministry. We finally said, 'Let's ask Dale to come. If he does any good, we'll get the benefit; but if he fails, he will be in the hands of his best friends!' " O, brother! That still brings tears to my eyes. What a greathearted man was Lester Shields! I have prayed many times to be of similar encouragement to the young preachers who come my way.

Ian MacClaren used to tell of the early days in his ministry when he was trying to preach without notes. He was pastoring a small church somewhere in Scotland. Once in awhile, right in the middle of his sermon, his mind would go blank. Embarrassed, MacClaren would stop and say, "Folks, I know this isn't very clear, but if you will excuse me, I will start over again." At the close of such a service he was at the door when an elderly brother took him by the hand and said, "Pastor, when you are not remembering your sermon, just give out a hymn, and we'll be singing while you recall it. For we are a-loving and a-praying for you all the time." I imagine that MacClaren felt toward that church just as I have felt toward the Stanford church down through the years.

In October we took in another $135 at Omaha, Nebraska, but had to pay out too much of it for train fare. We had no dates for November and December. I took a job in Indianapolis helping to wreck a big frame building at fifty cents an hour. With my father forgiving me the rent for those two months, somehow we got by. Christmas came, but there was no money for gifts. We were broke and I was sick, probably from worry about our situation. A Sunday school class from the northside church in Indianapolis sent us a basket of groceries and seven dollars in cash. One could buy food for a week with seven dollars. Our total income for 1924 was $1,092.

It is interesting to look back and see how the good Lord had to take me to school in order to teach me certain things I needed to learn. For example, the church in Middletown, Ohio, had outgrown the Young Street edifice and had contracted with Jim

Denny, Tom Steenbergen's father-in-law, to build larger quarters at the corner of Crawford and Logan Streets. With the new building completed, dedicatory services were scheduled, to be followed by a week of evangelistic meetings featuring F. G. Smith as speaker and newcomer Arthur Lynn as soloist. I was in charge of the music and Polly at the piano. The new building seated seven hundred persons. I had not been told in advance that another soloist was being imported for the week. The Middletown church had not previously found this necessary, so I was a bit apprehensive even before meeting Lynn. I was about twenty-four at the time and enjoying a certain amount of success in my work. But I was not at all prepared for Arthur Lynn, a middle-aged Scot with a great tenor voice. He could sing higher and hold onto a note longer than any man I have ever heard. Besides, all his music had been transcribed in what looked like hen scratches. My wife was bothered no end in reading it and in accompanying Lynn whose interpretations of every solo were unpredictable. In addition to all this, he called my wife "Beloved."

The fact is, Arthur Lynn sang like a professional and from the very first service was the talk of the town. The people would say, "Isn't he great? Did you ever hear such singing in your life? I tell you, I could listen to that fellow all night." I would answer with a hesitant "Yes," or something weaker, for inside I was burning.

These were *my* friends. These had been *my* people through several meetings in Middletown. These were the very folk who had always complimented *me*. Now all the compliments were for Lynn, and something began to grind away inside my heart.

I *had* to confess that Lynn was a great singer and that he could sway a crowd with the masterful use of his voice. But in all honesty I also had to confess that I was jealous. This was a brand-new experience for me and I didn't like it. One night as Polly and I were walking toward the home where we were staying, I confessed to her exactly how I felt and how ashamed I was to have to admit it. The week of meetings was about at the halfway mark.

Some young people had been invited to the house for refreshments and a social hour, but I said, "Polly, I don't feel like mixing with them. I'm ashamed of the way I feel about Arthur Lynn and

I want to get victory over it. When we get to the house, you visit with the young people. I'm going to our room and pray. I'm going to stay on my knees until I have licked this thing. When I come from our room, you will know that I have won the battle."

I'll never forget that experience. In our room, I dropped to my knees by the side of the bed and told the Lord honestly just how I felt and what I wanted him to do about it. He reminded me that *I* also had to do something. I must have prayed for half an hour or so when the Lord heard and answered. I came out of our room delivered from that awful feeling of jealousy.

After that night I could brag honestly about Arthur Lynn both in public and private. A thousand times I have thanked God for the victory gained in that time of soul travail. Since that hour I have never heard someone who could sing or preach better than I but what I have said, "Pour it on him, Lord. Bless him. Inspire him. Use him." The better they sing and preach, the better I like it. Honestly! And that's the way I want it to be forever.

About fifteen years ago, as I was preaching in union pre-Easter services in a certain Indiana town, the young pastor of the Church of God took me aside for a talk. Noting the expression on his face, I was curious to hear what he had to say. We were no more than seated in a small classroom before he began to vent his spleen on me. "I just wanted to tell you to your face that I don't like you," he said. "I never did like you. In fact, I hate your guts. I wouldn't walk across the street to hear you preach. I stay away when you are preaching at camp meeting, and I refuse to tune in on the Christian Brotherhood Hour."

I asked, "Have I ever done anything or said anything to hurt your feelings?" He had to admit that I had not. But as we talked on he began to weep. Finally he tearfully confessed that my every success made him the more jealous and envious. After he had said all there was to say, we got down on our knees side by side. I put my arm around him and prayed, asking the Lord to deliver him from this spirit which could so easily wreck his life and ministry. No man can make a spiritual success while being spiritually defeated. When we arose from our knees, he seemed a different person and we have been friends ever since.

132

Singers, church musicians, and preachers are especially susceptible to such inroads by Satan. No man can successfully do Christ's work without Christ's spirit, and the spirit of Christ causes us to love our brother and give him the preferences. Paul wrote to the Roman church, "If any man have not the spirit of Christ, he is none of his" (Rom. 8:9). The spirit of envy and jealousy is not the spirit of Christ.

In March of 1925 Polly and I rode the train to Cincinnati, Ohio, to be with William Drew in evangelistic services to be held in a church pastored by Russell Olt. Drew was one of the keenest students of the Old Testament with whom I ever labored. His sermons were interesting and helpful. Even more important was our fellowship with Russell Olt, a man who would throughout the following years make a tremendous place for himself in Church of God educational history.

In 1925 he was pastoring a church, taking classes, acting as assistant professor at the University of Cincinnati, and in addition was Dean of Wilmington College. All of this indicated even then his capacity for work. Later Russell Olt moved to Anderson to join President Morrison in a most successful educational partnership. As a team President Morrison and Dean Olt led a very ordinary school into North Central accreditation and saw its enrollment multiplied. Russell Olt was academic Dean of Anderson College from 1925 until 1958, thirty-three years. He loved the students, although his brusqueness frightened many of them, especially when they found one of those little blue slips in their mailboxes reading, "The Dean would like to see you in his office at 3:30 today."

Since I've brought the Dean into my story, let me tell you more about him even at the risk of injecting an anachronism into my narrative. The Dean was quite a fellow in many ways. He taught psychology at Anderson College in addition to his duties as Dean, although Dr. John used to say laughingly that the Dean taught more psychology and practiced less of it than any man he knew. But the Dean could practice psychology as well as teach it.

When I was managing what may have been the first Church of God youth camp held in Indiana, the Dean was one of our teachers. I had more trouble with him than with all the kids put together. He would put a sheet over his head at two o'clock in the morning, slip over to the girls' dormitory, and scare the daylights out of them with his ghosting. Afterward, of course, they loved him for his pranks. One day a girl hid his coat and refused to tell him where it was. He said, "That's no problem. I can find it." When one of the girls confessed to knowing where the coat was hidden, the Dean said he could find it blindfolded. No one believed him, of course, so he was blindfolded. He took this girl by the arm and, guided by her reflexes, went right to the coat. The youngsters thought him a genius, and perhaps he was.

Forty-five years ago many of us had little understanding of the psychological basis of hypnotism. However, since the Dean taught psychology, he was naturally interested in the psychological aspects of hypnotism. In fact he experimented a bit with hypnotism and became convinced that he could hypnotize almost any willing subject. Downtown was a dentist friend with whom the Dean discussed hypnotism, saying he thought it would be possible to painlessly pull the tooth of a hypnotized person without applying an anesthetic. The dentist was of the same opinion. One day when the Dean's secretary complained of a bad toothache it seemed a propitious time to launch their experiment. To this she agreed. The Dean hypnotized her as she sat in the dentist's chair; the tooth was pulled painlessly; the patient awakened, smiled, went her way; and that was that.

It was? Within hours it began to spread out all over the church that Dean Olt had hypnotized somebody. Everyone was sure that hypnotism was the work of the devil, so Dean Olt had to be a servant of Satan! Something had to be done about it! You just couldn't let a man like that go on. No telling what he might cause someone to do while hypnotized! Finally matters got to the point where a conclave of ministers was called to meet in Anderson, there to sit in judgment on the Dean. Although still in my twenties, I happened to be chairman of the sesssion. Testimony began. "Did you or did you not hypnotize that woman?" As the minutes passed, emotions mounted steadily. Static was in the air. At one particularly electrified moment during the hearing I believe that if someone had shouted, "Let's lynch him," half a dozen preachers would have started up from their chairs before realizing what they were doing.

Finally, however, as some of the better educated, more intelligent, and less inflammatory brethren began to make their presence felt, emotions began to subside. The Dean was rebuked and warned but permitted to go on with his job. Incidentally, I think the Dean was less moved by the proceedings than anyone else. When it was over he chuckled and went merrily on his way. In fact, I think he rather enjoyed the whole affair because it gave him a rare opportunity to observe psychological phenomena at work.

When I think of Dean Olt, I like to remember that day in March of 1925 when we rode in his Model T from Cincinnati to Wilmington, stopping halfway at a little roadside restaurant operated by a woman who could panfry chicken exactly how the Dean felt it ought to be done. I also remember how the Dean enjoyed a midnight snack of limburger cheese and garlic bologna. Bless his memory!

The Dean was little understood by those who had no opportunity to know him well. However, his friendships were warm and lasting and his heart tender toward human needs. He constantly inspired his students to work for those social reforms which a changing day began to demand. He espoused the cause of the black man when few in the Anderson community would do more than admit there was a problem. He was active in the Anderson Urban League, where he fought constantly for human rights. He led the fight to open up restaurants, hotels, and theaters to the negroes of Anderson and the fight was finally won.

Following World War II the Dean went to Europe almost every summer and gave endless hours in efforts to relieve the plight of countless displaced persons. He helped many of these to come to America and then saw to their getting settled and finding employment. To many he gave gifts of money to alleviate their acute financial distress, although he had never too much of this world's goods. He was embarrassed with public thanks and often gave a gift with the stipulation that no one should be told about it.

When dread cancer finally overtook him, Dr. Olt put all of his enormous will into a determination to live. But there was a certain

135

inevitability in the progress of his disease. When he finally realized he was not to recover, the Dean turned from a will to live to a will to die. In three days he was gone. But he was not forgotten, for he will live through years to come in the hearts and lives of those he helped, particularly young people to whom he gave not only wise counsel but himself as well.

After the Cincinnati meetings, where they gave us $100 for three weeks, we experienced another financial drouth for a couple of months. To help us out, Tom Steenbergen organized a music class for me to teach in Middletown. Such classes were not uncommon back then. Those interested in learning to read music would come together each night except Sunday for a couple of weeks and be given an intensive course in sight-reading. The Middletown class went so well that another was organized for me to teach in Dayton.

Then about the first of June Polly and I rode the Louisville and Nashville train to Cynthiana, Kentucky, to take charge of the music in a tent meeting to be held there in an effort to establish a congregation of the Church of God. Various men did the preaching— W. F. Chappel, R. C. Caudill, and W. H. Hunt. R. C. was pastoring at Morehead, Kentucky, and W. H. Hunt at Winchester. The meetings were fairly well attended and there were a few converts.

One day I was asked to bring the sermon. It frightened me—I was but twenty-two years old and sitting back of me would be three of the best preachers in Kentucky. However, I accepted the invitation, prepared my message, and at the appointed time arose to speak. I was literally trembling for a minute or two. I felt like the drunk who, standing on a bridge at night, looked down in the stream and saw the moon's reflection. After musing a bit, he said, "What am I doing up here?" That was the moment in which I formulated a philosophy with regard to the presence of preachers in my audience. I said to myself, "If these men are what they ought to be, they are praying for me. If they aren't what they ought to be, they aren't worth worrying about." Thus fortified, I delivered my message.

Chapter Twelve

Cynthiana,
Our First Pastorate

AFTER THE ANDERSON camp meeting was finished in June, at the insistence of the Kentucky brethren, Polly and I moved our scant furnishings to Cynthiana and proceeded to build a congregation. There wasn't too much to work with, but the people were kind and willing to cooperate. However, moving was painful, especially for Polly, because we were expecting our first child. We were terribly poor. A couple of men in the Indianapolis church owned a truck and hauled our few things to Cynthiana for not much more than the cost of the gas and oil. Polly and I rode the train to Cincinnati and then changed to the L and N for Cynthiana. With every turn of the wheels Polly's heart sank within her. She said afterward it was one of the lowest times in her life, and as we journeyed through unfamiliar hills she thought she would die.

In Cynthiana we found a little corner cottage which could be rented for twenty dollars a month. It stood up off the ground on stilts. We used to hear the rats running and gnawing underneath at night. We purchased on credit a five dollar matting rug for the living room and a four-burner kerosene stove for the kitchen. I bought a small misused teacher's desk from the Board of Education for two dollars. Someone loaned us a heating stove which would burn either wood or coal. Someone else stored a piano with us. We were in business. There was one water faucet in the house and it was, of course, cold. We had a nonfreeze toilet enclosed on the back porch. That is, the *water* didn't freeze!

When the weather turned cold, old Brother Lemons delivered 500 pounds of coal to us in his spring wagon and did not charge for the hauling. We had no car—not even a bicycle—and so we walked wherever we had to go. Cynthiana, county seat of Harrison County and located in the edge of the bluegrass region, had a population of 5,000 at the time.

Our new little congregation had no meeting place. Finally the city agreed to rent to us a hall located above the downtown fire station. It would seat about 100 persons. We accepted their offer, announced services, assigned teaching and other responsibilities to the most talented persons, and went to work. Sunday school was bedlam since all classes but one had to meet in the same room. The exception was a children's class which we located on the top landing of the stairway. Occasionally my sermon would be interrupted by the sounding of the fire alarm down below, in which case we waited until things quieted down again and then went on with the service.

But there was a growing enthusiasm in our little group. It was enough to cheer one's heart, and we were encouraged by the faithfulness and dedication of our people. Within a few months more than seventy were in attendance. These were mostly laborers and their families. They were willing to work and gave of their money as they were able. Every Sunday at the close of the evening service, our treasurer, Mrs. Herve Browning, would give me whatever money could be spared after expenses had been budgeted. Generally it amounted to ten or twelve dollars but I remember one wonderful Sunday when it was twenty dollars. I felt like Christmas!

Meanwhile, my lack of education was beginning to bother me. While still in evangelistic work, I had taken correspondence courses in high school subjects, but in Cynthiana I enrolled in school and sat in the back row of the seniors' assembly room. I was twenty-two and most of my fellow students were seventeen. It took a bit of courage to go back to school. Yet, attending gave me a feeling of progress and I was determined to obtain an education.

But we were poor, poor, poor. Bob Fields ran a small neighborhood store and sold groceries to me at a 10 percent discount. I budgeted four dollars a week for food, and, when it went to four-fifty, I was worried. This same Mr. Fields went to the local courthouse with me one day, having volunteered to post the $1500 bond demanded in Kentucky before a minister would be permitted to perform marriages. I had a wedding in the offing and never had a five-dollar fee looked larger.

Then came my first funeral. Of course, I had sung at many but now I would have to prepare a new kind of sermon. I prepared my message with care, selecting what I thought were just the right Scripture passages. Polly and I were to sing, and I gave special attention to the appropriateness of each selection. At the appointed time we went to the funeral home for the service. I felt that everything went quite well, but, as we prepared to sing our final song, Polly whispered something to me. Unfortunately, I did not catch what she said. Later I wished that I had.

When the service was concluded, the funeral director and his assistant wheeled out the casket, the people went to their cars, and Polly and I rode with the undertaker. Only then did I discover what it was my wife had whispered. She had said, "Pray." What a sinking sensation developed as it dawned on me that I had not offered a single prayer during the entire service! No invocation, no general prayer, and no benediction. No entreaty on behalf of sorrowing relatives and friends. I cannot remember ever being more embarrassed; in fact, I was *so* embarrassed that I prayed about three times at the cemetery before dismissing the people. They say we learn by trial-and-error methods. That day it was *both* trial and error. After this sad experience, whenever I conducted a funeral I typed out copies of the order of service, kept one lying on the pulpit, and gave others to the funeral director, instrumentalist, and singers.

As the time drew near for the birth of our child, Polly experienced a heightening of nervous tension. I was away one evening attending an evangelistic service with another pastor. Shortly after we left, a dog ran under our house and evidently made quite a bit of noise. He was probably chasing rats. But just that day someone had stopped at the house to warn Polly that a rabid dog was running loose in the neighborhood. The noise under the house convinced Polly that this must be that very dog and she became petrified with fear. She was afraid that when I arrived home the dog would rush out and attack me. When we finally drove up, she was at the door to call a warning. When I was safe inside, she nearly collapsed in my arms. I was very, very sorry for her and felt guilty for having left her alone.

One day there came an insistent knocking at the door of our little house on Wilson Avenue. Upon opening it I found a young man standing in a high state of agitation. He said, "Can you come quickly? My mother is dying. We children have all been called in. The doctor doesn't expect her to live over night." He drove fast as he took me the several miles out to his mother's farm home. When we arrived, we found the entire family in tears. Someone whispered, "I don't think she will last another hour."

I was taken to a bedroom where the pale face of an old lady lay upon an even whiter pillow. She was breathing as elderly people often do before making the final crossing. It seemed to me she was unconscious, but I was not sure. Without further ado I dropped to my knees by the side of the bed and earnestly petitioned our heavenly Father to spare the good woman's life and give her a few more years with her children. My prayer was scarcely finished when the sick woman, with a shout of praise to God, threw back the covers and got out of bed. Then in flannel nightgown she walked up and down the room praising God for her healing. I can see her yet, weeping, waving an arm, and crying, "Praise the Lord! I'm healed!" And she was! She lived for several more years before being called to her eternal reward.

I wasn't too surprised at her healing. As already noted, we in the Church of God were brought up to believe that God hears and answers prayer. We were told that since the Lord made these bodies of ours he is perfectly able to restore them to health when we are sick, just as the man who makes a watch is able to repair it when something goes wrong. My mother brought all four of her children into the world without benefit of hospital or doctor. A neighbor served as a midwife. In such cases, if anything went wrong or an emergency arose, death frequently ensued. But the Lord did heal us in answer to prayer.

Of course, there were some radical preachers among us to whom doctors, medicine, and hospitals were anathema. Some boasted they had not taken even an aspirin in forty years or more. Of itself this never seemed to prove very much to me. You aren't necessarily a person of faith because of something you don't do. I once met a man who had broken his arm while cranking his car. Refusing to go to a doctor to have it set, he said, "I just held my arm with the other hand and asked the Lord to heal me and he did." But the arm was crooked. As I walked away I told myself that if ever I broke my arm I would go to a doctor and have him set it. *Then* I would pray and ask God to heal it. The healing would be the same, but I'd have a straight arm where his was left crooked.

There were no medicine bottles in my boyhood home. No aspirin, castor oil, or spirits of camphor. While traveling with various preachers I used to listen to their conversations with sick people who had called them in for prayer. The preacher might say, "You can't take medicine and trust the Lord at the same time. If you want him to heal you, get rid of those medicine bottles."

You can understand how I felt when called to pray for a Cynthiana woman who had suffered a heart attack. When no one answered my knock, I opened the door, called out, and was directed by a weak voice to a bedroom where the sick woman lay. "I thought I was dying last night," she said. "Thank God, I was ready. The doctor doesn't seem to be helping, so I felt like having you pray for me." But I was stymied, for about all I could see was a bedside table literally covered with medicine bottles. How could I pray the prayer of faith with all those corks staring at me? Nevertheless, as earnestly as I could I asked the Lord to touch the woman. I left hoping for the best. Next day she was downtown shopping and telling everyone how she had been healed. In fact, she was still alive forty years later. That experience was good for me. It taught me to pay no attention to medicine bottles.

You may remember what witty "Uncle Bud" Robinson of the Church of the Nazarene said to the woman whose question was, "Brother Robinson, when I am sick should I go to the Lord or to the drugstore?" "Uncle Bud" replied in his lisping voice, "Sister, if you are living closer to the drugstore than you are to the Lord, you'd better go to the drugstore."

How scarce money was in Cynthiana! During the months before our baby was born, the only clothing I was able to buy for Polly was a bathrobe and a pair of house slippers. I borrowed twenty-five dollars with which Polly purchased a layette for the expected little one. We really didn't have enough food. I remember saying to the butcher on Saturday, "Give me fifteen cents worth of beefsteak and slice it thin." At home we would cut the meat into four small pieces, eat two for supper and save the rest for Sunday dinner. Our people brought us half-gallons of wild raspberry preserves, but we were hungry for green beans and potatoes.

November arrived and Thanksgiving was but a day or two away. We weren't sure we would have a Thanksgiving dinner. Polly said, "There is a family down the street in back of us who are even worse off than we are. I think we should take them their dinner." So we spent a couple of precious dollars and filled a basket with staple groceries and decided to forego our own dinner. When we went to deliver the basket, it was received gratefully.

A glimpse inside the house revealed no beds or chairs. An orange crate served as a table. A mattress lay on the floor in one corner of the front room. But the place was spotlessly clean. Here was a mother who kept her self-respect through hard work and cleanliness. We received quite a blessing through our giving. Later that afternoon a member of our little church came to the door with a plate on which were two large slices from a turkey's breast. Since neither Polly nor I had ever eaten turkey in our lives, this was a real treat for which we thanked both the donor and the Lord. Thus we had a Thanksgiving dinner after all, plus a blessing.

Shortly after arriving in Cynthiana, we began to inquire about a doctor for Polly. Several women recommended the same one. It was said, however, that occasionally this doctor took time off and went to the hospital where he stayed drunk for a week. The women would add, "Most of us would rather have him, even when drinking, than any other doctor who is sober." Thus advised, we chose the drinking doctor and hoped for the best. He gave Polly the usual tests from month to month and said he saw no reason why she should have any difficulty in delivering her baby. How expectantly we looked forward to the little one's arrival! No one ever wanted a child more than we. Dean Elmore Oldham arrived December 18, 1925.

Since poor women couldn't go to the hospital to have their babies, our doctor came to the house. Thus Dean was born in the front bedroom at 414 Wilson Avenue on a cold winter afternoon. While the doctor worked with my wife, I walked back and forth in the adjoining room, praying. Polly did not have too bad a time of it and before long the baby was born, a plump ten pounds. When he did not cry, the doctor picked him up by the heels and spanked him. But still no sound came from those tiny lips. Another long minute passed with the doctor working feverishly. Then I knew something had to be wrong. The baby was dead, in fact, had been dead for a day or two the doctor told me afterward. Why? Nobody knows. No RH factor was involved and it seemed unlikely that my wife's "mad dog" scare a few days previously could have caused this result.

Did you ever lose a long-wished-for child at birth? A *first* child? It seemed like a nightmare, a bad dream, such a reversal of what we had hoped and planned for. Unbelievable, until we stared at the hard, cold facts. Our child was dead! It seemed it just *couldn't* happen to *us*. Weren't we God's children? Weren't we down here in Cynthiana, Kentucky, hundreds of miles from our folks, sacrificing for the Cause, even going hungry in order to establish God's church? "Lord haven't you made a mistake? Surely you mean to perform a miracle. Let us see that tiny chest inhale and those brown eyes open. Surely, Lord, it can't end like this! It just can't! Not after all we've been through for you. Not after the way we've waited and waited for little Dean's arrival. O God, why? O, God, why? Why? Why?"

But nothing changed. After that something seemed to die inside of Polly—and me. It is *so* hard to go through a valley that deep when you are young and inexperienced. You have no mature experience or philosophy upon which to fall back. Polly turned her face to the wall and refused to be comforted. I tried; reminding her that there could be another time. But she didn't want to live. On the third day she nearly died. As the long, dark hours passed, my own heart filled with resentment. How could the Lord do this to us when we were giving every minute and every last penny in his service? It wasn't right. It wasn't fair. Where was God's love now? Wasn't our little one worth more than sparrows? I got hard-nosed about it and went into a spiritual nose dive for three days. during that time, of course, we had the funeral.

The graveside service was held on a snowy, cold, blustery day. The wind cut through the cemetery with chilling force as W. H. Hunt, pastor from Winchester, read from the Book, made brief comments, and offered prayer. I stood there weeping, shivering, and resenting the whole thing. When I saw the little casket being lowered into that cold, cold ground, I thought my heart would break. I could hardly stand it. That frozen ground! And then the clods were shoveled in. Never, never, never have I felt so alone. Polly was back at the house, refusing to be comforted. Bless her broken heart! She, too, was all alone, even with her mother there to comfort her.

After three days both of us moved out from under the worst of the emotional wreckage and were able to think more rationally. God hadn't taken our beloved baby away from us. This was just one of those accidents of nature which happen to people. This time it had happened to us. Were we any better than the others? We realized that God still loved us, wanted us to take his hand, and let him lead us out of this dark valley. Dean's failure to live had nothing at all to do with God's love for us. I comforted my wife and she comforted me. Then, as the days passed and she was able to leave her bed, we joined hands and started down a new avenue of life together. We had always stood solidly together, but now there was an ever-warmer nearness in our relationship.

Many times during the intervening years I have gone out to the silent city of the dead with an undertaker and a young father. Always a little wooden box lay cradled on the back seat of the funeral car. With the young mother still in the hospital, the three of us sometimes made up the entire funeral assembly. Standing there beside an open grave, time and again I have slipped my arm around some young father's shoulder and said, "It's all right son; it's all right. You can't understand now, but don't be bitter about it. Just give it up to God. Trust where you cannot see." I have been a more understanding comforter to lads like that because of what happened to an immature couple in Cynthiana, Kentucky, in December of 1925. But when we left Cynthiana, we left part of ourselves up there on the hill in old Battleground Cemetery.

Chapter Thirteen

Back to the Field

HAD LITTLE DEAN LIVED, we probably would have shifted before long into another pastorate. Instead, a few months later, we turned the Cynthiana church over to another's care and returned to evangelistic work. We had grown a bit, suffered a bit, and were more mature. In looking back, it seems to me that people are never at their best for God until their hearts have been broken. Love is refined and deepened through Christian suffering.

There followed revival meetings in Indianapolis; Lima, Ohio; Bemidji, Minnesota; and a return to Stanford, this time with that great preacher R. C. Caudill. During the Stanford meetings, I wrote to my friend Claude Townsend to see if he would be willing to arrange for us to buy a small automobile. Train fare was expensive for two persons and schedules were inconvenient and time consuming. Townsend was the successful oilman who had furnished the tent for the Paintsville meeting. He was a consecrated Christian businessman with high principles. He had financially assisted many a young struggling preacher. It pleased us when he wrote that the money was waiting us at a Winchester bank. R. C. ordered the car through a relative's dealership in Morehead, Kentucky.

When the Stanford meeting closed, we went to Winchester, signed for the money, and then went on to Morehead and proudly took delivery of our brand-new 1926 Chevrolet coupe. Price, $680. How happy we were with that little car! It had no gasoline gauge. I had to watch the odometer and, when 200 miles had been traveled, fill the tank. When in doubt, I measured with a ruler. The four-cylinder car had a top speed of fifty-six miles an hour. We kept it three years, got it paid for, and it gave excellent service. It was of great help in our work.

Evangelistic work has certain drawbacks. For example, you always hate to see the Thanksgiving season arrive. It means you are going to be out of work for about six weeks. No church wants a meeting Thanksgiving week, or between Thanksgiving and the first of January. About December 1, 1927, I spoke to my old friend in the personnel department at Marmon's and he gave me a job which I stayed with for three months in order to get squared around financially. But March found us back in revival work, this time with my father's church in Hickory, North Carolina.

As observed previously, my father was not a pulpit orator; nevertheless, he was a good pastor and a solid builder. Wherever he served, the church prospered. His youth groups always flourished. But he was somewhat of a plodder and did not expect a mushrooming type of growth to take place. However, when a person was converted under his ministry, he generally stayed converted.

The previous summer dad had written from Hickory concerning a tent meeting he had conducted out in the country in which twelve persons had found the Lord. At the time I was singing in some fairly large meetings in which we would see a hundred or more converted during a two-week period. So I felt a bit sorry for dad, thinking of how he had labored on hot evenings for three weeks to see only twelve brought to the Lord. In all truth, it needs to be confessed that in some of the places where an evangelist and I had held those big meetings one might have gone back a year later and been able to find a dozen of our converts holding true.

On my first Sunday morning in Hickory, dad and I were sitting up front as the congregation drifted into the sanctuary from their Sunday school classes. While they gathered, my father began to point to this person and that saying, "He was converted in that tent meeting I wrote you about." He identified all twelve converts and then said, "They all seem to be doing well spiritually and are present in every service." After that I quit feeling sorry for dad.

148

The final test of a man's ministry is not the number of persons who make a profession of faith but in how many of them really find the Lord and settle down to serve him.

It is too bad I can't tell you everything I would like to about those early years. We had some great preachers but also some pygmies. There were smart men and ignoramuses. There were men who loved everybody but a few who just loved the women. There were courageous men and self-pitying weaklings. Some men managed their finances well; others were head over heels in debt, expecting a miracle to extricate them. There were men who stood on their own two feet and slugged it out with life and others who ran at the first smell of gunpowder. There were valiant souls who decided to be true to Christ and his blessed truth until death called them home. But there were others who quit when the going got tough. They dropped out of sight and were never heard of again.

Most preachers were honest, but a few were phonies, playing upon the weaknesses of the people as a pianist manipulates a keyboard. They were indeed manipulators. Someone told me of seeing a certain preacher's sermon outline which was lying on the fellow's desk. Two-thirds of the way down the page he had written in the margin, "Cry here." On another preacher's outline there was scrawled in the margin. "Argument weak here. Shout and pound the pulpit."

But at least once it was someone else's scribbled-in comments which threw the preacher. Tom Steenbergen and George Blackwell were in a revival series somewhere, but they had played too much golf during the day. George traveled as an evangelistic singer for a few years until financial necessity shunted him off into the insurance business. Anyhow, these two were playing the Tippecanoe Country Club in northern Indiana one day. Out on the course they were joined by a member of the Indiana legislature. Both wished to impress the legislator not only with their personalities but with their golfing skill. During a running conversation Tom importantly mentioned that he had played golf all over northern Indiana. But George spoiled the anticipated effect by adding, "Yeah, and never once left this course."

Tom and George played thirty-six holes one day and it was seven o'clock when they hurriedly returned to the home where they were staying. While Tom freshened up, George picked up the sermon outline Tom planned to use that evening and rearranged it a bit. Taking a pen, he wrote on the outline just ahead of point one, "Tee off here. First hole, 485 yards." Then here and there all through the outline George inserted more "helpful" advice. Tom stood up to preach that night, read his text, and then said pompously, "Tee off here. First hole 485 yards." It broke up the congregation, most of whom knew his love for golfing. But it so confused Tom that, after glancing down over what was to come, he folded the outline into his Bible and preached without it, remarking, "Somebody's been fooling around with my sermon." George thought it was a huge joke, and so did I, seeing it was perpetrated on someone else.

George enjoyed telling of a meeting in which he sang for the late J. Lee Collins in Lexington, Kentucky. "J. Lee" was an orator of the first rank, and seldom lacked something to say or knowledge as to the best way to say it. I always enjoyed hearing him, if for no other reason than for the pure pleasure of listening to the way in which he turned those choice phrases. What figures of speech rolled glibly from his experienced tongue! He used to read books of famous orations for the express purpose of discovering how the world's greatest speechmakers said it in other days. Then he would memorize and use some of their choicer phrases. Give J. Lee a packed house with a row of preachers sitting behind him and he was at his best.

Such was the situation when we dedicated a new chapel in Mount Sterling, Kentucky, many years ago. Tom Farmer was pastor at the time. The place was packed to capacity with extra chairs filling the aisles. Six or eight preachers flanked Brother Collins on either side as he arose to speak. After five or ten minutes of warming up, he began to scrape oratorical stardust in every eye as he skillfully painted word pictures in a way which none present could duplicate. I loved the man and years later invited him to our church in Dayton for meetings.

In Lexington, as he and George walked toward church one evening, J. Lee said, "George, I'm in a fix. I don't have a thing to preach tonight. Pray for me." Because J. Lee kidded a lot, George didn't take him seriously. Then, just before George arose to open the song service the evangelist whispered, "Pray for me." And again as the pastor was introducing prayer, Brother Collins said to George, "I'm desperate. I simply don't know what to preach. What am I going to do?" And George realized that the preacher was really in trouble.

The unavoidable moment arrived, the evangelist was introduced and took his place behind the pulpit. His opening words were, "Friends, you see me tonight in the worst fix I've ever been in. I've been searching and praying today but still don't have a message for you. I am embarrassed. In my quandary I've decided to do this: I'm going to let my Bible fall open of itself; then I'm going to drop my finger on some verse, and whatever it is, I will use it as a text for tonight's sermon." You may be sure that by this time he had the full attention of every person present. Most thought his predicament both interesting and amusing. J. Lee closed his Bible, let it open of itself, then put his finger down on Romans 6:1, which opens with the question, "What shall we say then?" Fresh inspiration fired the imagination of this oratorical genius and he shifted into high gear. Afterward George said it was one of the greatest sermons he had ever heard.

J. Lee's ideas: What shall we say as we face life as a tender infant? Then as we advance into those perplexing adolescent years? What shall a young man say as he stands at the marriage altar with his blushing bride, this girl of his dreams, as they face an unknown future together? What shall the young couple say when their first-born is cradled in his mother's arms? What shall the middle-aged man say as he plods on through his forties and fifties, paying the bills, buying the house, seeing that insurance premiums are kept up? What shall the old man say when the sixties have given way to the seventies, and the seventies to the eighties; when sight and hearing dim and steps grow feeble? And last, what will he say when the death angel arrives on raven-black wings to carry him into the presence of God? I don't recommend this method of finding something to preach, yet I would give a great deal for a tape of that sermon. J. Lee was an orator!

Times change, and with those changing times preaching forms change, also. Read the sermons of fifty and sixty years ago and compare them with the style of today. The difference is not only in the basic preachments but also in the way they are presented. There is little place in today's pulpit for horse-and-buggy illustrations. In changing times, some preachers intelligently discover new and better ways of presenting the gospel while others continue in the same old hackneyed way.

As my friend W. F. Chappel grew old, he found himself invited less frequently to speak in our Anderson convention. I don't think he particularly resented this as he was an intelligent man of good spirit; but something prompted him to do a very unusual thing there one evening. With someone else scheduled to preach, the chairman called on Brother Chappel to pray. Remember, I told you how he could pray!

Well, he stepped to the podium, closed his eyes, opened his mouth and began to inform the Lord as to the state of the church, the nation, and the world, plus the needs of the present camp meeting. In his prayer he reviewed the glories of North Carolina during the days of his boyhood and the privilege of having been brought up by a sainted mother. Warming to the occasion he reminded the Lord of the times when his mother used to brush the ashes back from the bricks on the fireplace floor, and then pour cornmeal batter over the hot stones to make hoe cakes. He almost smacked his lips as he reminded the Lord of how good those cakes were.

By this time really inspired he proceeded to thank the Lord for that momentous day when he found Christ as Savior and the old life slipped away from him like a worn-out garment. He praised God for the day he was called to preach, for the day of his ordination, and for almost every other important event in his lifetime. He thanked God for the church past and present and for missionaries on foreign fields. When the smoke of battle cleared, he had prayed for thirty-five minutes and it was probably time to dismiss the service. It happened twenty years ago, but once in awhile people still mention the longest prayer ever offered during the Anderson camp

152

meeting. Whoever preached that night was probably irked by the delay, but most of the people seemed far more blessed than critical. However, I think that was the last time Brother Chappel was ever invited to pray, preach, or pronounce a benediction during an Anderson camp meeting. Nevertheless, I always felt that he had had the last word.

Preachers of half a century ago generally had a sprinkling of stories available with which to illustrate their sermons. The late H. M. Riggle not only had stories but knew how to tell them. During my first year at the Bible Training School while H. A. Sherwood was pastor at Park Place church, Dr. Riggle came for a two-week evangelistic series. He was then at the height of his preaching power and had no difficulty in holding the attention of the people. Most ABTS students attended every night. Singing in the choir near me one evening was Giles Jump, a student from Fort Wayne, Indiana. Giles was a bit on the emotional side and whatever he did he did with enthusiasm.

During the sermon on this particular evening Dr. Riggle told of a big bully who was forever inflicting pain on a smaller boy. Every time he came into the neighborhood the bully would punch the smaller lad in the nose or slap him around. There seemed nothing his victim could do about it. Naturally, he became weary of such treatment. One day he decided that next time the bully mistreated him he would give him one healthy poke in the nose if it was the last thing he ever did on earth. Giles, intently listening to every word, was sitting on the edge of his seat. Riggle continued, relating how the bully hove into sight and how the smaller boy's resolve strengthened with every accelerated heart beat. Then the two were face to face and the little fellow, clenching his fist, drew back almost to the ground and then let fly with a well-aimed uppercut which caught the bully right on target. When Riggle said this, Giles cried out, "Praise the Lord!" It broke up the meeting. Riggle laughed until he had difficulty continuing. Giles sat back in his seat, a bit embarrassed, but mostly tickled at how he had been caught off base.

The late I. S. McCoy used to tell of a meeting he and Dr. Riggle conducted in a rural community early in the century. In our group manufactured wafers were never used when communion was to be served. Instead some good woman in the church, often the pastor's wife, would make a small, flat, brown loaf of unleavened bread. This was sufficient for the entire congregation. For this particular communion service some dear sister volunteered to bake the bread, but she had evidently not had much previous experience in this field. When Dr. Riggle stood before the congregation and quoted the words, "And Jesus took the bread, and blessed it, and brake it," the bread simply would not break. Embarrassed, Riggle applied greater pressure but the loaf was stout and would not yield. In desperation he turned his back to the congregation, held the loaf along the edge of the communion table, and applied more pressure. No luck.

Irishman McCoy quickly perceived that the situation called for reenforcements. Slipping to Riggle's side he whispered, "Give me the bread. While I am gone you sing "His Yoke Is Easy and His Burden Is Light." McCoy found a hammer in a back room, took it and the bread out behind the church where there was a rock to pound on, and a couple of minutes later re-appeared, solemn as a judge, with the bread broken in a hundred small pieces. Thus the "solemn" service continued.

Dr. Riggle should have written his own autobiography. He certainly had enough material to produce a good one. One day he was on a fairly high platform addressing a group of veterans in a home for old soldiers. As he orated in high gear, his false teeth flew out and landed in the sawdust a few feet in front of the platform. The oration ceased suddenly and there was quite a pregnant silence. Then an aging veteran in the front row slowly left his chair, retrieved the teeth, and soberly handed them up to the speaker. Riggle turned his back on the audience, slipped them back into his mouth, and proceeded with his address.

On another occasion, the high platform on which he was standing had apparently suffered either from age or termites. As Riggle "got blessed" he jumped into the air a foot or two and when he came down he went straight through the floor into an area so dark he had difficulty finding his way out. Someone finally opened a door for him and the shaken speaker emerged, little the worse for

154

wear and tear, to go on with his speech. But one may imagine that from that point on his delivery was a bit more subdued.

Dr. Riggle was a really talented and successful preacher and in demand everywhere. He wrote some twenty books and was a debator of proven quality. He was also a health faddist, periodically experimenting with this and that diet. During one of these times he told me that his breakfast consisted only of grapefruit and coffee. Not just ordinary coffee in an ordinary cup, but the real thing. His coffee was strong enough to float an egg. Into a quart cup he would pour half a pint of coffee cream and then fill it up with that super-strong coffee.

He and his wife came to lunch at our house about forty years ago. Polly, knowing his yen for strong coffee, invited him into the kitchen to make it for himself, which he did. Later, Sister Minnie put a cupful to her lips, took a swallow, nearly choked, and blurted out, "O my! I can't drink that. It is too bitter." Polly smiled and said, "Your husband made it." And sister Minnie replied, "I might have known. I might have known." Dr. Riggle broke into that famous smile and, emptying his cup, called for a refill.

His physician finally forbade him to drink coffee, but Dr. Riggle would brew it anyhow when his wife wasn't around to check up on him. One evening when he did not appear on a camp meeting platform when due to preach, I found him in his room enjoying a final cup of coffee. As we walked toward the auditorium, he said with a laugh, "I like a good, strong cup of coffee the last thing before I am to speak. It makes me preach like a house afire." We all loved Dr. Riggle. There was never a dull moment with him around.

We were all saddened when the action of the years began to tell upon his body and memory. He was a faithful soldier of the cross, dedicated to the truth, and fought a good fight. Thousands will be in heaven because of his labors.

Chapter Fourteen

Akron and Rochester

IN THE FALL of 1928, after my wife had experienced a crisis in health, we felt it would be too much for her to continue in evangelistic work. In September we accepted an invitation to pastor the Churches of God in Akron and Rochester, Indiana. We decided to live in Akron, population 930 persons.

Rochester was larger but had a smaller congregation. I would preach in Akron on Sunday morning and Rochester in the evening, reversing the order the following Sunday. Record Sunday school attendance in the Akron church was 138—not large considering it was one of our oldest congregations. In it were men who had been present at Beaver Dam United Brethren Church about 1880 when one of our pioneer leaders, D. S. Warner, had "taken his stand for the truth."

One or two friends warned me not to accept this pastorate saying, "R. N. Gast will chew you up and spit you out in little pieces before you have been there six months." Gast was one of the old timers, an ordained minister, then well up in his seventies. But those prophets of doom were wrong, because R. N. Gast became one of my best supporters, lending sound advice and counsel. He was always helpful, and I came to love and respect him highly. Polly and I enjoyed some delicious meals in the Gast farm home a couple of miles north of Akron.

On moving to Akron about the first thing I did was to open a series of evangelistic services. I preached for two weeks and there was no response; three weeks; then four. In that entire time two children and one adult were the only converts. I began to wonder just what kind of church I was sentenced to serve. Aging Brother Ferree confided, "Brother Dale, you can't have a revival here. This is an old burnt-over field. You can't raise a crop on it." After four nearly fruitless weeks I was almost ready to believe him.

The following November T. J. Steenbergen came for a revival meeting. You already know from what I have written that Tom is not like anyone else. When he came to Akron, it was not to fit into anyone's pattern. Tom's methods and ways of saying things never brought him an accusation of plagiarism. Forty years ago he was unique and uninhibited. At Akron he came, he saw, and he conquered. Steenbergen was a nine-day wonder to our community and the people flocked to hear what he would say next. One evening, however, near disaster struck. As I have said, my friend R. N. Gast was old. He was also extremely hard of hearing; a fact which Tom had not as yet discovered. Brother Gast often sat on the front row, the better to hear. Occasionally he had been known to nod sleepily during a sermon.

On this particular night, however, he was not sleepy, but ill, and he sat with his eyes closed. Having arrived at about point two in his message, Evangelist Steenbergen thought Brother Gast had gone to sleep and something ought to be done about it. Taking a thin songbook which lay on the pulpit, Tom sailed it through the air intending that it should slap the floor at Brother Gast's feet. Unfortunately his aim was a bit off and the book hit the old man on the foot, arousing him with quite a start. In a few minutes he got up, went to the basement, and was sick. That night at home Polly took Tom to task over what he had done and kept at him until he reluctantly agreed to apologize, which he did.

Next evening there was a big increase in attendance. It had gone out all over town, and for miles around, that old man Gast had gone to sleep in church and that Kentucky evangelist—the one with the big scar across his cheek—had thrown a songbook at him. The crowds increased until we had to move into the high school gymnasium. The last Sunday night our ushers counted 917 persons in attendance. There were twelve converts during this meeting. In the next series, with W. C. Gray as evangelist, there were twenty-eight.

After that we had conversions like any other church. The old burnt-over field had begun to sprout new growth.

During the Steenbergen meetings Sunday school attendance jumped to 225 and a few weeks later to 265 and never dropped back down. I soon afterward relinquished the Rochester charge to give full time to Akron. Tom Steenbergen took the oversight of the Rochester church.

The month of the Steenbergen meetings in Akron also witnessed the collapse of the stock market ushering in the Great Depression. All of a sudden money was scarce; then scarcer still. Farmers in our church were hit hard. Yet we had to build an addition to our building or lose what we had gained. The Board of Trustees agreed we should have the new addition; the question was how to obtain it. Finally, the chairman said, "Pastor, we'll erect the building if you will raise the money." To which, in my innocence, I agreed.

I had never raised a dollar for any such project in my life. The next few weeks found me covering the countryside in search of pledges. I would see a farmer at work in his field, park my car, cross the fence, talk to him about weather and crops, and then bluntly ask, "Have you decided how much you are going to give on the new building?" Some were not too happy to see me but with every new pledge the total grew. One thing was in our favor. Since the cost of building materials had sunk to an all-time low, the estimated cost of the addition was correspondingly at a minimum. Our men agreed to do most of the work. R. N. Gast would supervise the job.

As was to be expected, not all our men were enthusiastic about pledging to the building fund. I found one brother riding his tractor and finally said, "I suppose you want to give something toward the new building." He replied, "Well, I don't particularly *want* to but I guess I'll have to. Otherwise, all the rest would talk about me." He was probably right. In any case I accepted his modest pledge with thanksgiving and went on to the next farm. In spite of the depression the neccessary money was soon raised and we erected the much-needed, two-story addition.

It was in Akron that I first met Forrest Higgins who was to become a lifelong friend. His was an engaging personality which

159

made friends on contact. Forrest had an almost limitless supply of energy and was always helping somebody. If a barn burned in his neighborhood, Forrest was the one who called farmers on the phone and saw to it that loads of hay and grain were brought in and that a crew was on hand for the new barn raising. Forrest had a boat available for the pastor's use and a good rabbit dog, which unaided, could force rabbit after rabbit out of the briars.

I used to go out to the Higgins farm when potatoes were ready for digging just for the pleasure of watching the big ones roll out of the black muck. A time or two I helped the threshing crew and that was enjoyable, too, except for that day when one calculating farmer decided to give the young preacher a workout. I was pitching bundles from the ground to the wagon. We happened to be harvesting rye which must have grown to the height of at least four feet on the level. The bundles were large, long, and heavy. That particular farmer came into the field driving a big team of mules hitched to a wagon equipped with wide, steel wheels calculated not to sink easily, even in this rich soil.

He must have decided to see how high I could pitch those heavy bundles. As he started his load, he extended the bundles on each side of the wagon bed. This tipped me off to his plans. Then he began to build. Higher and higher went the load and higher and higher I pitched the bundles. I decided to pitch them to the moon if need be before ever uttering a word of complaint. Finally, the driver realized that if he loaded on any more he would never get out of the field. With a chuckle, he spoke to his mules and headed for the threshing machine. I had discovered some new muscles but on the whole felt pretty good about the match.

On my pastoral rounds one fine November day, I stopped at the farm home of a family where the wife was a good Christian but the husband left a bit to be desired at that point. However, he did attend church with some regularity. It was a good farm with gently rolling land and produced well. I stopped at the door for a moment. The lady of the house told me her husband was back in the fields but was due in soon. I had gone no farther than the barn when I met him coming in with his heavy team. He was in a curt frame of mind and apparently not overjoyed at seeing me, which

160

My Father
W. H. OLDHAM
(About 1912)

My Mother
MYRTLE OLDHAM
(About 1912)

The only picture of our whole family (l. to r.): W. H. Oldham,
Faith, Hazel, Dale, Etha, and Myrtle Oldham. Taken in 1923 or
1924.

Bill Bowser, Sr., took this picture of Polly while she was a telephone operator at the Gospel Trumpet Company (1922).

The first picture of Polly and me when we began going together. I was eighteen, she sixteen (1921).

Here I am at the Anderson Bible Training School in 1920 (age seventeen)!

The first A.B.T.S. male quartet (l. to r.): Charles Smith, first tenor; Dale Oldham, second tenor; Homer Byers, baritone; and John Settlemyre, bass.

The A.B.T.S. senior class of 1921. STANDING (l. to r.): Giles Jump, Hazel Kleeberger, Mamie Wallace, J. S. Ludwig, Gladys Horton, Eva G. Loofburrow, —————————, Carl Kreutz, ——————————, Stella Frazier, Ed Harding, Eva Laucamp, Burd Barwick, Conrad Ebert, ———————————, Mona Moors, Dale Oldham, Jewell Torkelson, Julius Boetcher, Harold Míller (hidden), Hope Nelson, Harvey Barnes, and Charles Smith. SEATED: Ralph M. Shaw, Lawrence Hatch, Jay M. Bentley, Elver F. Adcock, John H. Kane, Emil Ratzlaff, and Walter B. Crowell.

This photo of several early Church of God leaders was made on the steps of the Gospel Trumpet Company in Anderson, Ind., sometime in the early 1920s. FRONT ROW (l. to r.): Charles E. Brown, R. L. Berry, D. W. Patterson, H. M. Riggle, A. T. Rowe, Noah H. Byrum, J. E. Campbell, J. Grant Anderson, and W. E. Monk. BACK AND MIDDLE ROWS: J. T. Wilson, E. A. Reardon, W. A. Sutherland, Fred Bruffett, C. E. Byers, Earl L. Martin, W. F. Chappel, W. D. McCraw, G. R. Dodge, F. G. Smith, Andrew L. Byers, J. W. Byers, G. T. Neal, E. E. Byrum, and Barney E. Warren.

C. W. NAYLOR

D. OTIS TEASLEY

A. L. BYERS

At a tent meeting in Middletown, Ohio, about 1923 (l. to r.): W. F. Chappel; John Chappel, pianist; and R. C. Caudill. I led the singing.

E. L. Bragg of Marion, Ind. (1920). I sang for him in several good meetings, 1921-1924.

The gymnasium-auditorium at the Anderson campgrounds, built in 1910.

R. C. Caudill speaks at Anderson, 1945.

CHARLES E. BROWN   A. T. ROWE

John A. Morrison speaks at the Anderson camp meeting. Although a strong man physically, Dr. Morrison was stricken by arthritis and never fully recovered. Seated on the platform (l. to r.): T. Franklin Miller, A. T. Rowe (A. F. Gray behind him), Adam W. Miller, Clarence Hatch. Lola Thompson at the piano.

Inside the wooden tabernacle at Anderson.

Homer Rodeheaver and I at the International Young People's Convention, St. Louis, Mo., on September 1, 1934. Homer led the singing while I spoke. For many years he was·a song evangelist with Billy Sunday.

Gospel Trumpet Company members and the board of directors, 1942. SEATED are the directors (l. to r.): William Bowser, Oscar Flynt, Noah H. Byrum, Charles E. Brown, H. M. Riggle, Dale Oldham, A. T. Rowe, and Steele C. Smith. Other members of the company are (SECOND ROW, l. to r.): D. W. Patterson, R. L. Berry, W. O. Moon, L. W. Guilford, Andrew L. Byers, M. A. Monday, W. D. McCraw, H. C. Gardner, Elmer Rich, A. F. Gray, and Barney E. Warren. BACK ROW (l. to r.): W. E. Reed, G. R. Dodge, E. E. Shaw, Carl E. Reynolds, C. Lowrey Quinn, Hillery C. Rice, Raymond Jackson, Warren C. Roark. Earl L. Martin was also a company member, but absent from this picture.

The old Park Place church building, located at the northeast corner of College Drive and Eighth Street in Anderson. It was torn down in 1972.

LEFT: Richard L. Meischke and my son, Doug, who worked together on the Christian Brotherhood Hour for several years. Richard now uses the radio name, "J. Richard Lee."

RIGHT: Everett A. Hartung, a great Christian layman. Everett was chairman of the finance and building committees while I was at Park Place. He died in 1972.

LEFT AND BELOW: A special fellowship dinner was held during the 1941 Anderson convention to honor E. E. Byrum, Noah H. Byrum, and Barney E. Warren, the three oldest pioneers at the Gospel Trumpet Company. Shown at the head table are (l. to r.): C. E. Byers, John A. Morrison, H. M. Riggle, Noah

H. Byrum, E. E. Byrum, Barney E. Warren, A. T. Rowe, E. A. Reardon, Charles E. Brown, Raymond Jackson, F. G. Smith and Dale Oldham.

The Anderson College choir, directed by Robert A. Nicholson, was regularly featured on our early radio broadcasts.

Our silver wedding anniversary (1949), celebrated at the old gymnasium-auditorium on the Anderson campgrounds. About 1,000 persons were present.

At an early recording session for the Christian Brotherhood Hour. Our first broadcast was over KGGF in Coffeyville, Kan., in January of 1947. Since then, the program has expanded to nearly 400 English stations and 60 Spanish stations around the world. R. Eugene Sterner is now the speaker for the English broadcasts, while Fidel Zamorano is the Spanish speaker.

"To higher ground . . . ." Leading the ranks in our move to the new Park Place sanctuary in June, 1960 (l. to r.): Elbert Jones, youth minister; Dale Oldham, senior minister (with the pulpit Bible); and Ray Tuttle, associate pastor.

A reunion of four old friends, 1954 (l. to r.): Clifford Hutchinson, E. E. Caldwell, T. J. Steenberger, and R. C. Caudill. I began my work as an evangelistic singer in August, 1921, in Hinton, W.Va., with Dr. Caudill.

My son, Doug, and his family, 1972. In recent years Doug has been a radio and television soloist for Dr. Jerry Falwell of Lynchburg, Va., and has become widely recognized as a Christian recording artist.

Dedication of the first full-color press at Warner Press (formerly the Gospel Trumpet Company) in June, 1971. On the platform are (l. to r.): T. Franklin Miller, Clarence Patterson, Dale Oldham, and Steele C. Smith.

was about what I had expected. Since next day was Thanksgiving, I said, "It is a good thing to have one day set aside in which to especially thank the Lord for his goodness." He answered gruffly, "I don't see anything around here to be thankful for."

A few evenings later, just about deep dusk, this farmer hooked a small stock trailer to his car and drove west along a field where he planned to load a hog which was ready for market. It was a rolling road and the dips were deep enough for an approaching car to be completely hidden from view. My friend parked his car and trailer at the edge of the narrow gravel road and was crossing toward the field when a car came from the west at high speed. It hit my friend squarely; threw him clear over the fence and killed him almost instantly. It was difficult to conduct his funeral. As I stood before the people, all I could hear was, "I don't see anything around here to be thankful for." There is always *something* for which to be thankful.

Our son, Douglas Reed Oldham, was born in the Akron parsonage on November 30, 1930 and was a healthy baby. Forrest Higgins and I made a quick trip to Huntington in his Model A Ford, to bring Polly's mother. It was a dangerous drive, for the high crowned gravel roads were a glare of ice following a freezing rain. At one unexpected turn we skidded a hundred feet into a very propitiously located schoolyard, spun around, then without stopping proceeded shakily on our way.

Esther Shakespeare, R.N., came to care for the baby and Polly and stayed a full two weeks. At last we had a child. I treated the men to coffee next morning at a local restaurant. Doug was born about ten o'clock on a Sunday morning. I neither went to church nor sent word, so they had Sunday school and dismissed. Dr. Ferry and nurse Esther were well-trained and did a good job. Esther's was a labor of love. But neither did Dr. Ferry send a bill. Doug's arrival turned our program upside down and our emotions right side up. Polly was frightened at the prospect of having a baby in her care and was at first afraid to bathe him lest she should drop him. But how beautiful she was with a baby cradled in her arms. Our home was now complete; with my very own madonna and child to photograph.

177

With Akron in mind, I recall an observation made some years ago to the effect that a wise God always puts at least one critical person in every church to keep the pastor humble. Sometimes the critic is an old woman but it can be an old man or even a cantankerous teen-ager. Sometimes it is a good sister who waits until you are dead tired at the close of the Sunday evening service and then unloads all her troubles and gripes on you. Things were going well in the Akron church, but now and then I felt a burr under my saddle, placed there by one of our leading members who was critical, sarcastic, and judgmental. His sub-Christian attitude spoiled the spirit of the entire congregation and I resented it.

The Akron church had the bad habit of voting every year on whether or not the pastor should stay. I think this is an abominable practice because it gives a wonderful opportunity for a split to get under way. In any case, each year I received every vote but one and was always quite sure as to who had cast the negative vote. After three years at Akron, chiefly because of this one man but also because I was young and not accustomed to standing up against people, I submitted my resignation and accepted the pastorate at Lima, Ohio. The Akron church didn't want us to leave and we really didn't want to go. They had a farewell reception for us during which my thorn in the flesh said with a smile, "I suppose you know that I am the one who always cast the opposing vote in the annual election." I was glad to admit that I did know. "Really," he continued, "I don't want you to go. I like you. But I just don't like for things to be unanimous."

I really didn't expect the annual voting to be unanimous, but I did expect the people to vote their convictions and not their prejudices.

Chapter Fifteen

Lima

ABOUT OCTOBER 1, 1931 we reluctantly moved on to Lima, Ohio, a city hard hit by the depression. The wheels in the big Lima Locomotive Works had come to a complete halt. Men walked the streets looking for work; jobs were almost nonexistent.

I found a dispirited congregation hardput to keep up with the church's running expenses. The former pastor had left under pressure and I inherited a problem or two. My salary was to be thirty-five dollars per week, out of which I would pay all of our expenses including rent, utilities, and automobile upkeep. Part of the time I received twenty-five dollars a week but one week it dropped to fourteen dollars. Basically, however, it was a good church with kindly people and we had a spiritually profitable time together.

Twenty-eight of our families were on the relief rolls at one time. It was hard on their self-respect. When a man has been accustomed to taking good care of his family, it is hard on his very soul to have to line up with other poverty-stricken people to receive the government's handouts of rice, flour, lard, bread, and potatoes. It was interesting to observe the various ways in which hard times affected people. Some leaders in the church fell by the wayside. Other members of the congregation who had never demonstrated any particular inner strength blossomed forth into new spiritual life.

There were twenty or more unemployed young men in our Lima church, ranging in age from eighteen to twenty-four. Time hung heavy on their hands and their morale was low. Some had lost confidence in their abilities. They sat around their homes making life difficult for their parents and occasionally getting into trouble on the streets. Something had to be done to help them. Since I was active in the program of the YMCA, I asked permission to bring the boys into the gymnasium and swimming pool once a week without charge.

To this the secretary finally agreed and so to the "Y" we came and had some great times together. We played volleyball, basketball, handball, and swam in the pool. Since the fellows took their own soap and towels the "Y" had small expense because of them. I felt it did the young men no end of good. They would come out of the "Y" laughing and joking with each other, better able to face up to life and its disappointments.

I attended high school one year in Lima and was at long last awarded an Equivalency Certificate by the State of Indiana in lieu of a diploma. I joined the city ministerial association and was soon elected secretary-treasurer of the group. I was still very green, so far as my preaching know-how was concerned, and had formed the habit of speaking too loudly from the pulpit. Preachers so often seek to make up in thunder for what they lack in lightning. This fault was brought pointedly to my attention one day in a monthly meeting of the Ministerial Association.

At the opening of the fiscal year I had been assigned the task of addressing the group some time during the winter on the life of St. Francis of Assissi. In the Lima and Springfield public libraries I found out a great many things about this remarkable man of God. In due time I put together what I considered a fairly good paper. When the time to speak arrived, I was ready. The chairman introduced me and announced my subject, whereupon I arose and launched forth nervously with a voice loud enough to be heard by hundreds. Since only about twenty were present, the noise must have been quite disturbing to the brethren. But not for long. One of the more courageous soon held up a hand, stopped me, and said, "Brother, I think if you will lower your voice to a more conversational tone, we will enjoy your paper much more." Humbled, I turned down the volume and learned a valuable lesson. Subsequently I discovered that in almost every ministerial group there is one brother who doesn't mind turning *anybody's* volume down.

Lima was a rough and wicked city with an above-average amount of immorality and crime. One night the whole south end of town was rocked by a terrible explosion. I thought the gas works had blown up. Neighbors flocked into the streets to find out what had happened. It was some time before we had the answer.

With poverty so general in the city there was bound to be a considerable amount of theft and larceny. Even before hard times came, however, Lima had earned a reputation for being a hideout for the lawless. On this particular night, one or two men had apparently planned to blow a safe somewhere, and for this purpose had buried a container filled with nitroglycerine in a wooded field, a quarter of a mile or so from our home. When they went that night to dig it up, the shovel must have struck the container with sufficient force to set off the explosion. Actually, no one could ever say with certainty what happened. All we had to go on was a hole in the ground and little spatterings of human flesh in the surrounding trees. Next day as I returned from visiting the scene, all I could think of was, "Be sure your sin will find you out."

Forty years ago the FBI listed John Dillinger as Public Enemy No. 1 and organized a nationwide search for him. Dillinger had robbed various banks and once held up a police station. With one or two henchmen he held at bay the officers on duty and then robbed the place of shotguns and rifles. He served time in Ohio and Indiana penitentiaries but escaped from both, once with a make-believe gun. Captured again, he was being held temporarily in the Allen County jail at Lima. Jess Sarber was sheriff at the time. Since Dillinger had arrived, Mrs. Sarber, a motherly soul, had been trying to soften his heart with kindness, sending in with his meals pie and cake baked in her own oven.

One evening a henchman unceremoniously entered the sheriff's office, shot him without a word of warning, took keys from his desk, opened the cellblock door, and liberated Dillinger. Mrs. Sarber came rushing in just as Dillinger emerged from the cellblock. She said afterward that as he passed his head was down and he averted her gaze. Thus was her kindness to a murderer repaid.

Dillinger went on in his ruthless ways until the FBI set a trap for him in Chicago into which he was led by "the woman in red."

181

They shot him down as the two emerged from a movie. Dillinger's face had been lifted and his fingertips mutilated in an effort to destroy his fingerprints, but destiny finally caught up with him and he died without time to pray. Since Indianapolis had been his boyhood home, he was buried there in Crown Hill Cemetery.

Years later, we were in that same cemetery because of the death of a friend. We looked up Dillinger's grave and were amazed to find not a blade of grass growing on the outlaw's grave. Contempt for the man and what he had done caused visitors to stamp out in anger every green shoot that dared to appear. A man dies as he lives, but history generally remembers him, not for an occasional kindness but for the bad things he did. In Dillinger's case I'm afraid that list was longer than average.

It was said that some of Dillinger's rebelliousness came from an incident which took place in a Sunday school class when he was about twelve years old. His class was meeting, typically enough, in a basement room, the only window of which was set fairly high in the wall. Bored with whatever the teacher was saying, young John decided to leave. Mounting a bench, he was in the act of climbing out the window when the teacher caught and shook him soundly for his brashness. Dillinger became angry and never returned. He never rejoined society but remained a rebel to the end of his colorful but disastrous career. "Whatsoever a man soweth, that shall he also reap" (Gal. 6:7).

Long before my tenure, S. L. Wingert, of whom I have already spoken, had served several years as pastor of the Lima church. In fact the church experienced its greatest growth under his leadership. His quick laugh and ingratiating smile made him beloved by saint and sinner alike. When a local newspaper offered a Hudson automobile as first prize in a subscription contest, Wingert went to work and won the car, which he needed badly. Syd was a persuasive preacher with an evangelistic turn to his pastoral ministry.

During the Payne, Ohio, meetings with E. L. Bragg, Wingert wrote inviting me to come to Lima for a few days. I was staying in Pastor Ira Kilpatrick's home. His son Harold operated a ham radio, something quite unusual to my way of thinking. At lunch one day I spoke of calling Wingert to tell him when and how I would be arriving at Lima. Harold volunteered to get the message to him by radio, since he often talked with a Lima operator during the noon hour. Upstairs he went with my message and returned a few minutes later with the answer. I considered the transaction a very smart one, for it was very unique back then.

In Lima, Pastor Wingert shared with me a chilling incident which had recently taken place. The girl involved attended the Lima church, married the wrong man, and her marriage drifted into trouble. Pastor Wingert counseled with her, insisting that what both she and her husband needed was an old-fashioned experience of salvation. She continued attending church even though she had to come alone. One Sunday evening during the invitation Pastor Wingert left the platform to speak personally to the girl about her need of Christ. As she listened she wept, but finally she shook her head saying she could not yield now but planned to do so later.

However, as her domestic problems worsened, her anger mounted. When news came that her husband was running with other women, she decided to show him a thing or two. In church a night or so later, the pastor again invited her to surrender to Christ, but this time there were no tears, only a certain hardness on her countenance. Looking Wingert in the face, she said bluntly, "You know how my husband has treated me. He's not going to get away with it. In fact, I'm going out and go to the devil as fast as I can." With this she turned on her heel and left the church.

The following Sunday afternoon she and another young married woman dated two married men. The four went for an automobile ride and must have had quite a time. The ride took them eventually into a wooded lane where they spent an hour or so together. To exit from this lane to the highway it was necessary to cross double tracks of the Pennsylvania Railroad. The tracks next to the wooded area were being used for the storage of empty boxcars. A long line of them had been broken just wide enough to leave access to the lane. Finished with their good time, the young people cranked up the Ford and headed out of the woods. I imagine they were laughing and talking as they came to the blind crossing.

They should have sent someone ahead to see if all was clear. Instead, they drove between the box cars and across the main

183

track just as a crack Pennsylvania passenger train came through at seventy miles an hour. The Ford and its occupants were ground between freight cars and passenger train, leaving only unrecognizable remnants of them all. Again it came to me, "Be sure your sin will find you out." I do not believe God sends such things to those who disobey him. This accident came about through pure carelessness which sin promotes and from which it collects its toll as people give themselves to do evil.

We had a friendly group of pastors in Lima. I enjoyed their fellowship even when I did not agree with their theology. Reverend Thom, the Congregational-Christian pastor who had toned down my St. Francis speech, was my golfing partner on Monday mornings at the Country Club. They allowed local pastors to play free, which is certainly the only way I could have done it.

I had been forced by stark necessity to borrow a hundred dollars from a loan company and their excessive interest rate of 3½ percent a month caused me to become an avowed enemy of loan sharks ever since. My payments on that one-hundred-dollar loan were seven dollars a month. I shall never forget the indignation which was mine as I made the first payment and saw the girl credit three dollars and fifty cents on the principal and charge three dollars and fifty cents to interest. I finally paid off the loan, but believe me, I have never again patronized such a place. I paid interest at the rate of 42 percent a year on that loan. "There ought to be a law . . ."

Doug was about two at the time and was the delight of our lives. Polly showered him daily with TLC, as the doctors call it, Tender Loving Care. Then Doug began to experience frequent earaches. One ear was lanced twice to relieve the pressure. The other one once broke of its own accord. We were afraid he would develop the type of ear which drains constantly and is so odorous.

Then, while I was off somewhere in a series of meetings, Polly called long distance to say that Doug had pneumonia and it was serious. I was home in a few hours and vividly remember standing by his bedside· apprehensively watching his labored breathing. There were no sulpha drugs in those days—no penicillin, or myacins. The little fellow would have hard coughing spells now and

184

then which sapped his waning strength. The crisis neared. The doctor said that within the next few hours Doug would make a turn either for the better or worse. "If he can keep from coughing during the night, I think he will make it," he told us.

There was an extra earnestness in our prayers that night as Polly tucked the covers around our son and turned down the light. Sometime after midnight we were awakened by the child's coughing. My heart began to beat more rapidly as fear mounted. The doctor had said that the lad must *not* cough—and he was coughing. Quickly Polly and I came to his bedside. If I have ever prayed with my whole heart, I did so then. Having lost our first child at birth, were we about to see our second taken from us? When the prayer was finished, Doug turned over on his side, went back to sleep, and never coughed again. In a few days he was well and we had another testimony to the healing power of a loving God.

On Monday mornings at Lima during the winter some of the preachers would go to the "Y" for volleyball. There was always a considerable amount of ribbing and kidding over plays—well or poorly made. We had fun and the recreation and exercise were good for us. As two pastors joined me in the locker room one morning, the older of the two asked, "What kind of service did you have last night, Oldham?" I replied, "Great! We had a full house, a fine meeting, and seven persons were converted." At this my preacher friend grinned and said, "Well, Fred and I quit trying to convert our people long ago. Now we just bring them up as best we can, turn them loose, and hope for the best." I said to myself, If that is the philosophy of the leaders what can be expected of their people? Is this what Jesus Christ died to do for men?

Since the Lima church had no parsonage, Polly and I rented a house within a block from the church for $22.50 a month. This was really more than we wanted to pay in such hard times. It was a two-story house, the typical square kind with two bedrooms upstairs and a small study. There was a coal-burning furnace. One day I placed in it a small newspaper-wrapped package of garbage to be burned. I had done this before but this time the fire was not burning briskly. The garbage caused an accumulation of gas to form after which the furnace gave a big, solid puff strong enough to blow out a couple of chimney thimbles. A chimney thimble is a covering set over a stovepipe hole in the chimney wall. Most homes where heating stoves were once used were later converted to furnaces, but the old stovepipe holes were not bricked in. Instead decorative metal covers on spring-tension mounts were inserted.

As a result of the explosion we had soot all over the house. It was everywhere and on everything. We were away when the puff occurred and on our return dared not even enter the front room for fear of tramping the filthy soot into the rug. Polly suggested lighting a match to the house and burning it down, and I was tempted. Instead we borrowed a vacuum sweeper from a neighbor. We started at the front door and kept on until we had cleaned every floor, every wall, every picture, and every piece of furniture in the house. Believe me, from that time on I did not use the furnace as an incinerator unless I had a brisk fire going.

Financially, times grew no better with the passing months and soon $22.50 rent was a heavy burden. We moved into a little remodelled schoolhouse on Fourth Street, owned by the Shriner family. It had thick brick walls, a full finished basement, and a good furnace. The rent was reduced for our benefit to $16.00 a month. The house was located on half an acre of ground.

Since this back lawn had served as the school playground, the sod had not been broken for at least forty-five years. Nevertheless, when turned by a plow the soil proved rich and productive. So we put in a big garden and my father assisted during a visit. We planted rows of Burpee's Stringless Greenpod beans, Stowell's Evergreen sweetcorn, and a few long rows of yams and Yellow Jersey sweet potatoes. I dug enough sweet potatoes that fall to take care of us and several of the neighbors (Nine bushels). Those I kept I rubbed free of dirt and laid them out in the sun to dry. Afterward, in the dry basement, I laid them out on papers and spread them out so that none was touching another. They kept perfectly all winter.

As cold weather came on, I obtained a five-gallon crock, filled it with salted sauerkraut, placed an old plate upside down over the filled crock on our cold back porch, and weighted it down with a rock. When I wanted sauerkraut, Polly cooked it with smoked

186

sausage. She ate only the sausage, but I ate both, which she generally served with mashed potatoes. So you don't like it?

I sympathize with you. Neither did I until that day when we were visiting at my wife's grandmother's out in the country from Huntington. Polly's brother, Glenn, worked in town but had a long trapline which he visited daily during the winter. He collected enough hides to add considerably to his income. One cold day I offered to run the traps while he was at work. It was a good three-mile walk. Several inches of snow were on the ground and I misjudged the amount of time the trip would take. When I arrived back at grandmother's, lunch was over. My wife said, "Sorry, fellow, but all we had was sauerkraut, sausage, and mashed potatoes." I had never liked kraut, but that day I took a second helping and have enjoyed it ever since.

I find great pleasure in gardening. There is something elemental in getting your hands down into the soil. There is pleasure in planting seeds and watching them grow. It thrills me to transform a weed field into rows of vegetables. You remember the man who, observing a beautiful garden, said to its owner, "You and the Lord have certainly made a beautiful place of this." To which the gardener replied, "Yeah, but you should have seen it when the Lord had it all by himself."

During World War II, I planted a full lot with vegetables to supplement our food budget. When Polly became ill and continued in poor health for several months, I took her and Doug to our cottage on the shores of Yellow Creek Lake in northern Indiana. There they stayed for ten weeks. That left me with the question of what to do with all the produce coming on. Finally I said, "If a woman is smart enough to can green beans, peas, and such, so am I." Obtaining a government bulletin on how to process vegetables, I canned peas and picked, snapped, and canned green beans—bushels of them. Before Polly and Doug returned I had canned 108 quarts of green beans. They lasted us for nearly three years.

That fall in Lima, Polly told me to bring in everything which was left in the garden. Since it was late in the season, I didn't expect to find much, but I brought in carrots, cabbages, and onions to which she added celery and tomatoes. We canned thirty-five quarts of this stock. After that, all we had to do was add a good piece of beef to enjoy delicious soup, and it was just as good the second day as the first.

The depression resulted in much personality damage to some of our folk, but it also led to revival. Our Lima church attendance grew until we had to purchase a portable schoolhouse ($180) and set it up on the back of the lot. When we first went to Lima, Sunday school attendance was about 225, but only 75 persons remained for church services. This didn't suit me at all. After thinking it over for some weeks, I resolved a way to change things.

Glenn Herring was Sunday school superintendent and had charge of the "opening exercises." One morning I said, "Glenn, this time when you come to the place where you usually say 'We will now go to our classes,' I want you to say instead, 'Our pastor will now bring us the message.' " So instead of 75, I spoke to 225 that morning and enjoyed it so much that we kept right on having preaching before Sunday school. After that we had 225 in both services.

Strangely enough, this new order of things evoked criticism from one or two of my Ohio pastoral brethren. During our state camp meeting at Springfield, while I was off somewhere finishing another camp meeting, one of our preachers had quite a field day speaking about worldliness, which was one of his favorite themes. He lambasted the way women were dressing (I wonder what he would say if living now), took a crack or two at the men, and then said, "Some of our *churches* are also following after the world. I know of one church where they even have church ahead of Sunday school!" My, my! The people all shouted "Amen!" When I arrived a day or two later, someone told me of the sermon. Since I was the only one in our entire movement who scheduled preaching ahead of Sunday school, I knew I had to be the bad, bad boy to whom he had referred.

Meeting this preacher a day or two later, I said, "I've been wanting to see you. I have a very important question to ask. Since you are so much older than I and have had far wider experience in the ministry and know your Bible far better than I will ever know mine, I felt you might help me." He gave me serious attention and answered, "Sure, Dale, what is it?" Thus, having put him solidly out on a limb, I proceeded to saw it off by saying, "My question is this: Did Jesus have Sunday school before or after church?" My friend turned red in the face, sputtered, and finally said with a forced laugh, "It *was* foolish of me, wasn't it?" I replied, "You didn't seem to think so while you were up there preaching in such a big way."

He and I remained friends and sometimes hunted together; but that wasn't the end of his potshots at me. His basic problem was that he had been forced to drop out of school after the fifth grade and ever afterward was uncomfortable in the presence of educated men. He was coinstigator of one anticollege thrust which came near to bringing disaster to our chief educational institution, Anderson College.

Years later he and I were both on the program at our Ohio state ministers' meeting. I spoke in the morning session and he was scheduled for the evening. I had taken a layman with me to the conference, promising to get him back that evening in time for work. During the afternoon I went to the evening speaker to carefully explain why we had to leave. He said he understood perfectly and that it was all right with him. In fact we had a good talk together. I asked him why he felt he had to take a shot at me every once in awhile. Tears were in his eyes as he said, "Dale, I don't know why I do it. I really like you and appreciate your work. But you school men give me a feeling of inferiority. I suppose this is my way of compensating for it."

My layman and I headed for home, only to hear afterward that when my friend arose to speak that evening, he prefaced his remarks by saying, "The devil doesn't want me to deliver this message tonight and some of my brethren don't want me to deliver it. In fact, when I said I was going to speak up anyhow, one of the pastors left and has gone home." After that I decided just to love the man as he was and thank the Lord for the great work he had done down through the years in behalf of Christ's kingdom. I knew then that he would never change.

One day as I returned from hospital visitation in Lima and turned the corner toward our church, I was surprised to see fire

189

trucks and a crowd in the street. Firemen were directing streams of water onto and into our church building. My heart sank within me. My first thought was, Where will we have services next Sunday?

It was quite a shock to see curls of smoke issuing from under the siding. Firemen were breaking windows to spray the burning section. Our church auditorium was heated by an old-fashioned one-register furnace located under the center of the sanctuary.

The day of the fire, someone had probably by chance, closed the shutters in the register. The custodian came to warm the building for the evening service, built a good fire, set the thermostat, and left. But with the airflow shut off, the furnace built up heat until the floor and boxing around the register caught fire. Now where would our classes meet? Where would services be held? Would some of our people drift away during the rebuilding program? Actually, the fire proved to be a blessing in the long run. The insurance was paid promptly and was adequate. We installed a better and safer furnace, remodeled the burned-out basement to provide more Sunday school rooms, and repainted the building both inside and out. But in spite of all of our cover-up efforts the smell of fire stayed with us for months.

With the building again fresh and bright the yard needed attention. It needed sod and shrubbery, but with the depression still on there was no money with which to purchase it. But "where there's a will there's a way." Mother Shriner offered sod from the old school ground. We put one crew to work cutting it and another to hauling it over to the church on a small farm trailer. We began to cover the old lawn.

One older brother stood by watching the young men lay sod, but didn't think they were doing it properly. He said, "No, that isn't the way. Let me show you." We ended by letting the good man show us how to do the whole thing. He seemed uncommonly tired when evening came. Other people donated plantings. With the lawn sodded and new shrubbery in place our newly painted church presented a much better appearance. You can tell a great deal about a congregation just by looking at the building in which they are content to worship.

The Lima church was quite demanding. The people had been spoiled and thought nothing of calling me at two o'clock in the morning to pray for their headaches. I lost considerable sleep while pastoring there. However, there was one young man in the church who thought my pastoral job was a snap. He would say, "Here is the man who works one day a week." Since he was young and single and had no family responsibilities, one day I said, "Look, I want you to go home with me for a week. You will eat when I eat and sleep only when I sleep. You will go when and wherever I go." That suited him fine because he had Polly's cooking in mind. He also enjoyed driving a car and that job would be his also.

It just so happened that the following week was exceptional as far as night calls were concerned. This lad was a sleepyhead anyhow and when I would rouse him at one or two o'clock in the morning he would not come up smiling. One night we were up from one-thirty until five and he came back bushed. He had stuck it out for three days and nights; but after breakfast, with a wry smile, he bade me adieu, saying he was going home to get some sleep. That was the last time he ever wise-cracked about my one-day-a-week job.

Money may have been scarce in the Lima church but the Lord was at work in the hearts of the people. E. E. Caldwell was pastor at Fourth and Neal Avenue in Columbus and a good friend of mine. Since neither his church nor ours could afford to import an evangelist, he and I decided to exchange meetings. I would go to Columbus for three weeks and Caldwell would come to Lima for three weeks. Each would receive $25.00 for travel expenses. It was the best we could do.

We had a good meeting in Columbus but an exceptional one in Lima. The people had no other place to go so they went to church. The Holy Spirit began to work and they began to surrender to the Lord by the dozens. The kneeling altar across the front of the sanctuary was filled again and again with penitents seeking forgiveness and new life in Christ. We had three or four "landslide" altar services during the three weeks. One came on the last Saturday night. Afterward the evangelist said to his host, "Well, we've had such a large response in the meetings, I have a feeling that my work is about done." But the answer came back, "You mustn't feel like that. There are many more who still need to find the Lord." On the closing night the altar was again filled with those seeking Christ.

About this time Charles Hartung, of Fort Wayne, and Von Chesterman of Pierceton, Indiana, decided to broadcast a series of radio programs over Fort Wayne station WOWO. They began to solicit funds for this purpose. None of our preachers were broadcasting at the time and this seemed a bold, brave venture. The Fort Wayne station had excellent coverage and a large listening audience. I was pleased when, a couple of months later, Reverend Hartung wrote asking that I prepare a sermon for broadcast. I was to speak for fifteen minutes. Prior to this time I had never written a sermon out in full, although I always used extensive notes. This time everything had to be written out; word for word and what a job it was! It was but a foretaste and training for the 1160 Christian Brotherhood Hour sermons which years later I had to write.

I remember sitting at my desk looking at the outline I planned to use as a basis for my manuscript; wondering if it had the quality it ought to have. I began to type and the further I went the more I realized just how much "sawdust" or stuffing had been going into my pulpit delivery. A sermon which took thirty minutes to deliver in the pulpit boiled down to ten when committed to manuscript. I worked four days on that message and still remember what a gigantic task it was. Finally I delivered it as scheduled over WOWO. I had been initiated into sermon writing. I could now understand a bit better what it does for a preacher to write out his sermons even though he does not plan to take the manuscript into the pulpit with him.

Every preacher ought to write out many of his sermons in full, if for no other reason than to be able to look at them objectively. There is a great deal of difference between a written sermon and one delivered from notes. There is no better way to discover how much you have been repeating yourself or how inadequate your sentence structure has been. The next step is to record your written sermon and then listen to the play-back.

A few years later, as I studied homiletics under Dr. D. H. Gilliatt in the seminary at Dayton, recording machines were just appearing on the market. Some time during the winter every student had to deliver a sermon before the class and it was recorded. Afterward the class would criticize the message. It took courage to speak before a group composed entirely of critics. Afterward Dr. Gilliatt met privately with each speaker and the two would listen to a play-back of the recording. Then the instructor would point out ways by which the order of the sermon or the manner of its delivery could be improved.

One young fellow did such a poor job that we all felt sorry for him. In fact, we said almost nothing in criticism of his very futile effort. But after hearing the play-back he packed up and left the seminary, explaining that the recording proved conclusively that he would be miscast in the ministry. And he was right.

I will always remember the Lima years as times of "bitter herbs and unleavened bread." Times were hard and money scarce. One could buy jowl bacon for seventeen cents a pound, but we could seldom afford it even at that price. I remember being downtown one day walking past a drugstore from which emanated the smell of good coffee. Coffee was but five cents a cup, but I did not have even a nickel. I walked a great deal in Lima to save gasoline money. The five-dollar bills received for conducting funerals or weddings were like gifts from heaven. We lived frugally of necessity; eating cheap but filling foods, like rice, potatoes, and beans. Meat was a luxury we could afford about once a week.

We were in Lima from 1931 until 1934 and then accepted the pastorate of the First Church of God in Dayton. Before leaving Lima the church treasurer asked if I felt the church was in debt to me for the amount of my salary which had not been paid. I told him that as their pastor during those three years I had felt I should share their poverty and so they were not in debt to me.

Early in my ministry I felt there were certain churches I would pastor some time during my life. One was in Dayton, Ohio; a second in Anderson; a third in Fort Wayne, Indiana; and a fourth in South Bend. I did pastor in Dayton and Anderson but missed out at Fort Wayne and South Bend. However, I shall always feel we should have moved to South Bend at the time we went to Lima.

My friend, W. C. Gray, had done a fine work in South Bend for several years and had built a beautiful new sanctuary before leaving. I felt definitely led of the Lord to succeed him. We had worked with the South Bend church in evangelistic meetings and knew the people well. Many felt that the Lord was leading us their way. I heard later that my name was presented to the Pulpit Committee and all but one man favored my being invited. He vetoed fhe motion and the matter was dropped. But I still feel the Lord wanted me in South Bend at that time. In the days that followed the church came on hard times, lost that big new beautiful building and had to move into a much less desirable structure. It was years before the congregation again became solidly established.

Chapter Sixteen

Dayton

IN MAY OF 1934 we moved to Dayton, Ohio. The church promised to pay us forty dollars a week out of which we would furnish our own living quarters and pay all other expenses. First Church was running about three hundred fifty in Sunday school with fairly good leadership on its various boards and committees. Miss Mae McAlpine was director of youth and Christian Education. She was a faithful, intelligent worker. She and the custodian were the only other salaried employees.

The depression was still on and the church was going through difficult times financially. There were unpaid bills amounting to twelve hundred dollars; a huge amount in those rugged times. The church had failed to make five of its last twelve building payments. Offerings were running about ninety dollars a week which did not cover expenses. Yet I felt definitely in the order of the Lord in going to Dayton and entered this new field with a bright feeling concerning the future.

I had come to Dayton on a split vote, and knew it. There had been ninety votes for me and sixty for a friend of mine who had relatives in the congregation. This somewhat lopsided vote worried me very little. I had faith in God and felt that things would straighten out and all would be well. I began preaching and loving the people, acting as if I had come to Dayton with a unanimous vote. A spirit of enthusiasm soon made its way into the church— but we still had those pesky bills staring us in the face.

In one of my first meetings with the Board of Trustees, I asked how much the church had given to missions in the preceding year. The question evidently embarrassed him but the treasurer answered, "Nothing. We couldn't even pay our own bills, so how could we give to missions?" I irritated him further by remarking, "You know, I think this may have something to do with the fact that all these bills remain unpaid. This church has become ingrown. We need to give to something outside ourselves." The board wanted to know what I would suggest. I told them we could begin by giving one Sunday school offering a month to foreign missions. To this they somewhat hesitantly agreed. It amounted to only fifteen or eighteen dollars a month at first but then increased to one hundred dollars or so.

During this time our general offerings also increased. Before long all of our assessments and outstanding bills were paid and offerings were running about five hundred dollars per week. When the inward look was replaced by an outward look, revival came to the church and we began to experience conversions in our Sunday services.

There had been good leadership in the Dayton church in the years prior to our coming. Among former pastors were John Turner, who also owned a toy factory; E. E. Caldwell, genial Irishman beloved by everyone; W. D. McCraw, who never seemed well, yet lived to the ripe old age of ninety-five. All three were better than average pulpit men. McCraw was also in demand as a camp meeting and revival preacher.

I also inherited a Board of Elders which was something new in my experience. The Board consisted of three elderly men: C. C. Conyers, F. W. Grisso, and Charles Pfeiffer, all of whom have long since gone to their final reward. The elders were a help to me; first in outlining the directions the church should take but also in giving advice when appointments to certain responsibilities needed to be made. I valued their wisdom and judgment, but there were a few in the church who resented it every time I announced that I would like to see the elders for a few minutes at the close of the service. They felt they were being left out of something or that their judgment was not considered to be of value. On leaving the Dayton pastorate it was my judgment that having a board of elders was not good for a church. I could have sought the same advice from the same men unofficially and it would not have been resented.

In 1935 radio was of considerable importance in the homes of the people; about as much so as television is now. We had been in Dayton less than a year when some of the trustees suggested that we should put on a weekly radio program. The idea appealed to me also. Although the Board had taken no official action, I visited station WING and signed up for thirty minutes each Sunday afternoon. We had superior musical talent in the church and I knew their singing would appeal to the public. On the following Sunday morning I told one of the trustees what I had done. I said with a smile, "Now, all you have to do is raise the money." Twenty dollars a week. The program would have to support itself because there was no money in our budget for it. We appointed a radio treasurer to whom the people handed their weekly donations. In this simple manner the program was supported for over ten years. In fact, the Dayton church still broadcasts every Sunday.

We could put on an attractive musical program because of a first-class male quartet, ladies' quartet, and featured soloists. My wife and I sang together occasionally. She also played the piano and on a few occasions during my absence stood in for me as announcer. The program was well received from the beginning and made many friends for us. It helped substantially in building our Sunday evening attendance.

Soon the church was full. Our first-class choir sang on Sunday evenings instead of mornings. People from many denominations joined in times of real refreshing. We also reaped from several excellent evangelistic meetings. The Sunday school grew until we were averaging five hundred twenty-five in attendance. This packed our inadequate building to capacity. On a hot, July Sunday morning a panoramic camera photographed the congregation on the sloping lawn outside the building. There were seven hundred twenty-five present.

In 1939 Hitler entered the Corridor and before long war in Europe brought increased production in American factories. The depression slowly subsided as money began to circulate more freely. We burned the mortgage on our church building and began putting a thousand dollars a month into a building fund. Then came Pearl Harbor, followed by restrictions on building, so we could not enlarge our plant.

During my thirty-four years as a pastor, I wasn't much of a dictator. But, in Dayton I once came very close to railroading a project. You could almost hear the whistle blow. In 1940 not too many of our churches had installed organs. Most used pianos in public worship but Polly and I felt that an organ would lend itself much better to the spirit of worship. We made inquiries and found an electrically operated reed organ which sounded fairly good to us (although later on we were glad to trade it on something better). A special price had been posted on this instrument. The salesman also offered to place the organ in our sanctuary and provide an organist for our next Sunday morning service. Polly and I were excited over the prospect. It was a nervy thing to do but we ordered the organ sent out anyhow.

That Sunday morning while our people assembled for worship the organ filled the sanctuary with lovely melodies. The shocked people sat listening—surprised looks on their faces. Just before the benediction I explained the situation, saying I had been sure they would want the organ once they had heard it and had seen what it could do for a worship service. Did they enjoy the organ? (Amens.) Would they like to have it remain with us so we could use it in all of our services? (Amens, nods, and smiles.) Then I told them that all we had to do to keep it was to pay for it. Special sale price; twelve hundred dollars. I concluded, "If you like the organ and want us to keep it, say it with dollars, right now. The ushers will pass the offering plates." We received about half the money that morning and our youth organization promised to take over the remaining payments. I drew a long sigh of relief. What a blessing that organ proved to be and what a difference it made in services of reverent worship! It was especially appreciated during funerals and weddings and in creating the right mood for the midweek prayer meetings. Thank God for organs!

Sometime during 1943 the manager of station WING called me into his office to engage my services as a news broadcaster. So many young men were away in the Armed Services that adequate help was hard to find. Most radio stations carried fifteen-minute news broadcasts about four times a day. The manager liked my voice and thought that my sincerity led people to believe what I said. He asked me to take the 6:00 P.M. and 10:00 P.M. newscasts for the munificent sum of twenty-five dollars a week. Since my salary at the church had risen to only sixty-five dollars and war prices had continued to climb, I welcomed the opportunity to supplement my income and began my news broadcasting immediately.

I loved it. Every single minute of it. In the first place the necessary preparation for every broadcast kept me well informed on what was going on in the world. Second, I was forced to check the correct pronunciation of every word and name. Third, news broadcasting sharpened my ability to handle a manuscript in front of a microphone. Fourth, I met many persons I would never have met otherwise. Some of them I interviewed for our listening audience.

The newscasts went well. At 6:00 P.M. we were sponsored by the Rike-Kumler Company, Dayton's largest and best department store. I heard never a word from their advertising department to indicate whether or not they were pleased with my work. The station manager told me to relax; that I was the only one who had ever done the Rike-Kumler newscast without bringing complaints from them.

A few months later the station manager asked me to take on the 8:00 A.M. and 12:00 noon editions of the news, also. But by this time I was discovering some of the job's disadvantages. It limited several of my general church activities. I couldn't speak outside the city except on Sunday. I could not accept invitations to address youth conventions, ministers' meetings, evangelistic crusades, or camp meetings. The station manager was insistent at wanting to build me into a public personality. I addressed luncheon clubs and civic organizations. My photo appeared in newspaper display ads and in the Rike-Kumler elevators. Wide publicity was given my broadcasts. The salary would be three hundred dollars a month, which was more than the church was paying. I was tempted, but while discussing it with Polly, she wisely remarked, "I suppose this

199

is as good a time as any to decide whether you are going to be a preacher or a newscaster." I rejected the offer and also gave up the other newscasts in order to pursue my real calling unhindered. In their next board meeting the trustees voted me a twenty-five-dollar-a-week increase in salary.

Shortly afterward I received a call from WING which informed me that President Roosevelt had just died. He asked that I prepare, as soon as possible, a special prayer suitable for the occasion for broadcast. I was deeply moved by the death of the president and realized the crisis it brought to the nation. My prayer apparently reflected the sentiments of many WING listeners. With radio now in my blood, I dreamed of presenting a literary program in which I would read poetry, essays, and other items of value, interspersing these with my own comments. I would call it "Bob Elmore's Notebook," borrowing my grandfather's name for the purpose. After preparing a fourteen-minute pilot program, I took it to radio station WHIO where my work would have to stand on its own merits. The program director gave me an audition and the response was so exciting I thought I was launched on a new avocation. But no sponsor was immediately forthcoming and I had to drop the idea, but I still think it was a good one.

With my Equivalency Certificate from the State of Indiana in hand, I now turned to see what possibilities Dayton offered for furthering my education. Someone referred me to the United Brethren Seminary. I drove over to make inquiries. As I parked my car, Dr. J. R. Howe came by and stopped for conversation. Dr. Howe was a professor of systematic theology. I explained to him my wish to take courses which would equip me to teach leadership training to my Sunday school teachers. He told me if I would complete their prescribed diploma curriculum, I could do that and much more. Fortunately, this Seminary offered a three-year diploma course for the benefit of students lacking a college education. Without further waiting I enrolled and began a six-year relationship with United Theological Seminary; then known as Bonebrake Seminary.

It was my first experience in the liberal approach to theology. It was quite a shock to my conservative mind and conscience. A time or two, I became so upset over the teachings of the New Testament instructor that I got up and walked out of class. I had yet to learn how to simply reject what did not appeal to me as being reasonable. Another professor elevated my blood pressure now and then. On one occasion I challenged him before the whole class, which I shouldn't have done since it was not a Church of God school.

Historically the Church of God has taught that we can not only be saved from our sins but subsequently be filled with the Holy Spirit. Our fathers called the experience sanctification. Many of the United Brethren used to believe and teach this doctrine but most of them dropped it somewhere along the line.

One day as I sat in class about half asleep, the teacher began to speak disparagingly of the experience of sanctification, ending his cute criticism by saying: "My grandfather used to say that when he heard a sanctified man was in the community he always put a second padlock on his chicken coop." I exploded! "Doctor, this is the first unkind and unreasonable thing I have ever heard you say. It seems to me most unfair and intolerant in the light of other things you have been teaching. Do you mean to say you would put an extra lock on the chicken coop if I were to come your way? Just because a man differs with you theologically? I've been in the Church of God all my life. My father is a preacher in this group. I have aunts, uncles, and cousins who are also preachers. I've been surrounded by Church of God people all my life and know them well. Many are saints. In fact, sir, I'll stand our Church of God people side by side with your United Brethren folk any day you suggest and will compare them for honesty, decency, and integrity."

Wow! Like the man said, "I hadn't oughta done it!" But I was riled and talking fast. Finally I ran down and sat back with some trepidation, for this particular professor could be caustic and blunt. I waited, expecting him to unload on me like a ton of bricks. I can see him yet, sitting behind his desk, looking down, whirling his horn-rimmed glasses with one hand. At long last he looked up and said, "Well!" and went on teaching. Strangely enough, after that we were the best of friends and he was a great help to me in many ways.

201

My diploma work was finished in the spring of 1937. The following year I commuted the one hundred miles to and from Anderson College every Monday, completing work for a Bachelor of Theology degree. In the fall of 1938 I petitioned the United Seminary faculty for graduate standing for some of the Diploma School credits I had not used on my Anderson degree and they granted it. Then I entered the Graduate School of Theology and completed work for the Bachelor of Theology degree during the next three years. I was graduated in May of 1941 when I was thirty-eight years old. Now they call it a Master of Divinity degree.

As I look back over my seminary years I realize afresh how much they have meant to me. Had it not been for the seminary I could not possibly have filled certain positions or accepted certain invitations. I owe a deep debt of gratitude to the professors who put up with me in my greener years. For this reason I never let a year go by without sending at least a small gift to United. I was a stranger and they took me in.

The Dayton pastorate was a joy to me and so was the city. I enjoyed the association with my people, with the merchants, with WING personnel, and with my handball partners at the "Y" where I went for a workout about three noon hours a week. I kept in good physical condition; at one hundred and seventy-five pounds. The church was growing. However, several of our people had to drive across the city to meet with us. This took time and was also expensive. There were no through boulevards; the days of freeways and interstate highways had not yet arrived. We hadn't been in Dayton very long until a few people from the south side wanted to start a Sunday school for underprivileged children in their community. I objected; chiefly because I didn't want to lose any adults at a time when we were having such difficulties in paying our bills. In 1935 we were still in the depths of the depression.

But these good folk said, "We don't want to start another church; we just want a Sunday school where these street waifs can be taught the gospel." Finally I relented and the Sunday school was started in a small store building. But, as I had anticipated, it wasn't long until guest ministers were being brought in and regular services of worship instituted. I could have fought and perhaps terminated the project, but it seemed wiser to "jine 'em if I couldn't lick 'em." Soon afterward I installed their first salaried pastor, gave the church my blessing, and before long they had an attendance of three hundred in Sunday school.

Three or four years later, when some of the east side people indicated they would like a church in their part of the city, we gave them their first teachers and leaders—about thirty-five of them. In a couple of years, they, too, had a Sunday school of about two hundred and fifty. Now there were three white congregations where formerly there had been one. Attendance was diminished a bit on the west side, but from a financial standpoint I could never tell we had lost anyone. Explain that if you can.

Competitive sports have always appealed to me. For thirty years I enjoyed handball. It is a fast game and I could get a first-class workout in forty-five minutes. In the noon handball sessions with three other select players we had some great games. I have told many a young pastor that it is far better to take out your gripes on a handball than on a Board of Trustees. Being left-handed was to my advantage, especially in doubles play. My friend and seminary teacher, Dr. J. R. Howe, an excellent tennis player, teamed up with me in handball doubles. We have a few trophies tucked away somewhere, which were won in Dayton and southwestern Ohio YMCA competition.

One fall, Secretary Friermood asked me to teach a beginner's class in handball. In the group was a young fellow who showed unusual talent. I never saw anyone take to the game more rapidly. He was tall, slim, rangy, and very nimble. In addition to all this, Red proved to be ambidextrous. He could serve the ball equally well with either hand. Within a year he was beating me at singles. He went on to become Ohio State YMCA singles champion. I found satisfaction in having been his teacher.

After moving to Anderson, I occasionally entered handball tournaments with partner, Russell Hudson. I well remember the last match in which we played. It was held at the Terre Haute "Y" where we were defeated in the semifinals. Never had I played so hard or against more skilled competition. We really put our backs into it but weren't quite good enough. Immediately afterward I flew out to Wichita to conduct a series of meetings for E. E. Kardatzke. Next day I was on crutches. My arches pained almost unbearably. For two or three nights I entered the pulpit on crutches. A few years later my sacroiliac began to give me trouble. Dr. Wendell Kelly laughed and said, "Why not be your age and take up volleyball?" I replied, "Man, I'm not *that* old." But I had to give up handball and substitute with golf, swimming, and bowling. Yet no game ever satisfied me like handball; especially when playing in a good, fast, skilled foursome.

The Dayton and Montgomery County Ministerial Association was an active part of the Dayton and Montgomery County Council of Churches. I always enjoyed their monthly programs. We imported speakers such as Dr. Elmer Homrighausen, Dr. George Buttrick, Dr. Glenn Clark, and Dr. E. Stanley Jones. While I was chairman of the Evangelism Committee, we brought Dr. E. Stanley Jones to town as Holy Week speaker for our union meetings. Dr. Jones was one of my favorites. It was a pleasure to take him here and there to his appointments. During my final year in Dayton, I served as president of the Ministerial Association. I still count as my friends many with whom I cooperated in its fellowship.

One Monday our County Ministerium met in a rural church for an all-day retreat. We had a most refreshing time together. I mention it only because of a remark made by an Episcopalian rector as he led morning devotions. Speaking about "fits and misfits" in the ministry, he said that in his church district no divinity student was admitted to a graduate school of religion until he had been thoroughly examined by two psychiatrists for the purpose of discovering what were his motives for desiring to enter the ministry. His statement brought on considerable laughter. But I have often wondered how many ministerial misfits might have been weeded out and how many congregational difficulties might have been avoided had all of our churches followed a similar procedure. There are probably several men in the ministry today chiefly because mama always wanted them to be preachers. It takes balanced preachers to do balanced preaching. This in turn produces balanced congregations. The opposite must also be true to some degree.

In 1935 Polly's health was declining. After Doug's birth in 1930 she had developed pyelitis; a serious kidney infection. In Lima it had become worse. It was at least another fifteen years before penicillin and the sulphas were made available to the public. One day, while we were still living in the little remodeled schoolhouse in Lima, someone called me in from the garden, saying Polly was very sick. I found her in convulsions. Her hands and feet were literally turned up. I was alarmed. The doctor we called helped little, although the crisis did pass. In 1934, after moving to Dayton, we found that Polly had taken her sickness with her. She lost twenty pounds, felt ill most of the time, and was too weak to enjoy life.

One Sunday evening at her bedside I told her we would be having special prayer for her in the service. But after I left, Satan poured doubts upon her until she was wretched. Finally she said to Doug, who was nearly four, "Son, go into daddy's study and bring me every Bible and Testament you can find." Shortly he was back with half a dozen volumes. Polly laid these out in a circle around her on the bed and began to pray for help and healing. She said to Satan, "This is God's word. You can't get through the wall of promises I have laid around myself." That evening she was marvelously helped in answer to prayer, although still far from well.

Some time later we heard of a very intelligent and capable woman physician who had formerly been connected with a Vienna hospital. Dr. Vera Dreimer asked Polly if she had the will power to follow instructions to the letter. I could have answered for her: she did. A year later my wife was well and not a trace left of the old infection. The doctor said, "Mrs. Oldham, yours is a very remarkable case. Such a recovery does not often take place." The Lord and Dr. Dreimer had worked a miracle. We moved from a big square house into a six-room bungalow which made housework easier for Polly.

Meanwhile, the Dayton church was making solid progress. Doug was in school and at the age of eight or so was becoming quite a singer. He had sung in public since he was five. In school he was pushed to the front in musical programs. While still a boy soprano he sang with the Inland Children's Choir. The choir was organized in Dayton and had already been heard on a national radio network. Before long he was singing solos in church and on our radio broadcasts. Recently, in going over some of our old recordings I found one made from a Dayton radio program on which Doug, at ten, sang "The Holy City." He had emotional power even then and the ability to communicate. We took him to the Southeastern Youth Convention in Johnson City, Tennessee, in 1940. At the banquet Doug stood on a chair or table and sang "God Bless America," Kate Smith style, with the second ending. He was nine at the time. About that same age he was singing a solo in an evangelistic service, when suddenly he departed from the tune he knew so well and took off on one of his own. Polly was playing for him and almost had a nervous breakdown wondering what on earth he was up to. After soaring around for awhile on his own, he settled back down to the right melody and finished as he should. I suppose he had just given way to a moment of inspiration. He still does now and then!

One day I sat at a table in our bungalow counting up rent receipts. Polly was watching and said, "Instead of paying out all this money in rent, why don't we buy a house?" The question seemed absurd to me, for we were about four hundred dollars in debt on a car. I answered, "Buy a house without money?" She replied, "Other people do." I came back with, "How?" "I don't know," she confessed. "Why don't you go find out?" On impulse I crossed the street to where a war veteran in poor health lived with his working wife in a nice white two-story house. I told him of my predicament, and then asked, "How much does one have to pay down on a house?" He answered, "Five hundred dollars." "You couldn't buy much of a house with that small a down payment," I ventured. "I'll sell you this one," he replied. And he was serious about it.

When a member of our Board of Trustees heard of this opportunity, he and his wife volunteered to go to the bank with us and sign a note for five hundred dollars. Thus we purchased our first home in Dayton. Three years later we sold it at a profit and built a comfortable six-room brick house on a spacious corner lot about a mile from the church.

Polly and I pried flat stones out of a creek bed with which we built a two-foot wall along the back line between us and the neighbors. With Tom Steenbergen's help we also built a stone grill to match the wall and afterward fixed hamburgers there, and sometimes steak. We built a picnic table and enjoyed many an evening meal out there under the trees. We found a place in the country which had been beautifully landscaped but was now grown up in weeds. The owner said I could have all the shrubs I wanted for a dollar fifty cents each if I would dig and haul them. This added greatly to the appearance of our place. We had the yard sodded, planted shade trees, and began to enjoy the fruits of our labors.

It is a good feeling to own your own home, especially after you have made the final payment on it and it is all yours. It was a pleasure to care for the lawn and shrubbery while Polly gave her touch to things on the inside. Doug had his own room and I had a knotty-pine study on the second floor with built in bookcases. Who could wish for more? For companionship, Doug had a smart little Pomeranian, a red-haired Chow, and the children of the neighborhood. I had my rewarding work. Polly had the organ to play and all was well. How we loved Dayton!

About 1942 I was called to Vandergrift, Pennsylvania, to conduct evangelistic meetings for pastor Al Donaldson. It was my first experience in preaching to those stolid Pennsylvania Germans and for a time they really confused me. If I said something humorous in introducing a sermon, no one laughed. They wouldn't even smile. I thought I had lost my touch until Al told me these people had been taught from childhood never to laugh or even smile in church. What on earth is wrong with laughing if something is funny? I think after seeing giraffes, a rhinoceros, and a hippopotamus, Jesus probably laughed in church. I am sure that God has a sense of humor.

Donaldson's young daughter, Virginia Lou, contracted measles before the meetings were over but was not very ill. I felt immune because I had been very sick with the disease early in childhood. However, a few days after returning home Polly went into Doug's room, took one look at him and said, "Doug! You have the measles!" The telltale red spots were everywhere. Moments later as Polly stood before the bathroom mirror she exclaimed, "And Doug! I have the measles." I had carried home to my wife and son more than good news concerning those converted at Vandergrift. But they finally decided to forgive me.

As time passed I became more and more involved with our church work on a national level. I served for two years as president of the Anderson College Alumni Association and a number of years on the college Board of Trustees and its Executive Committee. I was fond of the college. It had made a considerable contribution to my life and I was glad to do what I could to advance its interests. In 1942, following the death of E. E. Byrum, I was elected to fill out his unexpired term on our Publication Board and so I continued until early 1973.

There has been a sense of satisfaction in helping to spread the gospel around the world by means of the printed page. At the time I joined the company, Dr. A. T. Rowe was General Manager and Dr. H. M. Riggle, President. Dr. C. E. Brown was editor in chief, and C. E. Byers, Chairman of the Directors. There were three hundred employees in the office and plant. Total sales ran less than a million dollars a year. The number of employees is still about the same, but sales have advanced past the six-million-dollar mark and are still climbing. Presidents Steele C. Smith followed by T. Franklin Miller have led in building and remodeling programs until today we have a modern printing plant with air-conditioned offices and press rooms. The former name, Gospel Trumpet Company, was changed to Warner Press, Incorporated, a few years ago, and our chief paper, *The Gospel Trumpet,* was renamed *Vital Christianity.* Dr. Harold L. Phillips, present editor in chief is doing a fine job leading an efficient staff in upgrading all our publications.

As has been said, we enjoyed living in Dayton, a city of some 275,000 persons. It was large enough to offer full opportunity for church growth yet small enough to cross from one side to the other in twenty-five minutes. Wright and Patterson Fields, operated by the United States Air Force, were but a few miles away. General Motors' Delco and Frigidaire plants boosted employment and the city's economy. The sprawling plant of the National Cash Register Company has been an important economic factor in Dayton's life since the turn of the century. More recently the Inland Manufacturing Company, a subsidary of General Motors, provided thousands of jobs for Dayton's citizens. There was a first-class Chamber of Commerce and several active civic clubs. No matter where you lived in Dayton a golf course was not too far away. The downtown YMCA was a crossroads and meetings of many varieties were held there. I played handball and swam there for eleven years.

One morning about six o'clock, as I started for Anderson, my wife decided to drop off at the church to practice on the organ for a wedding she had coming up. It was winter and still dark at that hour. I consented to let her do this only if she would take our Chow dog along. Church buildings are often broken into by drifters in cold weather as they seek protection from the elements.

I parked the car, went into the church with her, turned on the lights, and made a tour of the building to see that it was unoccupied. Then I drove on to Anderson. Polly began her practicing, the dog lying on the floor near by. Ten minutes later a man's voice, near at hand, shouted something, which nearly petrified Polly. The voice seemed to come from the pulpit area toward which Ching went flying, voicing her rage. But no one was there. Apparently a word or two from a passing police cruiser's radio had been picked up on the speaker of our electronic organ. Polly was so unnerved she put her music away and went home.

She was not in the best of health, but in Dayton Polly taught a junior class and for a time was superintendent of the beginner's department. Before long a greater need arose and she became youth leader. Under her direction the youth meetings enjoyed their largest attendance and best sustained interest. Polly's active imagination brought a considerable variety into the youth program. At the same time she was playing the organ for our Sunday morning services, helping out in our broadcasts, singing with me on occasion, doing endless counseling on the phone, and doing a good job as wife, mother, and housekeeper. But it was too much.

Her basement laundry brought on respiratory difficulties and her discomfort was intense and prolonged. We finally had X rays taken, thinking she might have developed tuberculosis. She experienced persistent stomach distress; probably the result of being a pastor's wife. Sometimes her energy would run out, and she would sit or lie for hours in one position, unable to exert the energy necessary to move. One afternoon I left her sitting on a hassock in the living room, looking out the picture window. When I returned three hours later, she was still sitting there in the same position. She said she simply had not been able to move. Actually she was suffering from nervous exhaustion. I took her hand and helped her to the davenport, where I sat for a long time with an arm about her. As she rested her head on my shoulder, I told her how much she had meant to me down through the years; how she had been such a great partner and helper; how I depended upon her wise counsel and good judgment. I told her how much I appreciated her Christian spirit, her work in the church, and what a fine wife and mother she was. She did not really weep, although tears made lines down her cheeks as I spoke, but I felt the tension draining out of her body. About six o'clock she arose, changed into a fresh dress, and prepared supper. Afterward she said it was as if she had been given a transfusion.

As a husband I learned a very important lesson that afternoon. I had always thought of Polly as being a very self-sufficient person; which she is. She would have made a good pioneer in the early days. She has the qualities of courage and daring needed then, and now. But I had never felt that she had any particular psychological need of me. She could stand on her own two feet and slug it out with life. But that afternoon I realized how deeply the lives of a loving husband and wife are merged, and that, no matter how self-reliant a woman may be, there are times when she needs to draw strength from a husband who understands and cares.

Chapter Seventeen

Of Home and Church

POLLY'S OBSERVATION of a felt need eventually led her to institute programs for ministers' wives, not only in our international Anderson gathering, but in state and area meetings as well. She also pioneered in presenting addresses aimed at preparing older people for retirement. When I was fifty or so, she began to condition my thinking, so that my sixty-fifth birthday would not come as a shock or find me psychologically unprepared for retirement.

She lectured Anderson College classes in Home Economics, wrote Sunday school lessons for Warner Press, and finally published a book titled *The Parsonage Family and You*. It has been widely used to advantage by many pastors in discussion groups to promote understanding between the church and the pastor's family. She gave instruction on the organ, and counseled, counseled, counseled, with college students, pastors' wives, and women in general. And some men. Her sympathy and wise counsel kept at least two women from committing suicide, and also healed many a marital relationship. She sat by sickbeds, carried countless pies and cakes to the neighbors, was diligent in her devotions and generous in her giving. Important to me has been her understanding of my needs and moods and her full partnership in God's work. The ministry is a lonely business. To be a pastor means that one must often stand alone. But in that aloneness I was never alone. Polly was always there. And so was the good Lord.

Although I have spoken millions of words from pulpits, I am not naturally a talkative person. Often when I came from my office or visitation the silence of our home was balm for my soul. On the other hand, my wife longed for more communication. Sometimes I would come in weary and tired to find a fire blazing cheerily on the hearth. Polly would turn down the lights as I stretched out in my reclining chair and then go to the organ to play softly the songs I love. It was healing to my soul. However, just to be near her gave me something I needed. To come home and find her out was enough to send me back to the office. After sharing with her since 1924 she has become an indivisible part of me. I am still head over heels in love with her and head over heels in debt to her. "Who can find a virtuous woman? For her price is far above rubies. The heart of her husband doth safely trust in her" (Prov. 31:10-11).

All too often married people fail to keep up their courtship as the years come and go. But to take each other for granted is deadly. And I mean *deadly*. For a husband to be so preoccupied with his work that he tosses but a fragment of his time, attention, and affection to his wife is to ask for trouble. Of course a man's work is important! And the more important and challenging his work, the more he is apt to give to it some of the time and attention which belong to his wife and family. Many a marriage has disintegrated simply through neglect. Friendship between husband and wife must be both respected and cultivated just like any other friendship. Friendship's fences must be kept mended or they fall into disrepair. It isn't enough to love; you have to *communicate* that love by words, deeds, attitudes, the touch of a hand. And by the giving of *time* to one another. Give *time* to the one to whom you are married just as you give time to a growing boy. Marriages can be weakened or strengthened just by our use of time. For years I was altogether too busy for my own good and the good of my family.

Sometimes I went for weeks without an evening at home, attending this meeting and speaking at that. It seemed necessary because a large church has a great deal of machinery constantly needing oiling. But it was *not* necessary. One day while changing clothes, I left my little red date book lying on the dresser. My wife found it and was taken with an idea. At her desk she wrote into the space allotted to Monday evenings, "No dates please." A day or two

212

later I was in a meeting with some of our men. At its conclusion each of us reached for the little red books to set a date for the next meeting. Someone said, "How about Monday night?" I opened my book, saw the notation, recognized the handwriting instantly and said, "Sorry, fellows, but I have a previous engagement for Monday evening. How about Tuesday?" It was just that easy! After that I found I could spend most Monday evenings with Polly. In fact this worked out so well that I added Saturday nights, also. The church went right on. The roof did not fall in because I dared to claim some time for my wife and home.

Many preachers and some business men need to follow this example. Marriages are strained, some of them almost to the breaking point, because of their everlasting busyness. Of course the preacher had a good alibi. He is busy at *God's* work. But he had best give adequate attention to his wife or his marriage—even a preacher's marriage—can drift into incurable difficulties. One neglected, bored minister's wife finally divorced her too-busy husband and married a man who promised her the time and attention she felt she deserved. I hope this won't happen to you.

As we continued in Dayton I felt myself developing and growing. It is sad to slip into a rut, but thrilling to climb out of one. The seminary opened whole new worlds in my thinking. It taught me how to study and how to say in a better way the things that were on my heart. I did not tell my people that I was going to school, but neither did I try to hide it from them. So I was somewhat surprised when the chairman of my board said, "I had no idea you were doing work out there." He had seen my name in the paper among the list of graduating seniors.

Those six years changed my way of thinking in many ways. The areas of my preaching had been quite circumscribed and narrow. Now I was exploring fields which I had not known even existed. The Lord's Prayer and the Sermon on the Mount took on broader, deeper meanings. As I preached expository sermons on these and other themes, the church was blessed even as I was blessed. Some of the social implications of the gospel began to hammer at my soul for attention. I came to understand why Martin Luther thought the Book of James should not have been included

213

in the canon of Holy Scripture. But I disagreed with Luther. The letters to the Corinthian church, together with the difficult Book of Hebrews, came to be much better understood. I could interpret them more effectively to my people. The Old Testament prophets came alive and began walking through the corridors of my heart as each took on his distinctive personality. I learned about Sunday school work and how to do a better job as pastor. My years at the seminary were *invested,* not spent.

Dr. George Buttrick, the then-famed pastor of Madison Avenue Presbyterian Church in New York, was our Commencement speaker and he did a characteristically fine job. He was indeed a preacher's preacher. A few days after commencement I met on the street a young pastor who had come to Dayton about the same time as I. He, too, had but a high school education. At first he had prospered in his church work. I said to him in 1934, "Let's go to seminary." He replied that he didn't have time. My comment was that my work was so heavy that if I didn't go to school and find out how to do it it would never get done.

He was young and single and pastored a church which boasted one-thousand in attendance on Easter Sunday. When we met on the street seven years later, he congratulated me on finishing my graduate work. I must have been in a contrary frame of mind, for I answered, "You know, the thing that bothers me is that those seven years went by for you, the same as they did for me." During that time he married the wrong girl, and his church had dwindled to a fourth of its former size. This is one reason I often say to young, aspiring preachers, "Go to school. It may seem like a long road to do four years of college and three years of seminary work—but go to school! The years are going to pass by whether you go to school or not."

In my first pastorates sermon preparation was the hardest kind of job. As I searched for a theme for next Sunday morning, it seemed as if I had already preached everything in the Bible. I had no preacher's magazines and almost no helps of any kind. In Akron, I remember rising on a few Sunday mornings at five, not having any idea what I would preach that morning. My sermons must really have been something! D. L. Slaybaugh finally introduced me to *The Christian Century Pulpit*. Later I stumbled onto the old *Expositor Magazine* for preachers. Then the Nazarenes began publishing *The Preacher's Magazine,* to which I immediately subscribed. It contained both sermon outlines and illustrations. During the depression I was able to purchase cheaply a set of the *Biblical Illustrator* which contained almost endless sermon material. After that, sermon preparation was easier. All a preacher actually needs for a sermon is a good idea. Reading the right books provides those ideas.

Today as I look at the sets of the *Interpreter's Bible,* William Barclay's commentaries, and the innumerable other books available, it seems to me that there is little excuse for a man to do uninteresting or innocuous preaching. I sympathize with the old preacher who said to a young man just starting his ministry, "Wear the old coat and buy a new book." You can't give out what you haven't taken in. "Reading doth make the full man." I have always examined the books on the shelves in the studies of hundreds of preachers. You can judge the nature and quality of a man's sermons just by observing what he has or has not been reading. A skimpy library results in thin preaching.

It is easy for a preacher to be lazy, especially if he is pastoring a small congregation. He can sleep late and put off shaving until noon. He can hunt and fish excessively without its being too well known. He can put off his sermon preparation until Saturday evening. But that *will* become known! A preacher once introduced his sermon by saying, "You'll have to excuse me for not being better prepared this morning. I have been awfully busy." He needn't have made the remark because the people soon found out how ill prepared he was. Pastoral visitation is important. Other pastoral responsibilities are important, but I have always felt that to enter the pulpit unprepared is generally inexcusable. It is cheating the people. I feel that a church has a right to expect something fresh and vital from its preacher on Sunday. If I had not given enough time or attention in preparation, I invariably felt guilty about it.

Never underestimate the power of preaching even in these days when preaching is being attacked. One of the reasons it is being attacked is that in many cases sermons have deteriorated in quality, relevance, and spiritual pointedness. One Sunday, while on vacation, my wife and I attended a prominent Community church where the sermon was utterly innocuous, without spiritual inspiration or value. There weren't more than half a dozen young people in that congregation of two hundred. We need preachers with burning hearts, vital messages, overflowing love, and a zeal to win the lost for Christ. We need preachers who know what preaching is all about and are willing to pay the price to excel at the task.

All through my years as a pastor I was an evangelistic preacher; always preaching for a verdict, always giving invitations, and always expecting a response. I am a firm believer in the power of the Word. Although a man could preach for fifty years using texts from Shakespeare, the results would be measured by Shakespeare's power, not Christ's. I wrote my Bachelor of Divinity thesis on "Biblical Characters and Teachings in Shakespeare's Plays." I have used quotations and illustrations from his writings again and again in sermons. Yet my central theme has always been, as with Paul, "Jesus Christ, and him crucified."

It is important also for a preacher to marry the right woman. Polly has been the greatest as a pastor's wife. Always circumspect in conduct and conversation, her ever-present sense of humor has brought a sparkle to many an occasion. Down through the years she has also been known for her culinary ability. One year she kept a record of those she fed in our home—meals or desserts. They numbered over five hundred during the twelve months. She has been a gracious hostess, with an interest in the comfort and well-being of our guests. However, she always felt that her husband and son were her first responsibility and has often said she keeps house for Jesus. Some wives of young pastors seem to feel that their first obligation is the work of the church. I would differ with them. Their first obligation is in the home caring for husband and children, entertaining guests, counseling on the phone, being there when school is out. Let the queen of the parsonage take care of her home duties first. If there is time left, she can help out in the work of the church. Too many preachers and their wives have saved the people of the community at the expense of their own children.

As Polly continued with the organ, she became more and more intrigued with its possibilities. In worship services the organ seemed to communicate with the very hearts of the people. Her preludes, offertories, and postludes received more and more attention as she became thoroughly at home at the console. Her love for the organ sometimes made her oblivious to the passing of time. She would come home late, saying that she had lost herself in the music. I used to scold her for sitting at the console for four or five hours at a time. But she was conscientious about her playing responsibilities. If a wedding was scheduled for next month, she would begin practicing for it today.

On one occasion she was practicing early in the morning for a wedding coming up that night. In between she ran home to do her laundry. Thirty years ago we had the old wringer-type washing machine. Suddenly her hand caught in a fold of clothing and was pulled into the wringer, flattening her fingers and injuring her most painfully. She quickly tripped the release but the damage was done. She was in agony and I was not at home. Anyone else might have served notice that another organist would have to be brought in for the wedding—but not Polly. She massaged her hand all day long, flexed her fingers again and again, even though it was painful to do so. That evening she played for the wedding, but next day her hand was swollen and stiff. For days while we drove on a trip through the east that hand was useless. Fortunately, no bones had been broken and within two weeks most of the soreness was gone. But that was Polly, whose motto has always been, "The show must go on."

Doug brought us a great deal of joy as a lad and as he grew on into his teens. He was a sunny-natured child and generally sang or whistled wherever he went. Since the doctor had advised us to have no more children, Polly gave Doug full attention. I suppose he was over-protected, but having lost our first child and suffering bad luck thereafter, there was probably the unconscious fear that something would happen to Doug and we would be left child-less. He had his share of childish woes; like the time when he was about two and came running into the house, saying, "A bee bit me." And the time when he was aimlessly hitting the shrubbery with a stick and disturbed a wasp which stung him seven times before we could get him into the house. Since he was allergic to stings, even those of mosquitoes, the wasp caused considerable swelling.

We bought Doug a bicycle when he was seven. In our relatively-protected neighborhood it gave him quite a bit of pleasure. He played with Ching, our female Chow, and sometimes wrestled with her. One day she got him down and stood over him while holding his arm in her mouth. She didn't hurt him, but she scared him. When he found he couldn't get up, he called for help. His mother had warned him about throwing stones into a neighbor's lily pond. In a day or two she looked out the window just in time to see him doing just that After a session with him about it, he went alone to Miss Clippinger, the neighbor, and apologized. That ended the stone-throwing business. We used a police whistle to call him in from play. One day Polly had to blow it a second time before he appeared. "Didn't you hear the whistle?" she inquired. And he replied, "I heard it the *second* time."

One December during the depression, when Doug was about five and Christmas was in the offing, Polly and I were discussing what to do about buying gifts. We must have painted a pretty sad word picture, because in a few minutes Doug came out of his room crying. Handing us his piggy bank, he said through tears, "You can have this, daddy." It broke us up. I assured him things weren't quite that bad.

When he was twelve or thirteen Doug began to work after school putting stock on shelves in a supermarket. I should have banked what he earned and doled out an allowance. But it wasn't much money, and we generally allowed him to spend it as he chose. I now know that was the wrong thing to do. About this same time Polly and I taught him to drive and to swim. He had already traveled thousands of miles with us to many parts of the United States, which added considerably to his education. He also learned from table conversations we had with visiting missionaries, preachers, and other dignitaries. Preachers' children have the advantage of meeting many prominent persons and hearing what they have to say.

218

But occasionally Doug did some of the talking. When he was about five, a visiting clergyman talked with him as they awaited the call to dinner. Later on this man said, "I didn't know you had another son. I thought Doug was your only child." Doug had been very seriously telling him about his "big brother, Ted, who was a fine athlete and rode a motorcycle." He had sold the preacher a bill of goods because of his loneliness.

No child should ever be brought up alone. We tried to adopt a beautiful little two-and a-half-year-old girl when Doug was four. But at the last moment the child's father decided he could not let her go. Her mother had died and there were three other children. The father remarried rather quickly in order to keep his family together. This was better for them but most disappointing to us. The last time we saw her the little girl ran down a corridor and leaped into my arms, hugging me hard around the neck. Not getting her was such a disappointment that we never tried to adopt another. So Doug grew up alone.

On our summer trips we kept the rear seat of the car clear so Doug could use it as a play room. He would play for awhile and then sometimes sleep. But not often. We thought it a pretty good setup for him. But years later—long after he had children of his own—he told us how shut off and alone he had felt there in the back seat and how he wanted a thousand times to climb up front with us but refrained from doing so for fear he would crowd us. Of course, he did ride up front with us some of the time but we hadn't the slightest idea he could be lonely riding along within inches of his parents. But a child wants to belong. He wants to be taken in, not shut out. I wish we could go back and do it over.

Doug was twelve when he and Polly spent those long ten weeks at our Yellow Creek Lake cottage recuperating. Although I was not with him very much that summer because of my daily news broadcast, I think Doug enjoyed the lake immensely. I had bought a second-hand twelve-foot aluminum rowboat and a three horsepower motor to propel it. Doug loved to operate the motor. After he learned how to swim well, I allowed him to go out in the boat alone and he was never careless. One day someone else brought the boat while Doug and I swam across the lake together, a distance of over half a mile. He was proud of his accomplishment and so was I. A couple of years ago in memory of that occasion Doug again swam this lake. But this time he had a daughter or two at his side. Time marches on! I taught two of his girls to swim just as I had taught their father, but they learned at six instead of twelve. A couple of years ago I taught Karen, then fourteen to water ski. To my delight she came up the very first time, skied around our Florida lake for half a mile and came back with victory written all over her face. "Now," she said to Polly, "I feel like a member of the family."

I was nearly sixty when I learned to water ski and I, too, was lucky enough to come up the first time. We saiied off down the lake and on our return I let loose of the rope and sailed in toward the pier, finally sinking in water thigh deep. The young people on shore were cheering and clapping their hands. As I walked up the bank, I asked importantly, "Anyone want my autograph?" But at seventy it seems good sense to turn this strenuous sport over to the young people.

Sports have always interested me. I've told you how I liked to run as a lad. At about twelve I took up lawn tennis which was played on grass courts. I also enjoyed baseball and played first base because I was left-handed. We kids formed a neighborhood team when I was eleven or twelve but we were so poor that none of us owned a decent baseball. We had a good pitcher and catcher. But you can't play without a ball.

One day we were understandably pleased when the son of a well-to-do man showed up wanting to join our team. He had, not only a ball, but also a catcher's mask and glove. We were delighted. Delighted, that is, until he said that if he played on our team he had to be the pitcher. And he couldn't pitch for sour apples! We allowed him to pitch for a few innings. Our opponents knocked the ball high, wide, and far and we lost the game. So we fired the rich man's son, even if he did own the equipment, and went back to playing with a ball I had made by winding string as tightly as possible into a sphere. You couldn't hit it very far, but, brother, you could put a real curve on it with a fast pitch. Later an older youth in the neighborhood presented us with a real "dollar-and-a-quarter" big league baseball and we were in business again. I wonder what those balls cost now?

In Anderson I used to collect one every once in awhile when we lived in back of the college baseball field. There was a grove of saplings between us and the field and some of the foul balls went through the trees into our backyard. I'd find them while working on my lawn. My conscience never made me give them back to the college because I thought the neighborhood kids deserved a break. I shared the balls with them, remembering my own childhood.

In high school I went out for football. In our first skirmish I was kicked so hard and so painfully that I lost about ninety-nine percent of my enthusiasm for playing the game. I did play basketball, handball, tennis, and squash, but always enjoyed handball and swimming more than the others. I never cared too much for spectator sports, with the exception of football. I always wanted to be in the game myself.

After my first disappointing experiences in Kentucky. I also enjoyed hunting. We hunted rabbits in Kentucky, but during the Dayton pastorate the opening of the pheasant season was a redletter day on my calendar. About 1940, "Nick" Powell introduced me to deer hunting in Pennsylvania. I bought a share in Hi-Rock camp where he and Dr. John Morrison, Steele Smith, and others told a thousand hunting tales while we sat around the big fireplace on those December evenings. Since then I have hunted deer with Nick in Colorado and antelope in Wyoming. I have also hunted deer with my good friend, Guy Whitener, in the South Carolina swamps where dogs drive the deer away from me more often than toward me. I'd still like to bag an Alaskan brown bear and fish for salmon up there. Who knows? I may yet have the opportunity to do it! I had an invitation from the Evangelical Ministerial Alliance in Anchorage to come for a one-week meeting, but I had to turn it down because of other engagements. They'd better not ask me again unless they really want me.

Our Dayton broadcast was going well and we received a good response from our listeners. One day a letter came from a Mrs. Myrtle Taylor saying how much she enjoyed the program. Her husband was a bedridden invalid and needed constant care. Our broadcast seemed to help her to carry the load. She asked for prayer and suggested that if we were in her neighborhood she would enjoy meeting us personally. Before we got around to making that visit, Mrs. Taylor called on the phone to ask us to come by that Sunday afternoon, which we did. Thus began our long and loving friendship with the Taylor family.

There were four sons and three daughters, and soon some of them were converted. I baptized five members of the family and they became staunch workers in the church. Madelyn married Marvin Hartman after he had been stationed in Dayton as chaplain's assistant during World War II. They have since pastored two or three churches with fine success. Marv served as an associate with me in Park Place for four years. He is now executive-secretary of our national Board of Church Extension and Home Missions. Ralph Taylor and his wife are pillars in the Dayton church as he continues in an executive position with a large Dayton firm. Barbara married Paul Clausen, minister of music, and later a member of the Christian Brotherhood Hour male quartet.

The quartet sang with Fred Waring for one season, and that was enough to get the star dust out of their eyes. While with Waring they sang for Queen Elizabeth and Prince Philip at the White House as guests of the Eisenhowers, so the boys met and sang for English royalty, but also for the Eisenhowers and Nixons.

Both Madelyn and Barbara Taylor developed into first-class secretaries. Paul Clausen's serious illness during the past few years has brought sadness to all of us. He still needs our prayers.

Glenn and Helen Taylor have given strength to the Dayton church for thirty years. Glenn has long served as announcer on the church's weekly broadcast. Mother Taylor, now in her eighties, gives daily thanks to God for what he has done for her children. Her eldest son, Carl, band leader and booker of entertainers for many years gave his heart solidly to the Lord a few years before his untimely death. Carl gave the Mills Brothers their start in show business and also launched the McGuire Sisters on their way to fame. I well remember when as teen-agers, the girls used to sing in revivals and camp meetings. Doug dated two of them a few times. I remember also that J. Richard Lee, who was then Dick Meischke, once made a recording of the McGuire Sisters with Polly at the organ. Carl Taylor once told Doug that if he ever decided to go into show business, he should come to him, and he would get him started in a big way. He could have done it, too, but how much happier Polly and I are to see our son using his talents for the Lord. Money isn't everything. A man who is reputedly worth two and a half billion dollars said recently in answer to a reporter's question, "No, I am not happy. I have too many things to worry about." I've often wondered what might have become of the Taylor family had they not found the Lord. One broadcasts always in faith, casting bread upon the waters, hoping it will return after many days. And it does!

Congregations I pastored were now and then irritated with me because of the speaking dates I booked outside the city, especially when these kept me from my own pulpit on Sunday. I could understand their objections, but I did it anyhow. I felt that I belonged not just to the congregation which happened to be paying my salary but to the church at large and to the world. After being absent to conduct evangelistic meetings somewhere, one of my Dayton parishioners on my return said rather sarcastically, "Well, you decided to come back, did you?" She really drove the barb home. During such absences I paid the supply minister out of my own pocket, so that the church was not disadvantaged financially. I continued to hold a couple of evangelistic campaigns each year, but never blamed my people for complaining about my absence. I don't suppose that anyone ever makes the congregation feel at home as does their own pastor. When he is away, things aren't quite the same, even if his pulpit supply is more eloquent than he. But it did me good to get away for a week or two, and I always felt that the congregation appreciated me more afterward. When I was away in meetings I could rest from the pastoral grind.

Our Dayton church was large but I had no pastoral assistant. Not even a secretary. I had to do all the visitation and pastoral work myself along with all the correspondence and mailing. I'm rather amused these days to hear the pastor of a church of one hundred fifty persons crying for help. Don't misunderstand me. I'm all for giving him the help. Two men can do more work than one, but why didn't the Dayton church bring in a pastoral assistant for me? I could have used one. But the thought never entered my mind.

We were in Dayton from 1934 until 1945. I was thirty-one when we arrived and forty-two when we left. It was a good ministry. Hundreds found the Lord through the years. Our radio work put the church on the map and made it known throughout the city and for miles around. Hundreds of visitors came and went, but some of them stayed. During the war years there was quite a population turnover in Dayton. We might see fifty persons transferred to other cities during a twelve-month period. So it took constant effort and revival to bring statistical growth to the church. We had that revival. Although our Sunday services were always evangelistic in nature, twice a year we would import speakers for two weeks of meetings: men like Ross Minkler, W. F. Chappel, W. O. Moon, R. C. Caudill, N. K. Powell, J. Lee Collins, Harvey Wright, Herbert Thompson, and F. G. Smith.

W. F. Chappel was evangelist for the first such series after we moved to Dayton. At the close of the opening service on Sunday morning among those who came forward in response to the invitation was Bill Peake, who was in real need of salvation. Bill was a tinsmith, and a good one. He was married to Marjorie, whom I had met years before in Middletown. Marj was a faithful Christian and had prayed long and seriously for her husband's conversion. Bill had been quite a rounder. He drank too much and used tobacco in every form. Several other sinful things had attached themselves to him related to both the flesh and the spirit. Bill used a pickup truck in his business. When his children would hear it pulling into the garage, they would go to the window to see whether or not daddy could walk the plank which led to the house. If not, they would run and hide under beds and in closets, because Bill was sometimes rough on them when he had been drinking. No wonder the whole family rejoiced at Bill's conversion! After he quit poisoning his body with nicotine and alcohol, he gained forty-five pounds in twelve months and regained much of his lost health. A couple of years later the church voted Bill into membership on our Board of Trustees. There he served well, especially in matters having to do with the upkeep of the church property. Bill had a friendly disposition, a quick smile, and a well-developed sense of humor.

About this time I accepted an invitation to speak at our South Carolina Youth Convention. When Bill heard of it, he decided it would be a good time to visit his parents who lived not far from Winston-Salem, North Carolina. He had not visited back home for nine years. After deciding to make the trip, he invited me to ride along in his car, which I was glad to do. Marjorie, however, was a bit worried over Bill's decision to visit North Carolina. While still living there he had been a member of a clique of nine drinking, gambling, carousing men. Marjorie wasn't absolutely positive that Bill could stand up under their combined influence. She took me aside to ask if I thought her husband was strong enough to meet with his old buddies and return unscathed. I assured her that I had the fullest confidence in him and that he would return an even better man.

Bill was driving a good Packard which was comfortable and fast and we enjoyed the trip together. I was to be gone only for the weekend, but Bill planned to stay for ten days or two weeks. However, before parting with him at the Winston-Salem bus station, I insisted that he should write down the address where I would be staying just in case he might decide to return to Dayton sooner than expected. Again he assured me that he would not be returning for at least ten days. But I insisted and he wrote down the address. He still didn't understand why I pressed him to do so. This took place on Thursday. On Saturday Bill called to say he would meet me at the Winston-Salem bus station about noon on Monday. I was not surprised, for I had guessed that Bill's stay with his parents would be rather short.

When we met at the appointed time and place, Bill's face lighted up with a grin as he said, "You rascal! How did you know I wouldn't be staying down here?" While we drove north, he told me what had happened. He had gone to his parents' home but within a couple of hours they had talked out everything they had in common. Then the conversation began to lag. Bill's parents were not Christians, if I remember correctly. Bill decided to take a walk and look up some of his old crowd.

He met with a surprise or two. A couple of his buddies were dead; two more were in the penitentiary. I don't remember what had happened to the other four, but Bill finally visited number nine, whom he found operating a shoe repair shop. They were glad to see each other and talking humorously of old times and the scrapes they had been in together. They talked of their wives and children and houses and work. But something was different. No profanity. No dirty stories or off-color jokes to share. These had been standard equipment in the old days. Finally, the shoe cobbler looked directly at Bill and said, "You're a Christian, aren't you?" When Bill nodded assent, his friend replied, "So am I." Then those two grown men, who had fought and drunk and gambled together, stood with tears running down their cheeks and shared what Christ had done in their lives and homes. Bill said it was the only really enjoyable hour he spent in North Carolina. After that he was ready to head back toward Dayton and was more than glad that I had given him a contact address.

As he movingly told the story, I was made to rejoice again not only in our Lord's power to transform human personality, but also in his power to *keep* that which we entrust into his loving care. Bill had returned to his den of lions, but they no longer had power to harm him. Marj's anxiety had been groundless. Nevertheless, I know she was relieved when Bill returned early and told of what had taken place. Isn't it wonderful what the good Lord can do by way of transforming sinners into saints? Thank God!

However, a pastor's life is made up of sorrows as well as joys and defeats as well as victories. Sometimes the defeats are very hard on him. The more that victories become a habit, the deeper the hurt when reverses come. We rejoice in someone's conversion and mourn when a good person drops by the wayside. In Dayton, after seeing two of my finest and most useful men make shipwreck of their family life, I went through a period of gloom and discouragement. First, it was hard on my ego as pastor. Second, I blamed myself for their failures saying, "If I were the pastor I ought to be, these men would not have failed as they did. I would have been able to persuade them to do differently. I would have been able to exert a healing, steadying influence over them during their times of temptation and trial." I was strongly tempted to resign and leave Dayton and accept one of the invitations now coming so frequently. But it wasn't the will of the Lord for me to move. I stayed, battling, berating, and belittling myself for their failures.

Before long the strain began to make inroads into my nervous system. One day Dean C. E. Ashcraft of the Dayton Seminary, after discussing certain courses for which I had just signed up, began asking me about my work. I told him of the growth of the church, of my frustrations and feelings of failure. It was well that I confided in him, and I shall not forget one or two things he said in return. He reminded me that every man has a will of his own and decides for himself the way his soul shall go. No other can decide for him and no other can keep him from taking the wrong turn in the road once he has thoroughly made up his mind to take it. The Dean continued, "Dale, you have some separating to do. You must learn to recognize the difference between the load God wants *you* to carry and the burdens he wants you to lay upon *his* adequate shoulders. If you continue to try to carry his share of the load as well as your own, it will break you down." These were words of wisdom, and I took them to heart.

I gave the two men and their problems over into the capable hands of God, lifted my head, and went back to work. I realized that some people can be persuaded and others, in spite of all you do and say, will take the bit in their teeth and do as they please. I was reminded of a sign I saw down in the southern mountains among the tortuous, unfenced curves above Hot Springs, North Carolina. Some wag had painted a crude sign and stuck it into the ground along a very dangerous curve. It read, "Speed up, big boy! Hell ain't half full."

227

Chapter Eighteen

The Transition
To Anderson

SOMETIME DURING 1943, while we were still in Dayton, Dr. John A. Morrison, president of Anderson College, informed me that his pastor Dr. E. A. Reardon had announced that he would be retiring in June of 1945. His eighteen years as pastor of Park Place church had been served in two separate terms of seven and eleven years respectively. The interim had been occasioned by the illness of Dr. Reardon's older son Willard, whose pulmonary disease had forced the family to move to Denver, a much drier climate.

Dr. Reardon was about seventy when he gave up the pastorate to spend a year in service abroad. In any case Dr. John informed me that upon Dr. Reardon's retirement I would be invited to the Park Place pastorate. How did he know? His statement irritated me. I told him so and added that I didn't like anything about Anderson, didn't want to be known as an Andersonian, and I would thank him never to bring up the subject again. I told him of the growth of the Dayton church and how happy we were with our people. Anyhow, who would ever deliberately choose to live at "headquarters"? A great deal of criticism comes to the head offices of any and every religious movement from all points of the compass. Thus to criticize its leaders is one of Christendom's favorite indoor sports. I had noted this not only while visiting Anderson but while mingling with the United Brethren students in their seminary. Men at "headquarters" are always the targets for the potshots of every Tom, Dick, and Harry across the nation and around the world.

I wanted none of it. Not that the executives in our general offices were often worthy of criticism. But this is just the way things are. It is the way they have always been, and always will be. Our Anderson leaders were of the finest quality. They were dedicated, consecrated, intelligent folk who were there because of a sense of obligation and urgency. Besides that most of them had been elected to office by the very persons who were shooting at them. Subconsciously, it may have been that I had no desire to become a part of the group which, *I,* at times had been free to criticize.

However, this was but one reason why we did not wish to leave Dayton. We had enjoyed our years there and the Lord had blessed the work. We loved the city. We had made many friends there since 1934 and didn't want to leave them. We had built and moved into our own comfortable brick home on an attractive corner lot.

I never took to the parsonage idea. A church moves you into its own house, then tells you your salary is so much "plus the parsonage" for which they make perhaps $125 a month allowance. You are supposed to accept this as part of your salary. The catch is that it is *their* house, but *you* are paying for it. The pastor lives there until he is sixty-five, but, when he is ready to retire, it is still *their* house. And heaven help the pastor who occupies a church-furnished parsonage until he is sixty-five! He then must enter retirement without having either a home or furniture. He actually paid for the parsonage but didn't get it. Let me underscore this again—*he did pay for it.*

An Indianapolis pastor asked a favor of me some years ago. He had been living in a poor little parsonage, but wanted to build his own·home. I wrote a letter to his board of trustees asking if they would rent the parsonage and give the rent money to the pastor to apply on his own home. They consented, and before many years had passed their pastor owned his own home clear of debt. And the church still owned its precious little seventy-dollar-a-month parsonage! Peace! The thing I am suggesting is that if

230

you have a pastor you would like to keep, it might be wise to lend him an interest-free down payment on his own house. He can pay you back just as anyone else pays off a second mortgage. He will feel as if you really have an interest in *his* welfare as well as expecting him to have an interest in yours.

I'll have to admit that the recommendations I have made here won't work very well with congregations or pastors which insist on a change every two years. Such churches and pastors remind me of that old bromide about the man who came running toward a pioneer log cabin shouting to the man working in his garden, "Luke, Luke! Come quick! A bear has attacked your wife." Without missing a lick with his hoe, Luke gave a sideward glance and replied, "If that fool bear doesn't have any more sense than to attack my wife, he'll have to look out for himself."

Before getting this off my chest I was describing our enjoyment of Dayton. The two new congregations were doing well. I had just been elected chairman of the Dayton and Montgomery County Ministerial Alliance. One of the city's leading civic clubs had voted me into membership. I had my top-flight handball buddies with whom I worked out two or three times a week. I was the pastor of an on-going church which had a mind to work and grow. In other words; our roots were down deep and growing deeper, and neither Polly nor I wanted to pull up, move, and plant again. Especially in Anderson.

However, since my own personal philosophy has always held that a person is morally obligated before God to invest his life where it will count for the most, I was duty bound to keep heart and mind open to the leadings of the Holy Spirit. In this case I'll have to admit that it wasn't easy because I was strongly prejudiced in favor of staying in Dayton. We would have been perfectly happy to spend the rest of our lives there and didn't want to move to Anderson or anywhere else.

But the Lord is quite clever in the way he manages certain things and certain people. It just so "happened" that during this time of inner struggle, Polly and I attended a retreat for young church leaders at Camp Jennings in Missouri. Attended by ninety young men and women, this retreat proved to be a turning point in our lives. Featured speaker was Charles V. Weber who brought to us his famous series of lectures titled "Living out of the Overflow." He dug deep, probing our motives and the depths of our dedication and devotion. All of us were forced to examine our hearts anew, to reassess the quality of our love for God and people. Following an unusually moving service, Polly and I were silently walking up the hill to our quarters when she turned to say, "I just told the Lord I was willing to go to Park Place if that is what he wants us to do." I had just told the Lord the very same thing. I think both of us felt a bit like rebellious children who have just had a spanking and are enjoying parental forgiveness. We had rebelled, but now repentant of our rebellion our hearts were at peace not only with God but with our own consciences.

When the Park Place pulpit committee asked permission to present my name to the church, I gave consent—but still reluctantly in spite of Camp Jennings. Secretly, I decided that we would not move to Anderson unless the vote was unanimous. Tacking on that one proviso made me feel rather good. To my knowledge nothing had ever been done by unanimous vote in Park Place church. But on a Sunday afternoon Dr. John called to tell me the church had voted unanimously for me to become their pastor. I felt good and bad about it at the same time. Some months after we moved to Park Place someone humorously told me about that business session, which had taken place at the conclusion of the regular morning service. As chairman of the pulpit committee, Dr. John had explained to the congregation that I was the committee's choice and he hoped I would be their choice also. After making his speech, someone made the motion that the recommendation of the committee become the action of the church. Dr. John said, "All in favor of Dr. Oldham becoming our next pastor, please stand." All over the church the people came to their feet. The benediction was pronounced and everyone went home without ever having been given the opportunity to vote against the motion. At least that is the story I heard. And, knowing Dr. John, I was inclined to believe it! True or not—it makes a good story.

The Reardons had always been underpaid at Park Place, but they were astute managers and had lived in their own home. So there was no parsonage for us to occupy. The church purchased a rather inadequate place for us on East Seventh Street into which we moved late in June of 1945, At that time quite a controversy was threatening to split our movement from coast to coast. The arrows were coming at Anderson from all directions, and now *we* were in Anderson. As the psalmist put it, "The thing that I feared has come to pass." We weren't to be installed until September and so I spent the summer in camp meetings and other evangelistic work.

On Sunday, September 9th, amid speeches by the president of the local ministerium and several other Anderson dignitaries, we were most properly installed as pastors of Park Place Church of God. The speeches were many and long, as my cherished recordings prove. But bless you, we were installed!

When the speeches were done, and I was theirs for better for worse, for richer for poorer, in sickness and in health, my first remarks in responding were, "Well! I really feel as if I had been installed!" Thus we began what was to become the most thrilling, challenging, exhausting, yet rewarding pastorate of our career. The salary was $3,750 a year, considerably less than I had received at Dayton, plus, of course, the parsonage. But we were where the Lord had led us and the rest was *his* problem. In only two of our pastorates did I know in advance what the salary was to be. My concern was to know that this was the place where the Lord wanted me to be. As the churches grew, salaries were always adjusted.

Park Place church was considerably larger than the Dayton charge. I approached my duties there with a mixture of confidence and anxiety: confidence, because the Lord led us there, anxiety, because this was a church altogether different from any we had previously served. There were a few times during the introductory months when I felt related to Daniel as he was tossed to the lions. And with the three Hebrews as they felt the heat of the fiery furnace.

Dr. John warned, "Dale, pastoring this church will be different from your past experiences. In your other churches you were probably the best educated and the most capable person in the congregation." (Flattery will get you everywhere.) "But in Park Place," he continued, "it will be different. Here we have a great many intelligent, well-educated, experienced people. Ph. Ds are a dime a dozen. So you will not be quite so extraordinary here. You will be one among twenty-five or so. You will be more like the chairman of a board." This didn't quiet my anxieties a bit. Most of the executives of our national church boards and agencies attended Park Place Church, as did a majority of Anderson College faculty members, plus a few hundred students from the college. What do you preach to a group like that? Certainly the old Dayton and Lima sermons wouldn't do.

However, I was encouraged by a remark made by a very talented, prominent Methodist pastor who recalled taking over an important charge in Ann Arbor, Michigan, a university city. He hadn't been there very long when he said to an elderly retired minister, "I am in a quandary as to what I ought to preach here. If I preach history, there sitting right in front of me, is a professor of history who knows more about the subject than I will ever know. If I preach in the areas of psychology, philosophy, or sociology the same thing is true. Teachers of all those subjects will be out there checking up on me." After hearing the young pastor out, the elderly minister advised, "Preach Christ to them, son. They don't know anything about *him.*" While that wasn't true at Park Place, I drew comfort from the story anyhow, realizing that my first job was to preach the Word with love and without fear or favor. So I determined to preach Christ, and him crucified.

In spite of the presence and helpfulness of many friends, there was a nagging feeling of loneliness during my first months in Anderson. Some of it stemmed from the fact that the installation service had not constituted my total welcome. There were a few "welcoming" letters sent to me also. Pointed letters. Unsigned. "Dear Dr. Oldham:

Why aren't you serving as chaplain in some branch of the armed services when so many of our dear boys are out there so far from home and in such dire need of spiritual guidance? Is it because the salary out there is so much poorer than what you will receive here?"

I didn't know who had penned this unsigned masterpiece, but the possible list of authors was quickly narrowed down as I realized that it couldn't have been written by a member of the Board of

Trustees or the Finance Committee, or their wives. They all knew of the inadequate salary.

"Dear Dr. Oldham:

How can you presume to take the place of our beloved Dr. E. A. Reardon, one of the humblest, godliest men we have ever known? Do you think you can take the place he has occupied in our hearts these eighteen years?"

(Dr. John, did you say that vote was *unanimous?*)

One dear sister came right out with it. To my face she said, "No one can take Dr. Reardon's place. He has been like a saint among us. His prayers contained such power. We were talking at home the other day and someone said, 'What will we do if one of us becomes ill or experiences deep trouble? Who will we call?' " I looked at her soberly and replied, "Oh, there are quite a few wonderful Christian ministers in this church. You could call on such men as Dr. A. T. Rowe, Dr. J. A. Morrison, Dr. Harold Phillips, or many others. Surely there would be *someone* to meet your need. Especially in an emergency."

I'd like to call back from the grave my good friend Raymond Black to tell him what I've just told you. When Raymond was young and in his first pastorate—doing a fine job of it in New Boston, Ohio—he told Tom Steenbergen that he would like to receive an invitation to conduct evangelistic services in Park Place church. Tom replied, "Raymond with the load you are carrying, you couldn't go if they invited you." "I know," sighed Raymond, "but it would give me prestige just to receive the invitation."

Which recalls the day in the Dayton Seminary sociology class when the venerable Dr. A. T. Howard, who had served as Missionary Bishop for the United Brethren for eight years, opened the hour with an observation. It seems he had just overheard a conversation in the hall in which two or three divinity students were discussing how wonderful it would be to be a bishop. Big house, big salary, big automobile, honor, glory, prestige. Said Dr. Howard, with a twinkle in his eye, "Gentlemen, you won't be a bishop fifteen minutes until all the glory and prestige will fade away and you will be up against the hard facts of life." Those first few months in Park Place certainly gave me no feeling of "prestige."

I was right up against the hard facts of life from the very beginning. This was no multi-pastored church. I was *it*. The entire pastoral function was mine, and mine alone, and I wasn't long in discovering the impossibility of doing the whole job alone. Miss Gertrude Little, now Dr. Gertrude Little of Anderson College, was Director of Christian Education. She also served as my secretary and office secretary. My old friend, Fred Pletcher, was custodian. That was the entire paid staff. Which explains how, from the very beginning, I became well acquainted with twelve- and fourteen-hour working days.

However, the church was growing and my job was both fascinating and exciting. You don't mind working hard when you can see results, and we were seeing results. The congregation sprang into new life and began to move forward. The students were a tremendous challenge and in turn quite a blessing to me. We opened each fall semester with Religious Emphasis Week —nightly evangelistic services held in the Park Place sanctuary.

In February there was another two-week meeting with imported preachers doing the speaking. On the list were Maurice Berquist, Clair Shultz, E. Stanley Jones, Mary Webster, Eugenia Price, James W. Blackwood, Dr. Roy Burkhart, Wilma Perry, Herbert Joiner, Ross Minkler, and others. Herbert Thompson, then at the height of his singing career, assisted in eleven or twelve such meetings before and after my arrival. With his beloved Lola at the keyboard, Herb's singing was enough to guarantee a good attendance. He was and still is one of Israel's sweet singers.

During such times of revival prayer meetings were scheduled each morning at seven o'clock in a college classroom. It was a thrill to see the students turn out in such numbers at this early hour. There were times when they filled three large classrooms to overflowing. My soul was blest as I listened to their earnest pleading with the Lord in behalf of their unsaved college friends. Our Father heard and answered their prayers.

In all such meetings we had the full cooperation of Anderson College. I would give the Dean at least a year's notice concerning the dates of all such special services. He, in turn, would cooperate by seeing that no major college functions were set up in competition with them. No athletic events were scheduled during church hours. Other events were placed on the college docket in such a way as to not force students to choose between them and our church services. This remarkable cooperation was appreciated very much and certainly worked out to the benefit of the students. Such cooperation is not always to be found in such situations. If it were, the moral and spiritual life of student campus groups would be maintained at a much higher level. I am sure that the Anderson College students were made to feel that the President and Dean considered one's personal religious experience to be of vital importance.

Park Place church was making progress in various ways. In 1945 the annual church budget totaled $29,500, of which $3,000 was designated for missions and other benevolences. Two years later the budget jumped to $59,000, then $69,000. When I resigned the pastorate early in 1962, Park Place church's income for the year was $214,000, and about $30,000 of this went for benevolences. When the good Lord blesses his people spiritually and revival warms their hearts, the giving to his work always increases.

Long prior to our coming the Park Place church plant had been quite inadequate. The Sunday school filled every available space to capacity. There was no room for expansion. When I urged teachers to go out after new students, they laughed at me. "We can't do a decent job with the ones we have now," they replied. "There simply isn't enough room."

But new people kept coming anyhow. We obtained permission to use college classrooms for Sunday school purposes. We sent one large class across the street into Dr. Carl Kardatzke's basement activity room. We purchased the residence just north of the church and then the one north of that and converted them into a junior department and a youth center. Before long Sunday school classes were meeting in eight different buildings. I used to tell our people jokingly that we preached unity but practiced division. However, while we joked about the overflow, all of us knew that something had to be done soon about a new building. People will crowd in for awhile, but if comfortable quarters aren't soon provided they will drift elsewhere.

Our old building, erected in 1917, was constructed after the Akron plan. The chancel and pulpit were in the southwest corner, and balconies ran along the east and north walls of the sanctuary. The total seating capacity was about eight hundred. On special occasions we packed in more than a thousand, which made the fire marshall (and me) nervous. Since all floors were of wood, the building was a veritable fire trap. When an overflow crowd was present, I used to sit up front deciding exactly what I would do and what orders I would give if someone were suddenly to shout "Fire!" The Trustees installed new iron fire escapes to facilitate evacuating the balcony in such an emergency. During the winter months when the furnace had to be fired heavily, that old, dangerous building always made me nervous.

Nor was it attractive on the inside. The aisle carpets were faded and worn. The huge Monk's cloth drapes were dirty, sagging, and in some places torn. All were badly faded. And this was our "headquarters" church, attended by most of the dignitaries. My wife and I wondered why the building had been allowed thus to deteriorate. We came to the conclusion that, although hundreds were attending our church, the loyalties of a large percentage of them were centered elsewhere. Their money was following their loyalties. Some of the college personnel were giving most of their donations to the college. Other executives and employees of the various Boards were tithing to foreign missions, home missions, or the national Christian education program. Many of our members were sending their tithes back to their home churches. Right then I decided to go to bat for Park Place church.

My wife, repelled by the appearance of the sanctuary, listed all the things which needed to be done to improve its appearance. Then in her characteristic "back of the scenes" way, she said, "I want you to take this list into the next meeting of the Board of Trustees and ask them to do something about it." Being an obedient husband, I did just that! The trustees immediately voted to spend $15,000 to improve things. Thanks, Polly! We bought new carpeting for the aisles, new burgundy velvet drapes for the huge windows, put a rail and drapes around the open front of the platform, and painted the sanctuary. What an improvement!

Speaking of Polly; we hadn't been in Park Place many years until the grapevine informed me that although I was a presentable speaker, I wasn't too much of a homiletist. One student whispered to another, "I have it straight that Mrs. Oldham prepares all her husband's sermons. He just delivers them. That's why he uses such full notes in the pulpit." Bless you, son! Polly did not prepare any of my sermons, although she did develop quite a homiletical mind and often shared ideas for sermons. She was also a great help in clipping illustrations for my use. At a drive-in sandwich place one evening she called my attention to a sign which read, "Don't toot your horn; turn on your lights for service."

Some pastors err by preaching their old sermons "as is" in their new pastorate. I tried this in Park Place, but it didn't work out well. Anderson was different from Dayton. The people were different. The whole situation was different. To preach old sermons would have been unwise. Most of them wouldn't fit even after thorough reworking. I filed them away in a drawer and faced the arduous task of preparing two new sermons each week. It was no small job, especially when you considered the nature of my congregation. Any man who ever stood in Park Place pulpit with little to say would wish five minutes later that he had given himself to a more thorough preparation.

One thing about Park Place church: if you did happen to preach a good sermon, there were people out front who knew it. They were just as quick to recognize mediocrity. I quickly learned to sympathize with the old pastor who was heard praying under his breath as he walked home after the Sunday evening service, anticipating the fact that another Sunday was just seven days away, "Lord, give me two more!" No matter how well you do this Sunday, next Sunday is already breathing down your neck.

As the church grew, the pastoral load increased unbearably. After three years, I said to Everett Hartung, a good friend who was a trustee and also chairman of the Finance Committee, "Everett, get me some help or I'll have to leave. I'm not going to work myself into a nervous breakdown." He smiled and answered, "Why didn't you say so? Who would you like to have?" I wanted Dewayne Bell, a young, ambitious, hardworking pastor who had served as an officer during World War II, having been commissioned on the battlefield. Dewayne had married Wanda Anewalt, formerly from our Dayton congregation. I knew him as a cheerful, talented, steady young man of balanced judgment and excellent spirit. The church quickly ratified our suggestion, and Dewayne and Wanda came to serve faithfully with us for three years. One of our large congregations stole him away.

Then we imported Marvin Hartman. Marvin, at the time we called him, was pastoring a church in northwest Ohio while completing his seminary work at Oberlin. Without advance warning, I drove up and caught the two of them in the midst of their spring housecleaning. We sat among buckets and mops as I extended the invitation to those surprised young people. The Hartmans came to help out for four years and did a very fine job of it. Soon we also added a full-time minister of music, a full-time minister to Youth, and a part-time Director of Christian Education.

The trouble with bringing in young pastoral assistants is that you can't expect them to stay with you for more than a few years. Give them the kind of training which the job, the program, and the total situation combines to furnish, and before long some church in California or Ohio recognizes their increased value, takes them as pastor, and you have to start all over again. The church at large eventually benefits, but the mother church must constantly train and educate newcomers. R. J. Tuttle was not a novice when he left his Traverse City, Michigan, pastorate to replace Marvin Hartman. Nor was David Coolidge when he became our valued minister of music. Nevertheless, even these two grew rapidly as they carried heavier burdens and assumed larger responsibilities. They were valuable and dedicated men.

It seems to me, however, that every seminary ought to have at least one course on how to be a senior minister and another on how to be an associate minister. In previous pastorates I had always served alone, as far as the pastoral function was concerned, and was not really prepared for the senior pastoral relationship. I'm afraid I was not too skilled in the fine art of communication at this point. If I could go back over those years, I could do a better job of it. I probably should confess right here that the church went forward under multiple leadership, not because of the guidance I gave to other members of the pastoral staff, but because they all were intelligent, of a good spirit, and had enough initiative to plan programs and see them through.

Dr. Dewayne Bell at present serves as executive assistant to the president of Azusa College in California. Marvin Hartman is executive-secretary of our Board of Church Extension and Home Missions. R. J. Tuttle has been pastoring a flourishing church in Oregon. Milton Buettner, who preceded David Collidge as our Minister of Music, is now following his first love, English Literature, as a professor at Anderson College. David Coolidge still serves Park Place church where his multiple-choir program, his four hand-bell choirs, and outstanding soloists are a delight to the congregation. David's wife, the former Shirley King, was one of our organists when David first met her, and they have made a great team. Shirley is an organist of exceptional ability and a master of the mighty Cassavant console.

In the fall of 1946 Dick Meischke was a student at Anderson College, earning his way by working part time at a local radio station. In Indianapolis Dick had worked for a year or two at a radio station while still attending high school. He had an excellent voice for radio, and in Anderson had already developed a first-class youth program which was being broadcast over WHBU weekly. One day in my office Dick asked with a smile, "Pastor, do you think it will ever be possible for us to produce a national radio program?" I had to think that one over for a moment, but finally replied, "I don't know why not, Dick. We certainly have the talent here. All we need is money. Why don't you see how much it would cost to make a beginning?"

I thought little more about our conversation until Dick returned one day to say that nineteen radio stations had already expressed a willingness to broadcast the kind of program we had in mind. To get started, our Board of Church Extension and Home Missions agreed to lend us $5,000. Before long we had a choir, male quartet, soloists, and accompanists in a recording situation. And I was the speaker. The new program hit the air the first Sunday of January, 1947, and some of those original stations still broadcast it weekly.

The Christian Brotherhood Hour is now heard over nearly 400 radio stations in English and about fifty in Spanish. It was my privilege and pleasure to serve as speaker for twenty-one and one-half years. The work was a happy responsibility which I carried along with my pastoral duties until 1962. The growth of both the church and the broadcast made it mandatory for me to decide which was to receive my full time. At the time I felt I should stay with the Christian Brotherhood Hour, not because of any desire to leave the pastorate but because I felt that my influence would be wider in broadcasting to the world. The job of Executive-Director for the Radio and Television Commission of the Church of God had been shunted off on me the previous summer. I was both the speaker and director of our international broadcast until my retirement on June 30, 1968. If I had it to do over again, knowing what I now know, I probably would have made a different decision as I stood at the crossroads in 1962. I would have stayed with the church and continued only as speaker for the broadcast. If this were not acceptable to the Commission, I would have turned the broadcast over to another. Park Place Church of God exerts a considerable influence upon the church at large. To stand in its pulpit and influence the leaders of the church, together with hundreds of college students, is to make one's ministry count in a really worldwide way.

The Radio and Television Commission invited R. Eugene Sterner to take over both of my communication jobs at my retirement. He has brought improvement to every phase of the work. Prior to my tenure Dr. Sterner served for seven years as Executive-Director for the Commission and so was not a stranger to the job's ramifications. Since he has taken over, the number of stations carrying both the English and Spanish programs has increased and the format of the English broadcast has been modernized and updated. Dick Meischke, who, in going into the radio and television advertising business several years ago found it to his advantage to change his name to J. Richard Lee, has been induced to return as producer of the broadcast he started. He has replaced Jack Odell who wrote and produced the Christian Brotherhood Hour from 1953 until 1971. The Christian Brotherhood Hour has exerted a unifying effect upon our movement, has given us identity among the people of our nation and the world, and has led many, many hungry hearts to Christ. It gives me considerable satisfaction to remember my years of service with our consecrated radio production staff.

How recording processes have changed since 1947! The first CBH recordings were made in our church sanctuary. We hired a Chicago recording company to do the work. The "company" was composed of two bright ambitious young men, one of whom was a radio engineer. He loaded his recording equipment into the trunk and backseat of his elderly automobile, brought it to Anderson, and set it up in the nursery (bawl room), located behind a glass partition opening into the sanctuary. Wires were run from this "control room" to the platform microphones through a hole cut in the wall near the floor. Music for the broadcast was furnished largely by singers and instrumentalists from the music department of Anderson College. We called our choir the Choralaires. Through the years they have always been a fine singing combination.

There were no magnetic tapes in 1947. We recorded directly onto sixteen-inch disks, "platters" they were called. Each side accepted fifteen minutes programming. Since ours was a half-hour broadcast, at the fifteen-minute break, the local station announcer came on the air with a brief statement while turning the "platter" over to side two. When we recorded, if anyone made any mistake, hit a sour note, coughed, sneezed, or if the speaker stumbled over a word, we had to go back and do that entire fifteen-minute section over again. One night we were still at it at three o'clock in the morning.

Then came that marvelous invention—a magnetic wire recorder. One couldn't splice it, but could erase it. Now when a mistake was made the engineer "wiped off" the wire and backed it up a bit. We then did the faulty part over and proceeded with the program. The magnetic wire was much better to work with than the platters; but still was not quite the answer to our needs. That answer came with the invention of magnetic tape. It is amazing what a good engineer can do by way of splicing magnetic tape.

In 1953, when Jack Odell joined our staff, we moved recording operations to the studios of the Universal Recording Corporation in Chicago. We took our entire broadcasting group there for program making four or five times a year. I remember the day Shirley Brewbaker, one of our best soprano soloists, came to Chicago with a bad cold which considerably affected her singing. She was scheduled to do an important number on one of the programs, but when she attempted it we knew she was in trouble. Her voice broke and she had to cough. It appeared that a substitute would have to do her number, but no one was prepared. We needed that particular song and Shirley had to do it.

Finally, Dr. Robert Nicholson, then in charge of our music, told the choir to take a half-hour recess. All except Shirley and the accompanists. When they came back into the studio a seeming miracle had been performed. In doing Shirley's solo, twenty-eight sections of tape had been made, edited, and very skillfully spliced together. As the tape was played back for us, there was Shirley singing her song beautifully without a single break in her voice. We all agreed that A. B. "Bernie" Clapper, our engineer, was a genius. We still feel that way about him.

Mail came from all over the world in response to the broadcast attesting to the effectiveness of the Christian Brotherhood Hour. Of course, the most thrilling letters were those which told of someone finding Christ through the program. But there were other encouraging reports. Marriages were healed, homes put back together, suicides thwarted. One deeply troubled man decided that life was no longer worth the living and he would put an end to it that very day. He drove his car up into the mountains, a loaded revolver on the seat beside him. As he rode along he listened to the Christian Brotherhood Hour and a gleam of hope crept into his soul. At the conclusion of the broadcast he drove down off the mountain, sought out one of our pastors, and gave his heart to the Lord. Such reports always thrilled me. Broadcasting is totally an act of faith. You never know who is listening.

Two high school seniors from Michigan decided to elope one Sunday morning because their parents would not consent to their marriage. As they drove happily along the Christian Brotherhood Hour came on the air, and they listened until the program was finished. I don't know what the sermon was about, but it caused this couple to abandon their plans to elope. They turned the car around and went back to finish out the school year.

People who will not go to church often listen to religious broadcasts. A woman wrote from Alaska to say that ours was the only program to which her atheist husband would listen. At first he ordered her to turn it off, but afterward began to listen. At the time of her writing, he was under deep conviction for sin and thinking seriously about religion for the first time. I am in favor of religious broadcasts, although I must confess that most of the religious radio programs on Sunday mornings are not the quality to interest the man on the street. In fact, some programs probably do the cause of Christ more harm than good, repelling instead of drawing. The radio or television exhibitionist needs to examine his soul for motives.

A bit of emotion mingles with my memories of the old recording days. Some of the sessions turned out to be deeply moving worship experiences. Even though we had a lot of fun together, there was always a note of seriousness to be felt as we produced the programs. I remember one particular day when the Choralaires preceded my sermon with that great hymn, "God of Our Fathers." You remember the words.

> *God of our fathers, whose almighty hand*
> *Leads forth in beauty all the starry band*
> *Of shining worlds in splendor through the skies,*
> *Our grateful songs before Thy throne arise.*
>
> *Thy love divine hath led us in the past,*
> *In this free land by Thee our lot is cast;*
> *Be Thou our ruler, guardian, guide and stay,*
> *Thy word our law, Thy paths our chosen way.*
>
> *Refresh Thy people on their toilsome way,*
> *Lead us from night to never-ending day;*
> *Fill all our lives with love and grace divine,*
> *And glory, laud, and praise be ever Thine.*
>   —Daniel C. Roberts

245

The choir was genuinely inspired that day. For the fanfare which precedes each stanza a trio of trumpeters had been imported. Together with the organ and piano the group thrilled me to my very toes. In fact they so broke me up that when the time came for my message, the recorder had to be stopped until I could get my voice under control. I never hear "God of Our Fathers" to this day but what I recapture some of the thrill and gladness of those recording sessions.

The entire group doesn't go together to the recording studios any more, and again we have magnetic tape to thank for the change. The musical sections are put together piece by piece according to the script from the tape library. It all works out splendidly; yet seems a bit mechanical as I compare it with those days when the entire broadcast group was in the studio together.

Doug began singing with the Choralaires and with the Christian Brotherhood Hour's second male quartet about the time he was being graduated from high school. He has served on the program as soloist for a number of years. Lately, however, his time is taken almost entirely by concert and television work. His big Geyhound bus may be seen almost anywhere at anytime across the United States. His albums are for the most part recorded in London where thirty or more members of the London Philharmonic Orchestra serve as his accompanists. His biography, *I Don't Live There Anymore,* written by Fred Bauer, a "Guideposts" editor, was recently published by the John T. Benson Company, of Nashville, which also produces and distributes his albums.

Chapter Nineteen

Growing Pains

WHEN THE NEED for a new building to house our Park Place church became more and more evident, I began to mention it from the pulpit with some frequency. Before long a Building Committee was appointed. Then the fun began. How can you plan for a new building unless you know where it is to be built? The longer we worshiped together, the more apparent it became that our present location would never be adequate for our growing needs. So another committee was appointed, charged with the responsibility of surveying the community to determine exactly where we should relocate. The committee shared some of its responsibility with Dr. Val Clear of Anderson College, who in turn called in Dr. Kinchloe, a sociology specialist from the University of Chicago, to assist in the project. After rather exhaustive research, this group advised us to move three blocks up the hill and relocate across the street from Anderson College.

Did you ever try to persuade an old established congregation to move? Did you ever try to persuade folk who live within a block of the old building to agree to walk three blocks up a hill to a new location? The hardest to convince were those whose parents had worshiped in the old church and whose funerals had been conducted from there. Objections came from others who had been converted and baptized in the old building. They could, and did, recall many sacred and happy memories of things which had taken place in the old sanctuary. "Why, pastor, it would be like desecration to walk off and leave all this"—especially since we planned to make a gift of the old building to the College and it would no longer be used as a place of reverent worship. To change the thinking of a large group of people takes time and a planned strategy. We took this fact into serious consideration. Trustees and Building Committee versed themselves well in every aspect of our need for changing locations. Meeting with one small group at a time—a board, a committee, or an adult Sunday school class, we sold the idea. After a few weeks of this, we took the matter to the entire church and received a solid vote favoring our move up the hill.

After a considerable amount of litigation and difficulty, we acquired the properties needed. A Philadelphia architect was commissioned to draw plans for the new structure. I wish I knew how many dozens of committee meetings were held during the planning and erection of that building. It wearies me just to recall the endless decisions which had to be made—all the way from drapes and floor coverings to roofing materials and window styles. An organ committee visited church after church before deciding on just the right organ for Park Place. They added an antiphonal organ, certain that if it were not worked into present plans, it probably would not be acquired for another fifteen years.

To make a long story shorter, the plans were drawn, the contracts let, and one Sunday morning in June of 1960 the entire congregation walked up the hill together to the new sanctuary where we sang "Praise God from whom all blessings flow." The new building was constructed to accommodate a Sunday school of 1475 under ideal Christian education standards. The sanctuary seated 1250, but almost from the first Sunday duplicate services at eight-thirty and ten-forty-five were necessary. Attendance jumped three hundred the first year. Dr. Roy Burkhart, then pastor of the famous First Community church in Columbus, Ohio, said he considered our new plant the best he'd ever seen from the standpoint of conducting a total church program. But it was fourteen years from the day I first preached about our need for a new building until we dedicated it. The building cost nearly $2,000,000.

A building program of these proportions presents a great many problems to a church. One is the danger that the church will become self-centered. Because a great deal of money is necessary for such a project, the church puts on financial campaigns, accepts special pledges, and asks for sponsors for special projects. As a result the money rolls in and before long the building fund looks impressive. Then someone is sure to ask if we can afford to give as much to missions as formerly because the building needs are so urgent. The only way to handle that problem is to *increase* the giving to missions. During the years while our building fund was accumulating our church gave a quarter of a million dollars to missions.

But that of itself was not enough to ward off self-centeredness. We financed the beginning of a new congregation on the east side, giving them $5,000 to help buy their lot, then loaning them $20,000 without interest for three years to assist in erecting the first unit of their building. A year or two later we cooperated with our other Anderson Churches of God in helping to establish a new congregation on the west side. I think we gave that project an outright gift of $9,000. Thus we staved off self-centeredness, while at the same time broadening the borders of the kingdom of God. As a result our people grew spiritually, and after we had dedicated our new building there was no backlash of conscience such as might have been experienced had we kept all and given nothing away.

On that memorable Sunday when we changed locations we had a short worship service in the old building. I picked up the large pulpit Bible, and with Milton Buettner and Ray Tuttle flanking me on either side led the congregation up the street and into the new sanctuary. Tears were in my eyes and joy in my heart. What a thrill to preach the first sermon in the new building to such an enthusiastic congregation! I thought of all the faithful men and women whose labors were invested in this glowing moment, whose giving and sacrificing had made this hour possible. The project had called for an investment of about $1,700,000, (more was added later), yet the largest gift we received was $30,000. The building belonged to God, but our people *all* had a liberal share in paying for it. Of course, there were the usual critics who said that all this money should have been given to missions. But isn't that what Judas said about the perfume which Mary poured over the feet of Jesus?

For years Anderson had been "home" to our church family and a center for our work. In Anderson are located the offices for our church boards and agencies. Our chief college and seminary are there. As already mentioned, in 1942 I had been elected to membership on our Publication Board, known then as Gospel Trumpet Company, to fill out the term of E. E. Byrum who had passed away. E. E. Byrum was one of the pioneers in our movement and had served the church for fifty years or more. He had been editor in chief of our publications and traveled all over the world. Not an eloquent speaker by any standard, he was nevertheless listened to when he spoke. His voice was not particularly pleasant and he sometimes spoke as if he had an impediment. He was too deliberate in his delivery and often paused too long to find the right word. But he had ability to inspire faith in his hearers and for this reason was called from far and wide to pray for the sick.

Such a healing took place in Mount Sterling, Kentucky, about 1922, and I recall it well. Following his message, E. E. Byrum invited those who desired healing to come forward for prayer. Among those who responded was an eighteen-year-old girl whose body was wasted away by the ravages of tuberculosis. She was so weak she had been brought to the service in a wheelchair. Fifty years ago tuberculosis was not only common, but deadly, and claimed thousands of lives. It was sad to see a beautiful young girl thus afflicted. E. E. Byrum prayed for her; a short, simple prayer, with no attempt at ecclesiastical oratory. No ordering of God, telling him what to do; just a gentle request, pleading with him for the girl's life. That was all. A year or so later when I was again in Mount Sterling, this girl was completely well, the bloom of robust health on her cheeks. Her transformation was miraculous.

I have always wondered why some persons are healed in answer to prayer and others are not. But I do know that E. E. Byrum had great confidence in James 5:15 which reads, "And the prayer of faith shall save the sick, and the Lord shall raise him up; and if he have committed sins, they shall be forgiven him."

In May of 1947 Dr. F. G. Smith, editor in chief of our publications for fourteen years and later the successful pastor of a large church in Akron, Ohio, passed away after slumping at his desk at

Warner Press. He served as president of our publishing house for several years and was a good friend of mine. I had conducted two or three series of evangelistic meetings for him at Akron. He had in turn served as guest speaker in our Dayton church. For two years he had given full time to the publishing house.

Dr. Smith was a man of considerable prestige, an engaging smile, and contagious personality. He had exerted a powerful influence in our church group for nearly half a century. Early in life he served a term as missionary to Egypt, and, at the age of twenty-five, wrote *What the Bible Teaches,* a book still widely in use among our people. He taught himself his own brand of shorthand and used it in writing the first draft of his manuscripts. Highly esteemed by most of our brethren, he was resented by a few who differed with him doctrinally. Dr. Smith stood staunchly for the truth as he saw it and felt that to do anything less would be in the nature of compromise. Dr. Smith was a good thinker, had an orderly mind, and was in wide demand as a speaker, especially in preachers' meetings. His voice was not robust and in the days before we had public-address systems he was handicapped in addressing large audiences. Dr. Smith was a thoughtful student of Bible prophecy. He published a widely circulated book titled *The Revelation Explained* in which he set forth his convinced theories on what he termed "The Last Reformation."

His sudden death was a shock to all of us. When the news was phoned to me, I rushed to the hospital to be at his side. As my wife and I entered the room, darkness was falling. There had been a power failure in that section of town. A nurse brought in a lighted candle and placed it on the dresser. I remember the silhouettes it cast on the wall from the persons of Dr. Smith's wife and Gerald, his older son. All of us knew that the end was near. As I gazed into the unconscious face of this noble soldier of the cross, I thought of his faithfulness to the Word of God, his unshakeable confidence in the power of truth to win over error. I thought of the many sermons I had heard him deliver and of the great church of which he was so long the pastor. With the end but moments away, I suggested that we pray. In the middle of my prayer there was a short gasp and our friend was gone. The verses came rushing in, "Be

thou faithful unto death and I will give thee a crown of life."
"Blessed are the dead which die in the Lord, even so saith the
Spirit; for they rest from their labors and their works do follow
them."

I comforted the family, made an appointment to see them next
morning about funeral arrangements, and then Polly and I turned
toward home. As we rode along a fresh joy began to flow through
my heart in appreciation of the fact that the Lord had anointed me
to preach the gospel. What a privilege it is to comfort those who
mourn, to heal broken hearts, to speak peace to those in trouble!
If anyone has ever felt sorry for me because I am a preacher, he
wasted his time, because I wouldn't have traded jobs with anybody
on earth.

A week or two after Dr. Smith's passing, as I walked along East
Fifth Street in front of our publishing house, Dr. A. T. Rowe came
out of his office to inform me that the directors had just elected me
Chairman of the Board of the Company. It was quite a surprise.
I was to follow in the footsteps of Dr. E. E. Byrum, Dr. H. M.
Riggle, and Dr. F. G. Smith. In my heart was a bit of apprehension,
a feeling that the boots were a bit too large for me to fill.

Dr. E. E. Byrum's brother, N. H. Byrum, served as treasurer of
our publishing house for more than fifty years. These two brothers
were the ones who first located the large plot of land now occupied
by the printing plant, Anderson College, and our sprawling international convention grounds. The Byrum brothers should not be
forgotten by on-coming generations. They rendered yeoman service to the church for more than half a century and served sacri-
ficially.

Pastoring Park Place church was no small job. Where so many
talented folk are concentrated there are bound to be a number of
rugged individualists who not only think for themselves, but may
now and then insist on thinking for you, also. One of my seminary
teachers had said, "The only way to be a leader is to lead." But the
ability to lead depends largely on the effectiveness of one's personal influence. I don't have much respect for positional authority.
A pastor does not exert a strong influence simply because he has
been elected to the job. His authority seldom exceeds the range

of his influence. People must be led, not driven, especially if one is in a social situation where compliance is entirely voluntary.

Another thing which I observed was that even the most highly educated folk often need a pastor. Sometimes they need advice and guidance. One can be highly educated and still be faulty in judgment. Good common sense does not necessarily accompany the granting of graduate diplomas.

As pastor at Park Place I found myself in the center of a group of executives and junior executives employed by our various boards. Most of these boards operate through donations received from the church at large. This means that the income of the boards has to be established on a percentage basis, according to their needs. There never seems to be quite enough money to go all the way around and so power plays among executives have always been more or less common. "You vote for my project and I'll vote for yours." Occasionally in meetings of the Executive Council, where all boards had representatives, tensions would develop. In more than one instance tempers flared. I always felt it was good to have the pastor present in such meetings and others ratified my judgment. But men are human, even with the Holy Spirit in their hearts, and sometimes their zeal for a program they deem to be most important resents being frustrated.

Speaking about the Executive Council reminds me of the old days of its predecessor, The Associated Budgets. In the early years of our movement, The Gospel Trumpet Company guided and was responsible for nearly every operation of our work. Gospel Trumpet Company served as our first Missionary Board. Our Board of Church Extension and Home Missions found its beginnings in Gospel Trumpet Company offices. What is now our national Board of Christian Education was established by the Gospel Trumpet Company. I well remember when Miss Anna Koglin, then an instructor at Anderson College, taught mornings at the College, then crossed the street to the publishing house to give half a day as executive-secretary of our newly formed Board of Christian Education. The predecessor of Anderson College, Anderson Bible Training School, came into existence largely through the efforts of Dr. J. T. Wilson, who in 1917 was manager of the publishing house.

When all of these agencies were finally separated from Gospel Trumpet Company, they were faced with the necessity of raising funds for their various projects. The agency representative who was most persuasive in representing his board among our churches received the most money for its endeavors. The other boards had to subsist on what was left. So, there was not only competition among the agencies; there was also a bit of friction. The persuasive "Brother Jones" from the Board of Foreign Missions might make his pitch and take a big offering at the Centerville church this Sunday, only to be followed a week later by "Brother Smith" seeking to raise funds for the Home Board. The man there "fustest" generally got the "mostest" and the second fellow went back to Anderson unhappy. And the Centerville pastor and church were also unhappy.

It seemed almost providential when there came to our assistance, the Sage of the Ozarks, R. L. Berry, of Mountain Grove, Missouri. How well I remember him! He was a man of the soil and still had his home on the farm. Sandy-haired, shrewd, with a saving sense of humor, Berry did not hesitate to rush in where angels feared to tread. Yet he was the kind of man needed to bring progress into our business structure. In time, Berry succeeded in establishing the Associated Budgets, through which, as someone facetiously put it, our general agencies "put all their begs in one ask-it." Each church was urged to subscribe generously, after which the total amount received was allocated through a budget to which all board chief executives had consented. It was a big step forward for benevolences and also promoted peace among leaders.

R. L. Berry was quite a fellow with plenty of wit. Sometimes he added a bit of vinegar to the wit. And, as already noted, a touch of the soil now and then showed through. He could be candid to the point of bluntness and seldom used two words when one would do. It is to be regretted that he lived too early to read and apply Dale Carnegie's book on *How to Win Friends and Influence People*. In the early 20s, Berry was chairman of a camp meeting service in which I was leading the singing. Irritated because I took two minutes more than he had allotted for my part of the service, he told me off after the benediction. He said he was immediately taking steps to "hog tie" the music committee. Since H. C. Clausen and I were the only song leaders that year, it was easy to figure that he had us in mind. However, he soon simmered down.

I liked the man. He was amusing, humorous, and even lovable. He was also of considerable usefulness in the church at large. But even after retirement sent him back to his Missouri farm, he kept a watchful eye on what was going on in Anderson. Editor Harold Phillips received a letter from Berry one day, bluntly critical of something which had appeared in one of our publications. Apparently Dr. Phillips did not think the criticism warranted a detailed reply and so he sent Berry a letter containing just one word— *Relax!* By the time it was received, Berry had cooled off. Back came his answer to Phillips. It also contained just one word, *Relaxed!* I always felt that Berry's blood didn't circulate properly unless he could participate in a bit of an argument now and then. But when matters were settled with him, they were settled for good. He gave color to committee meetings. His humor eased tensions in many a situation.

I don't know how much I did for Park Place church, but its people did a great deal for me and I am appreciative. Dr. J. A. Morrison shared his wisdom with me on various occasions. One day he said, "Dale, you always think of preachers as making churches, but don't forget, churches make preachers, also." It is true that a great church causes a preacher to stretch to his full height. Dr. John was a keen judge of human personality. He could read men with a skill not given to many. He could go down the pages of our yearbook and predict with uncanny accuracy how various preachers would vote on a specific issue in the next meeting of the General Assembly. Dr. John would have done exceptionally well in politics, as he combined a native shrewdness with an unceasing flow of wit and humor. He was a delightful after-dinner speaker, much sought out by luncheon clubs. But he was also in demand in our ministers' meetings. He skillfully led the infant Anderson College through the awful years of the depression when money was so scarce that even the smallest contributions were sought after. He gave generously of his own inadequate salary to the needs of the college and wore out his own automobiles to forward its program.

Although his health broke in the process, he succeeded in keeping open the doors of his beloved college. Dr. John endured no end of opposition and misunderstanding, but he was finally rewarded in seeing the fulfillment of his dreams—the establishment of a fully accredited liberal arts college, plus a graduate school of theology.

Dr. John knew what he wanted and was like a clever chess player in planning the proper strategy to obtain it. He was always keenly aware of the direction in which the winds of public opinion were blowing. Loyal to his friends, he was also polite to his enemies. He loves his church. I remember how he complained when we were forced by growing attendance to begin holding duplicate Sunday morning services. He said, "I never know any more who is at church and who isn't."

All through the years Dr. John was subject to periodic attacks of flu and other illnesses. At one period a most painful form of arthritis persisted for months and almost took his life. It caused the greatest of physical agony. Only the mercy of God delivered him from this extended ordeal. After the affliction abated, Dr. John went back to give several more fruitful years to the college. Anderson College stands today as a monument to Dr. John A. Morrison and also to Dean Russell Olt who labored by his side for nearly thirty years. Both men lived out that quality of commitment and dedication which many of us talk about, but too few of us practice.

In pastoring Park Place church there was never a dull moment. What generous, talented folk are in that congregation! Of course, you would expect that among fifteen hundred persons there would be one or two who sometimes tempted me to resign. But on the whole it was a great church. There were about seventy ordained ministers in the congregation. This fact never caused the slightest problem. For the most part, these were either board executives, or retired pastors, and I felt their full support.

I was also fortunate in having in attendance most of the Anderson College faculty members, although I never prepared my sermons with them primarily in mind. I preached to the "common people" for the most part, and let the intelligentsia tune in. From a spiritual standpoint the problems of the educated and uneducated are quite similar. Both have hopes, fears, frustrations, and ambitions, many of which are thwarted. Both need the support of prayer and the power of a living faith in God. Both need to feel that someone is taking a personal interest in their welfare. I couldn't have made a greater mistake in Park Place than to have prepared my sermons week after week primarily for the benefit of the doctors of philosophy in the congregation. College folk are just people and should be preached to as such.

Whoever pastors Park Place Church of God will receive many invitations to speak in various places. The luncheon clubs want him, as do the Parent-Teacher Associations. Pastors invite him to dedicate their new churches, conduct evangelistic meetings, and speak to Christian Education groups. He will be asked to address ministerial associations, high school and college commencements, prayer groups, and city-wide preaching missions. With his hands full of his own responsibilities, it is not always expedient for a pastor to accept too many outside invitations. In 1945 Richard Lentz was pastor of the big downtown Central Christian church, and a very popular speaker. In fact, I thought that he and Dr. George Taggart, of First Presbyterian church, were the most eloquent preachers in town. Since I knew that Dick received dozens of calls to speak here and there, one day I asked, "How do you decide which invitations to accept and which to reject?" I profited by his answer. "When someone asks me to address this meeting or that," he said, "I ask myself if there is some particular reason why I, and not someone else, should address the group. If there isn't, I turn the invitation down." Let young preachers take note.

In addition to the usual pastoral burdens, I was also speaker on the International Christian Brotherhood Hour, and in almost every area where the program was heard there was a demand for a rally or a series of evangelistic meetings. I accepted what invitations I could but had to say no to most of them. Then came our Mid-Century Building Fund Campaign, carried on among the men of the church during the years 1953-54. During this time, in response to urging from our World Service organization, I addressed area meetings of men all over the United States in an effort to raise an extra two million dollars for capital funds for missions. Everett Hartung and I spoke in seventy-four such meetings all the way from California to New York, sometimes three and four a week. Twice I spoke in California on Saturday night and was back in Park Place pulpit on Sunday morning; not an easy thing to do before the days of jet airplanes. I flew over fifty thousand miles in 1953 besides traveling thirty thousand more by automobile.

You would be disappointed if I did not admit to hearing certain rumblings in the congregation. A few complained about my extra-curricular activities. In 1953, I also spent the month of August in Japan, first attending the Sixth World Congress on Evangelism, and then joining hundreds of preachers in covering Japan with evangelistic services.

About this time some of the leaders of our church held a retreat in what was then the home of my good friend Dr. D. Elton Trueblood, at Richmond, Indiana. In the course of our discussions the matter of my outside speaking dates was brought rather bluntly before the group. It was quite an interesting hour. My brothers and sisters really held me over the fire, but I rather enjoyed it. I can still hear one of our leaders as he said quite forcefully, "But doggone it, pastor, this is not a part-time job." True, brother, true! My chief argument was that all during this time the church was growing in numbers, offerings were increasing, and revival fires were burning. I told the group that if they were unhappy with me and preferred a pastor who was not as much in demand elsewhere, they should make immediate contact with him. They might even be able to obtain him at a lower salary, although, to be quite frank, mine was low enough. That ended the discussion.

I never felt I belonged to Park Place church just because they were paying my salary. I felt that I belonged to God, and to the church at large, and was duty bound to make my influence felt in as wide a circle as possible. I used my own judgment as to the use of my time and put in my best licks where I felt they would count for the most. Anyhow, who would want a pastor whom no one else wanted to hear? That would be like marrying a girl who appealed to no other man. Personally, I married a girl who was admired, respected, and desired by a great many men.

Every pastor's situation is different. He will have to use his own sanctified judgment in deciding what to do about the outside invitations. Some churches have their pastors so hog-tied they couldn't get away for a week if Gabriel were calling. Are preachers supposed to work for churches or churches for preachers? Is the church the pastor's field or his working force? I think some folk are crossed up in their thinking at this point. They seem to feel that the pastor's job is to spend most of his time in the homes of his people. Why should your pastor visit you unless you are ill or in trouble? The church will grow faster if the pastor spends more of his time ringing the doorbells of the unconverted. It will grow faster still if he can persuade members of the congregation to do the same.

Chapter Twenty

Sadness

In the Pastorate

I ONCE HEARD a medical doctor from another state refer to Indiana as "the cancer belt." He didn't elaborate but it certainly is a fact that cancer is prevalent there. We lost Dr. John Kane, Dr. Carl Kardatzke, Dean Russell Olt, and another prominent Anderson College professor, all within the space of months, from cancer. The three men named above were all active in Park Place Church of God and were exceptionally capable. Dr. Kane was executive-secretary of the Alumni Association at Anderson College after being a leading pastor for many years. Dr. Kardatzke was in charge of the training of school teachers. Dr. Olt had done a wonderful job as Dean. All three men were beloved of the people and all three were called to end their days in lingering affliction.

It is difficult to hide your feelings when you visit those who are in their final illnesses. However, all three of these men took the initiative in conversation when I called upon them. John Kane would share humorous clippings someone had sent or recall a pleasant happening of previous years. Carl Kardatzke was always cheerful. I well remember the day when, with death no more than a week away, he said, "Pastor, you are always praying for me. Today I am going to pray for you. You sure look like you need some prayer." I wish I had recorded that prayer. It was filled with faith in God, with Christian hope, and optimism.

When Dr. Kane was in the hospital in his final illness, he did not know at first the seriousness of his affliction. I had known for some time. One day in St. John's hospital, I met in the hall Dr. John Drake, one of Anderson's beloved Christian surgeons. Dr. Drake had operated on my mother when at an advanced age she had broken her hip. He said, "Do you know about John Kane?" When I nodded, he continued, "I am on my way to tell him the bad news." I replied, "Well, Dr. Drake, you don't need to hesitate to tell John the truth. I have known him since I was sixteen. He is a great soul and has always lived the faith he preached. He will take the blow like the Christian he is and so will his wife, Cynthia."

Dr. Drake spoke then of times when he had brought similar messages to other doomed persons. He said, "It certainly makes a difference whether or not they are Christians. I have seen relatives faint when the word was given about a loved one. I have had to administer sedatives to some who became hysterical and could not be comforted. It is a great thing to be upheld in the emergencies of life by a strong Christian faith."

The doctor went on his way and I continued my visitation rounds for an hour or so, coming finally to John's room. As I entered, tears were in his eyes and the eyes of his wife, but they were not really weeping. John said, "Do you know, pastor?" Then with a smile he told of Dr. Drake's visit. The doctor had opened the conversation with comments on the weather. He spoke of the nice corner room with its two-way view of the hospital grounds. He asked if John was being given adequate attention by the nurses. Then he ran out of something to say. That was when John spoke up to ask, "Doctor, was there something else you wanted to say to me today?" The doctor nodded. John said, "I thought so, doctor, and I am not surprised. I have been suspecting that something more serious has taken hold of me." Thus he lived, and thus he died, sustained in life and death by the Everlasting Arms.

> *So live that when thy summons comes to join*
> *The innumerable caravan, which moves*
> *To that mysterious realm, where each shall take*
> *His chamber in the silent halls of death,*

Thou go not, like the quarry-slave at night,
Scourged to his dungeon, but, sustained and soothed
By an unfaltering trust, approach thy grave,
Like one who wraps the drapery of his couch
About him, and lies down to pleasant dreams.
          —From *Thanatopsis,* by William Cullen Bryant

Why can't all of us live and die with a faith such as John Kane manifested? We all die as we live. We don't reach out at the last moment to lay hold on a great faith which we have been repudiating through all the years of health and well-being. At eighty-five Caleb could plead with Joshua to "give me this mountain" because he had been a great warrior for the Lord all his days. He was exhibiting at eighty-five a reflection of the faith which had been his at forty, when, with Joshua, he had brought in the minority report for the ten spies, saying, "Let us go up and take the land. We are well able to possess it." If you want to know how you are going to face death, take a look at yourself as you are right now and you will have the answer.

I am reminded of the woman who, after I had said something about dying, said, "I am simply scared to death of death." Why should a Christian say such a thing? To me, death is like going home to those you love at the close of the day. Death is like having your wife greet you at the door with a hug and a kiss. Death is like being graduated from the school of life into the thrilling realities of God's great, eternal heaven. Death is a turning away from the sadness, the heartbrokenness, the disappointments and sorrows of this world to enjoy the pleasures of an eternity where tears are unknown. I do not fear death. The one with whom I have walked hand in hand for more than fifty years will not withdraw that hand when my feet enter the chilly waters of the river of death. "O, death, where is thy sting; O grave, where is thy victory?" "If I go and prepare a place for you, I will come again and receive you unto myself, that where I am, there ye may be also." "Even so, come, Lord Jesus."

I have said that nothing breaks the heart of a pastor like the spiritual and moral failures of his people. To my knowledge, it was twenty-five years before any couple I had married ever went

263

to the divorce court. Divorce is such a sad, sad thing. It always speaks of failure. Divorce *is* failure. Someone has failed to keep his end of the bargain. Someone has failed to love as he ought. Someone has failed in patience, understanding, and a desire to cooperate. Divorce is not God's way. God's way is one man for one woman for life. Period! It is too bad we don't make his way our way. We would be a lot happier and get along much, much better.

It breaks a pastor's heart to see those who came up in his congregation, those who stood before him at the marriage altar and repeated those solemn, sacred vows together, now filled with resentments, animosities, and anger, eager to sever ties which have held them together for years. If love is blind, as some would have us believe, blind also are those who throw away in an hour of anger all the treasures they have accumulated during ten or twenty years of marriage. Life is never the same after a divorce, no matter where your steps turn or to whom you go. The pastor knows this, but it is hard to convince the tense couple sitting before him that it is true. People divorce so easily these days, scarcely giving the matter a second thought. We need to go back to the Book and take to heart what the Master said about divorce. Just because we are "moderns" we are not smarter than he, or wiser. We haven't outgrown the Sermon on the Mount and never will. We really don't break God's laws; we just break ourselves upon them. And like Humpty-Dumpty we never quite get put back together again.

Marry in the Lord. Establish your home in the Lord. Live every day in his will and spirit. Love as he loves you. Forgive as he forgives you and your marriage will withstand every shock which the world and the devil may throw against it. Marriage ought to ripen and deepen as the years come and go. It does, when husband and wife are both filled to overflowing with the Spirit of God. In such a case the children rise up to call their parents blessed. The elderly couple walk out into the sunset together, serene in the confidence which a solid love implanted in their marriage fifty years ago and which they never allowed to be interrupted.

When I began my pastoral ministry, I was often asked to remarry someone who had been divorced. Many times adultery had been involved. I was conscientious and always tried to find out

264

whether this divorced person who planned to remarry was the innocent party in the separation. I would remarry the innocent person but would not remarry the one who had been guilty of adultery. Thus I married divorced persons for some twenty-five years.

Then came a couple, both of whom had been divorced. Both were "innocent parties," so I married them. To my sorrow. It wasn't long until they were arguing and fussing. I was criticized severely by the church they formerly attended. That did it. I decided right there that I would never remarry another divorced person, since never in all those twenty-five years had I come upon any but the "innocent" party. Many had apparently pulled the wool over my eyes and I determined it would not happen again. From that day on divorced persons have had to go to someone else to be married.

I had always been bothered a bit by 1 Corinthians 7:10-11, "Let not the wife depart from her husband: But and if she depart, let her remain unmarried, or be reconciled to her husband: and let not the husband put away his wife." I had also been troubled by Matthew 19:9, "And I say unto you, Whosoever shall put away his wife, except it be for fornication, and shall marry another, committeth adultery: and whoso marrieth her which is put away (and this may often be the innocent person) doth commit adultery." Some of my ministerial brethren agree with my stand and some do not; but what another man thinks about this matter is his business. I must keep my own conscience before God, even though the mothers of a few sweet, young, divorced, darlings have thought me to be terribly old-fashioned and narrow-minded. Bless them!

It is my firm belief, based on a thorough study of both the Old and New Testaments, that if Jesus walked among us today he would forbid divorce for *any* reason. He said Moses allowed divorce because of the hardness of the people's hearts. We aren't under the Law, but under grace. Where the Holy Spirit abides in the hearts of both husband and wife, there will be no divorce. Don't tamper with the words of Jesus. Let him make the rules; then abide by them for your own spiritual, moral, and mental well-being.

Chapter Twenty-One

Retirement

IT WAS ABOUT 1953 that Polly said, as we sat reading, "Where do you think you would like to retire when you are sixty-five?" I answered that I hadn't given the matter any thought. She continued, "Yes, but if we were retiring right now, where would you like to live?" "Oh," I said, "I suppose it would be a toss-up between Colorado Springs and somewhere in Florida." Thus my wife began to force me to think about retirement, years before it took place. She was smart to take the initiative in these conversations. A man at the zenith of his career has little time, much less inclination, to ponder the problems of retirement. Really, he ought to begin thinking seriously about retirement plans when he is thirty, but most of us put it off for another thirty years or so.

Polly and I began storing up pertinent facts about retirement as we went along. I was in California perhaps ten times in the next ten years, and we were also in Florida several times. Colorado was a favorite vacation spot. We have always loved the mountains. In 1953 the ministers of Southern California tried to persuade me to head up Arlington College. But the more I was in California, the less I wished to live there. (My apologies to all native sons and other Californians!) The country was brown and arid, really a desert. The forest fires, mud-slides, floods, and predictions of earthquakes didn't appeal to me. Then, too, having been both places, examined the tax structures, and cost of living, I felt it would cost at least a hundred dollars a month more to retire in California than it would in Florida. A magazine writer drew this conclusion: "If you are interested in making money, go to California. If you wish to enjoy life, go to Florida."

After serious consideration we also crossed Colorado off the list. When you are old, you don't climb mountains. And although the Colorado Springs climate isn't severe, they do have some snow, ice, and cold winds off the Rockies. That left Florida. We had been up and down both the east and west coasts. Several places presented retirement possibilities. There was Fort Myers, with its beach a few miles away. My sister and her husband already lived at Bradenton, which is just nine miles from the Gulf. Saint Petersburg was known as Sun City. On the east coast Daytona Beach had long been one of our favorite places for a January vacation. In Fort Lauderdale and West Palm Beach we had several friends.

However, there is a dampness on the coast and hurricanes blow violently along its shores almost every year. They generally slow down before traveling very far inland. On the coast the salt air tends to rust the nails in the houses, and anything else made of iron. Houses need to be painted more frequently and that is expensive. The humidity is higher.

In 1957 Luther Moore, then pastor of the First Church of God in Eustis, invited us to hold an evangelistic series in his church. Eustis is located in Lake County, which contains fourteen hundred lakes. There is good bass fishing, and the specks (crappies to you Northerners) are caught by the thousands during the first two or three months of the year. We couldn't think of retiring in Florida with all those lakes, the ocean, and the Gulf, without living at the water's edge. That is how we happen to live at Star Route, Box 666, (the mark of the beast?) Eustis, Florida 32726, right on Lake Joanna.

We enjoyed our new home from the day we moved in, which was February 5, 1962. Twenty-nine feet of sliding glass doors give an unobstructed view of the mile-long lake. The house is airy and relaxed. The scent of jasmine is on the night breezes.

If you are thinking of retiring somewhere, take into consideration more than the climate. You need to know someone in the locality you have chosen. Preferably you should have some very good friends following, or already there. Otherwise, you may not be retired three months before you are overcome with loneliness. There should also be a good church available where you can meet and worship with like-minded people. You should give serious thought to what you are going to do with your time after retirement. You should have some interest in crafts, hobbies, fishing or hunting, or should plan to give many hours to the work of your church. Nothing is more deadening than for active persons to retire with nothing to do. Try that and you may be in the hospital within two years and in the cemetery in another two. Zestful living demands action.

Again, to be happy in retirement you should plan well in advance to be financially secure. Begin not later than age forty to save for the future. When you have a thousand dollars, invest it where it will bring a suitable income. Make a down payment on a piece of rental property. When this is partially paid off, get a loan and purchase another. The renters will pay for both of them. Make other investments on the strength of wise counseling as you are able to do so. Many elderly people are unhappy and grouchy simply because they do not have enough money on which to live. The time to do something about this item is at age thirty and forty, not sixty-five.

Polly and I live ten miles from our Florida state campground where church groups meet in special conclaves a few times each year. There we hear some of our better singers and preachers and meet with friends whose interests match our own. It all adds up to a pretty good life.

Isn't it sad to see a minister stay on and on at a church when his ministry is no longer leading to growth and progress? I hate to see a good man spoil all he has done by failing to see that it is time to retire. I quit while I was ahead; at Park Place, the Christian Brotherhood Hour, and Warner Press. It is better to leave with people wanting you to stay, than to stay until they want you to leave.

Chapter Twenty-Two

Spiritual Renewal

IF YOU THINK that a pastor's life runs month in and month out on a perfectly even keel, you don't know him. I know preachers. I've been one for fifty years and have counseled with preachers and preachers' wives for much of that time. They have poured out to me their hopes and fears, their heartaches and sorrows, their joys and successes. Occasionally their story has been one of shipwreck and failure. Preachers and their wives are people, very human people. They laugh and cry, become hungry and tired, irritated and sometimes angry. They respond to their environment, much as you do. They have their inner spiritual battles, just as you have yours.

But there is one thing which almost all preachers have in common. They long from time to time for spiritual renewal. A preacher may be looked upon as a professional "holy man," but deep down in his heart he constantly longs for a closer walk with God. That more intimate walk is not always easy to achieve. A pastor is so busy these days. When I think of the simplicity of my father's pastorate and the complexity of the job now, it almost makes me long for "the good old days." The modern pastor of a large church must be an executive, a counselor, an advertising expert, a financial genius, a fund-raiser, a first-class preacher, and a few other miscellaneous things if he is to succeed in his job. He doesn't punch a time clock. He is up early and late and works seven days a week. The sermons and other addresses he prepares each week, including those for funerals, take much more time than most laymen realize.

So, when can he find time for meditation and prayer? When can he find time to read the books which he knows would help to ripen and deepen his relationship to God? Often he is so busy preparing sermons on prayer and reading books about prayer that he scarcely has time to actually pray. He knows about Thomas a Kempis and Thomas Kelly but doesn't have time to saturate his soul in what they wrote.

Twentieth century churches almost force their ministers to become professional men. The touch of professionalism is the touch of death to a preacher as far as his spiritual life is concerned. He can preach as a professional minister, or preach as "a dying man to dying men." He can make hospital calls as a professional minister, or stand by the bedside of critically-ill, worried, anxious folk and exude the love of God. He can be a professional man as he conducts a funeral, or can be one whose heart is broken with the brokenness of the grieving. I detest professionalism in the ministry. I detest the ministerial tone of voice, the ministerial inflection, the professional smile and handshake. I cringe in the presence of domineering preachers who push people around. One reason I detest domineering preachers is because in past years I was one.

In 1955 I was pastor of Park Place church and speaker for the Christian Brotherhood Hour, but was pushing people around. Of course there has to be a certain amount of aggressiveness in any pastor who forges ahead. You nudge, you push, you persuade, you put the heat on. If you take a "business as usual" attitude, that's exactly what you'll have. The average preacher does an average job. Show me a fast-paced, swiftly growing church and I will show you a pastor who cannot be classified as an average person. He has to be a pusher to get things done. But when you have to push people, if you aren't careful you will get pushy. And folks resent it.

I didn't realize I had become domineering. How many people *do* realize it? Here I was telling everyone else how to live and act and all the while in need of spiritual therapy myself. After this shocking and humiliating revelation, I resolved to do something about it. I bought twenty-five books on prayer and began to attend Ashrams and Camps Farthest Out in an effort to change my personality. I prayed as I had never prayed before.

It didn't take long to discover what causes a person to become domineering. First, if you have been brought up in extreme poverty, as I was, you may tend to push people around in order to convince them (and yourself) that you are as good as they are. Second, if you have unresolved hostilities in your heart, they can make you pushy. Or if you have an unforgiven guilt in your soul. Certainly, to be domineering is positive proof that your love for people is insufficient. I said, "But, Lord, I *do* love people." And the answer came back, "Yes, but not half enough; and you don't love them nearly as much as you want them to *think* you love them."

It is one thing to realize what your spiritual needs are; it is quite another thing to change. Can an old dog learn new tricks? I prayed and agonized before the Lord. I walked the streets at night with tears running down my cheeks asking God to change me. I said, "I don't want to live unless I can change. I don't know whether you can change me or not, but if you can, I'm willing to do anything to cooperate in bringing it about." I meant it.

Can a man grow spiritually after he has been a Christian since boyhood and has been preaching to people for thirty-five years? Through those years I had kept up my private devotions. It had been a habit of long-standing to read the Bible through once a year, first in one translation, and then in another. It had done me a considerable amount of good, but had not actually returned the benefit I needed. So, I resolved to depart from this pattern and give myself for the next year to a serious study of the Book of Romans which I considered to be Paul's most important work. I began to rise an hour and fifteen minutes earlier than usual, which meant that I was getting up at 5:45 A.M. By 6:00 I was dressed and shaved, and had coffee on the kitchen table, together with my commentary. And so the months went by. I read slowly and thoughtfully the text, the footnotes, and the notes in the back of the book. I carefully read seven commentaries on Romans in seventeen months, and later added another to the list.

It was during this study of Romans that I began to change. It had not come about through prayer, the reading of the Bible, or my attendance in retreats. But, as I began to realize afresh the deeper meanings of Paul's teachings regarding justification by faith and what the love of God really means to a Christian, the change began. It seems to me that a great many "perfectionist" people, although they *teach* justification by faith, actually *practice* justification by works. They seem to be saying, "If I can be good enough, if I can toe the line and make no infringement of the rules, if I can guard my tongue and never talk out of turn, I will be saved." Paul did not teach this. He taught that none of us merits salvation. None can earn or deserve it. It is the gift of God, not of works, lest any man should boast.

This is almost too good to be true, but I decided to trust Paul and try him out. So I ceased my struggling. I ceased my everlasting straining to be good and began to relax in the arms of a loving God. To my great relief and satisfaction it "worked." I quit taking my temperature every morning to see whether or not I was "spiritual." Then the *Lord* began to keep that which I couldn't keep of myself. I began to *feel* the love of God as never before. I had always *known* God loved me, but had not been able to *feel* God loved me. There is a vast difference between the two. Now that I was open the love came pouring in and when God pours love in, you have something to pour out, something to share. As I relaxed, those about me began to relax. As I began to love others with a new quality of love, they began to love me as I had not been loved before.

I used to say to Polly, "Our people *respect* me but they don't *love* me. They like to hear me preach, but they don't particularly want me in their homes." All that changed when I changed. A few years later Doug experienced an even more radical change of heart and life. It shook me when he said one day as we drove along toward a meeting, "The fact is, dad, if you hadn't changed, I probably would never have changed either." What a frightening revelation! I can't help but wonder how many other young people would change *if their parents would change first.* How many erring husbands would be brought to the Lord if their wives would discover the secret of how to love in a thoroughly Christian way.

I changed and the church changed, and my last years at Park Place were the most enjoyable of all. When someone asked me to describe what happened during my pursuit of Romans, I told him it reminded me of a story I once read about the raising of a barge near the edge of the ocean. It was stuck so firmly in the sand that the stoutest tugs could not budge it. Finally they brought two barges at low tide and set them on either side of the sunken craft. Then they passed cables under the disabled craft and over both of the others. After tightening these cables they simply waited for the tide to rise. When it did, the barge let loose and floated. Well, the rising tide of Romans lifted me and set me free. I have never again been quite the same, although day by day I continue my quest. "My soul thirsteth for God, for the living God" (Ps. 42:2).

Many persons of fifty and over find spiritual ambitions stirring in their souls now and then but settle back and say, "What's the use?" Take heart. You *can* change. You don't have to go on as you are. The years which remain can be filled with a fresh love, a new delight in prayer, and a greater effectiveness as a winner of souls. That path is not short, and it leads uphill, but when at last you stand at the summit it will be worth it all.

Chapter Twenty-Three

Others I Remember

HOW DOES the writer of an autobiography know with certainty that his story has been fully told? In rereading what has already been written, I am shocked as I check certain lists, to realize the important persons whose names and deeds I have omitted. Of course, no book would be large enough to contain all that should yet be said, but I simply must mention just a few more names and facts.

There was Dr. A. F. Gray, for example, one of my predecessors as pastor of Park Place church and for long years chairman of our General Ministerial Assembly, and president of Warner Pacific College. In one of my darkest hours I flew out to Portland, Oregon, for a consultation with this calm, intelligent man of God. When I flew back to Indianapolis a few hours later a new assurance was in my heart. Thank God for men such as this! They have "gifts of the Spirit" which enable them to bless thousands. Dr. Gray's two volume *Introduction to the New Testament* is still in demand.

Fifty years ago there were few singing evangelists among us, so when Rachel Lord appeared to sing "A String of Empties" in our June meeting, she took the place by storm. What a sweet voice and what a sweet spirit! How many thousands she has blessed through the years as she sang in the Spirit. In June of 1972 we brought her back to sing again, in a special music program, the song which had first made her name known among us. At seventy, her voice is still clear and sweet and her spirit Christ-like.

For a few years, Dr. Earl L. Martin lived as our next door neighbor in Anderson, while teaching, and holding other administrative offices at the college and with our national Board of Church Extension and Home Missions. He was a step-brother to Dr. Morrison, and had some of that same Missouri wit and humor.

He was well past sixty when Dr. John became seriously ill. Our college leaders were pressing Dr. Martin to fill in as president pro tem, but this he refused to do. As he leaned across the back fence one day he said humorously to me, "The truth is, pastor, I just don't want to work that hard any more." At the present moment I know exactly how he felt. *I* don't want to work that hard any more, either. Dr. Martin has been gone for ten years, but just yesterday I saw one of his great books still on sale, *This We Believe, This We Proclaim*. The good which men do lives after them.

Then there was that good old brother from Virginia, the Rev. M. P. Rimmer, who became a fixture on the camp meeting platform at Anderson as he pushed his chair to within five or six feet of the speaker. He was there to pray for and encourage the speaker no matter his identity or ability. Unschooled, Brother Rimmer was nevertheless wise in the ways of humanity and lived close to God. As my personal friend he used to relate incidents which took place in his early ministry in the Virginia mountains where the walking was hard and the remuneration small. Meeting a poor old man who had no shoes one day, Brother Rimmer sat down, took off his own, and handed them to the other as a gift. When his new acquaintance remonstrated, M. P. said with that characteristic chuckle, "Go ahead, man, take them. I can get more, and you cain't."

W. T. Wallace was a Tennessee product but did most of his pastoral work in Kentucky, serving with distinction in Louisville during years when problems plagued our churches in that area. With native wit and constant humor wherever he sat was the head of the table. I do not remember that he enjoyed hunting and fishing as did Tom Steenbergen, W. H. Hunt, and R. C. Caudill. His chief sport was in finding some denominational preacher who happened to be in an argumentive frame of mind and debating with him on such subjects as the church, holiness, and healing.

He nailed to the tree the hide of many a man who thought he knew his Bible well. Soon none but the uninitiated dared challenge him. He was a strong doctrinal preacher with a decided flare for making a bit of money on the side. Before his pastoral days ended he had accumulated considerable property the income from which is, I hope, being of some comfort to him in his declining years.

A. J. Bixler was an artist. If you have visited widley among our churches you have seen his paintings adorning the front walls of certain sanctuaries. He seemed able to make the church's baptismal pool become a natural eddy in the Jordan's flow. Although he went on to his eternal reward a few years ago he will be long remembered, not only for his religious art but for the fact that he was treasurer of the newly formed Park Place Church of God, when that group erected their new sanctuary in 1917 at the corner of East 8th Street and Union Avenue (now College Drive).

Mrs. Nora Hunter was an ordained minister who with her husband served the church well for at least sixty years. During our Dayton pastorate we purchased a cottage at Yellow Creek Lake in northern Indiana, which her husband had built about the turn of the century from native lumber. It must have been during the later 30s that Nora Hunter called me down to the depot in Dayton where she was awaiting a train connection. There she confided that the Lord had definitely shown her that I was to go to Africa as a missionary. This came somewhat as a shock to me. After thinking it over for awhile I said, "Sister Hunter, a man's gifts make the place for him. Send me to Africa and you will cancel nine-tenths of my usefulness, for I am a preacher and know only English. Make me preach through an interpreter and you will handcuff me." That's how close I came to becoming a missionary to Africa. Nora Hunter went on to found the Woman's Missionary Society, and through that act probably advanced the cause of foreign missions more than any other person in the history of our movement. God bless her memory!

Dr. Charles E. Brown was pastor of Bethany Church of God in Detroit when I first met him in 1924. In fact I celebrated my twenty-first birthday anniversary during our March meeting in that church. John L. Williams (Jumping Johnny) was the evangelist and we had a good meeting with many converts. Dr. Brown later became editor in chief of our Church of God publications. He wrote several important books on points of doctrine and the history of our movement. He had a gift for editorial writing and the ability to observe and rightly interpret the signs of the times. I was his pastor for many years after coming to Park Place.

G. M. Byrd came originally from Kentucky and was a man beloved by the people. When I was just starting out in my singing career, we became friends and he gave me much encouragement. He surely must have been a school teacher before entering the ministry, as many of his children and grandchildren were afterward teachers and first-class ones at that. Looking back through the years I find myself remembering most clearly those men who were gentle and kind and had a quick sense of humor. Brother Byrd was that kind of person. Precise in manner of speech, he was always immaculately dressed; trousers well-pressed, and cravat properly tied and of the right color.

Polly and I stayed in the Byrd home during evangelistic meetings in Hamilton, Ohio. I still remember his wife's tasty cooking, especially her flavorful fried apples served with crisp bacon. Reverend Byrd owned a Chevrolet sedan. On Sunday morning when he pulled away from the house he was always wearing gloves to protect his hands from becoming soiled enroute. He was just as particular in his preaching of the gospel and had not too much patience with younger men who seemed to be compromising the truth or failing in their dedication. He left a vacancy in his passing that no one else was ever able to fill in our lives. His beloved wife is still with us at the age of 101. She is still alert and able and makes her home with her equally beloved daughter, Ida Byrd Rowe.

A word also ought to be written about Russell R. Byrum and his late wife, Mrs. Bessie (Hittle) Byrum, both of whom taught in Anderson Bible Training School for several years. Dr. Byrum had a brilliant mind and was an excellent teacher. He was self taught in Greek, and wrote one of our finest treatises in biblical doctrine and teachings. He also served for some time as book editor for our Publication Board. But fifty years ago, men were often forced to stand trial for trivial reasons, and following one such, in which the charge was most insignificant, Dr. Byrum withdrew from the Bible School and has since built hundreds of substantial homes in Anderson and vicinity.

When I was seventeen, I took a class in Christian doctrine from Dr. Byrum. He requested each of us to bring a sermon outline on the subject to class with us next day. I hadn't the slightest idea how a sermon outline should be formed. In the following class session I confessed to not having prepared the required outline. Dr. Byrum smiled and said, "Well, if you don't know how to do it yourself, go to someone else in the class and copy his." Thank you Walter Crowell, for letting me copy your outline and thus redeem myself. I never forgot the pattern and after that I found it much easier to make other outlines when required to do so.

After foreign missionary service, Bessie Byrum gave excellent service as a teacher in the Bible school. She was a first class teacher of church history. After fifty years many of the things she taught are still with me. She literally burned out for God and for the young people of the church.

Let me add another sincere word of appreciation for those who have served as my partners in making many foreign ventures for Christ possible through the liberality of their gifts: Arthur and Elizabeth Bunnell; Mr. and Mrs. Guy V. Whitener, Sr; Mr. and Mrs. Coleman Perry; Mr. and Mrs. Fred Leppien; Mr. and Mrs. Lowell Williamson; Reverend and Mrs. Ora Davis; Mr. and Mrs. Vernon Thomas; Mrs. Iva Caraker; Mr. and Mrs. Barry Richardson, and others. Without their generous assistance, most of our evangelistic thrust into the West Indies, Africa, Japan, and Europe would have been impossible. May God richly bless them all for their dedicated generosity.

I would also like to tell you about W. A. Lambert, David Leininger, Victor Lindgren, Harry Gardner, William Abel, Thaddeus Neff, Mattie B. (Oldham) Teter, E. E. Perry, N. K. Zazanis, S. L. Speck, P. B. Turner, H. French Wilson, Herman Babel, B. W. Barcus, W. F. Coy, John and Laura Ann Denton, Dr. and Mrs. David Gaulke, C. W. Hatch, Ernst Kersten, Gerhard Klabunde, Willi and Edith Krenz, Clair and Retha Shultz, Nathan and Ann Smith, and hundreds of others.

What a privilege has been mine and Polly's to walk down through the years shoulder to shoulder with these dedicated, courageous soldiers of the cross! May the coming generations find themselves worthy to follow in their footsteps. And may they preach and live the deathless Word in such spirit and power that thousands still unborn may hear the saving truth, and come to new birth in Christ.

INDEX

Krenz, Willi and Edith 281
Ku Klux Klan 87

Lambert, W. A. 281
Lane, S. J. 117
Larkin Co. 39
Lawson, B. F. 70, 72
Lee, J. Richard (Dick
   Meischke) 223, 241
Leininger, David 281
Lentz, Richard 257
Leppien, Mr. and Mrs. 281
Lima, Ohio 114, 178, 181ff
Lindgren, Victor 281
Literary Society 48
Little, Gertrude 236
Lord, Rachel 277
Lorton, George 95
Lovett, Hugo, Lloyd, Beulah
   111
Lucky Seven 53
Lykins, J. W. 90, 123
Lynn, Arthur 131

Madrid, Iowa 24
Martin, Earl L. 278
Maryland Camp Meeting 99
McAlpine, Mae 195
McCoy, I. S. 154
McCraw, W. D. 196
McGuire Sisters 222, 223
Merica, Merton 121
Mid-Century Building Fund
   257
Miller, T. Franklin 208
Minkler, Ross H. 224, 236
Monk, W. E. 83ff

Montague, H. G. 54
Moon, W. O. 224
Moore, Luther 268
Mount Sterling, Ky. 9, 123,
   150, 250
Morrison, John A. 47, 51, 91,
   133, 228
Murray, Mary 93

Naylor, C. W. 104, 107ff
Neff, Mildred 71
Neff, Thaddeus 281
Nelson, Hope 107
Nicholson, Robert A. 244
Nordyke and Marmon 41, 112,
   148

Odell, John P. (Jack) 242
Odell, Martin 55,
Oklahoma Camp Meeting 18
Oklahoma City 18
Oldham, Dean Elmore 143
Oldham, Douglas Reed 74,
   177, 184, 204ff
Oldham, John F. 15
Oldham, Karen 220
Oldham Mercantile Co. 16
Oldham, Myrtle (Elmore) 15
Oldham, William H. 15
Olt, Russell 47, 133ff, 256,
   261
Organ 198

Paintsville, Ky. 115
Pantlen, Miles 129
Paris, Ky. 87
Patterson, Clarence 55

Taylor, Myrtle 221
Taylor, Ralph 222
Teasley, D. O. 104, 107
Teter, Mattie B. (Oldham)
281
Thomas, Mr. & Mrs. Vernon
281
Thompson, Herbert W. 224,
236
Townsend, Claude 115, 147
Turner, Hazel 23, 124
Turner, John 196
Turner, P. B. 281
Tuttle, R. J. 240, 249
Trueblood, D. Elton 258
Tyler, Silas 24

Universal Recording Corp.
243

Van Hoose, H. M. 65
Vital Christianity 208

Wallace, W. T. 278
Warren, B. E. 103
Warren, Burd Barwick 53
Warren, Lottie Charles 53, 103
Warren, Nanny (Kiger) 103

Warner, D. S. 103, 104, 157
Warner Press, Inc. 54, 60,
208, 211
Weber, Charles V. 232
Webster, Mary 236
West Frankfort, Ill. 116, 118
WHIO Radio Station 200
White, Roger A. 101
Whitener, Sr., Mr. and Mrs.
Guy 221, 281
Whitinger Twins (Clarabelle,
Maybelle) 124
Wiles, Oscar 124
Williams, John L. 111, 279
Wilson, H. French 281
Williamson, Mr. and Mrs.
Lowell 281
Wilson, J. T. 27, 52, 253
WING Radio Station 197ff
Wingert, Bert 94
Wingert, Sidney L. 93, 182
Wright, G. E. 59
Wright, Harvey 224

Yellow Creek Lake, Ind. 219
Yourd, Principal 36

Zazanis, N. K. 281